D0205868

BURGESS
DT
746
.A32
v.1
1982

The African Liberation Reader

Edited by Aquino de Bragança
and Immanuel Wallerstein

Brother from the West

Brother from the West —
(How can we explain that you are our brother?)
the world does not end at the threshold of your house
nor at the stream which marks the border of your country
nor in the sea
in whose vastness you sometimes think
that you have discovered the meaning of the infinite.
Beyond your threshold, beyond the sea
the great struggle continues.
Men with warm eyes and hands as hard as the earth
at night embrace their children
and depart before the dawn.
Many will not return.
What does it matter?
We are men tired of shackles. For us
freedom is worth more than life.

From you, brother, we expect
and to you we offer
not the hand of charity
    which misleads and humiliates
but the hand of comradeship
    committed, conscious,
How can you refuse, brother from the West?

FRELIMO, 1973

The African Liberation Reader

WITHDRAWN

Volume 1

The Anatomy of Colonialism

Edited by Aquino de Bragança and Immanuel Wallerstein

Zed Press, 57 Caledonian Road, London N1 9DN

BuRGESS
DT
746
.A32
v.1

c.2

The African Liberation Reader was originally
published in Portuguese; first published in
English by Zed Press Ltd., 57 Caledonian
Road, London N1 9DN in 1982.

Copyright © Aquino de Braganca and
  Immanuel Wallerstein

Copyedited by Beverley Brown
Proofread by Stephen Gourlay, Rosamund
  Howe, Liz Hasthorpe and Anne
  Gourlay
Typeset by Margaret Cole
Cover design by Jacque Solomons
Cover photo courtesy of International
  Defence and Aid Fund
Printed by Krips Repro, Meppel, Holland

All rights reserved

U.S. Distributor
Lawrence Hill and Co., 520 Riverside
Avenue, Westport, Conn. 06880, USA

British Library Catalogue in Publication Data

The African liberation reader
  Vol. 1: The anatomy of colonialism
  1. Africa, Sub-Saharan — Politics and
  government — Addresses, essays, lectures
  I. Braganca, Aquino de II. Wallerstein,
  Immanuel
  320.9'67   JQ1872
  ISBN 0-86232-067-4

The African Liberation Reader

Publisher's Note

Zed Press gratefully acknowledge a grant from the WCC Programme to Combat Racism towards the cost of typesetting this project. Zed Press also wishes to thank the Swedish International Development Authority for making possible the gift of copies of each of these 3 volumes to the liberation movements of Southern Africa.

Contents

Preface

This collection of documents was originally assembled by the editors in 1973-74 and completed just as the revolution in Portugal broke out in April 1974. This event, completed in 1975 by the independence of all the former Portuguese colonies in Africa, transformed the political situation in Southern Africa. We decided to proceed with the publication of this book in its Portuguese version, since independence in the former Portuguese colonies constituted a clear turning-point in the historical development of their national liberation movements.

We hesitated however about an English-language version. The struggle was continuing in Zimbabwe, Namibia, and South Africa. Should the story stop in 1974? If today we have decided to publish this collection as it was constructed in 1974, it is because we believe that the Portuguese Revolution and the Independence, particularly of Angola and Mozambique, constituted an historical turning-point for the national liberation movements of Zimbabwe, Namibia, and South Africa as well.

Indeed so much has happened in those three countries since 1974 that all of us are tempted to forget the historical evolution of the movements in these countries as well as the importance of the early intellectual debates within the movements and their continuing relevance today. We wish to reinvigorate this historical memory which hopefully may serve as a tool of the ongoing struggle itself. It is in this spirit that we have decided to publish today the English-language version of this collection.

Introduction

National liberation movements do not emerge one fine day out of the mind of some superman or at the instigation of some foreign power. They are born out of popular discontent. They emerge over long periods to combat oppressive conditions and express aspirations for a different kind of society. They are, in short, the agents of class and national struggle.

Neither the classes nor the nations, however, have been there forever. They, too, are creations of the modern world and, in the case of Southern Africa, they were born in the crucible of the colonial experience. To understand the national liberation movements, we must first understand the social forces they represent and the ways in which these social forces were shaped by their historical circumstances.

The capitalist world economy came into existence in Europe in the 16th Century. Its internal functioning — the endless drive for capital accumulation, the transfer of surplus from proletarian to bourgeois and from periphery to core, the cyclical pattern of alternating phases of economic expansion and stagnation — combined to make necessary the regular, albeit discontinuous, expansion of the outer boundaries of the world economy. Slowly, over several centuries, other historical systems were destroyed and incorporated into this ever-growing octopus.

The forms of incorporation into the world economy have varied both according to the strength of the political systems in place in the zones undergoing incorporation and according to the internal configuration of forces among core states within the world economy during the period of incorporation. Sometimes incorporation involved direct colonial overrule, sometimes 'informal imperialism', and sometimes first this indirect mode of conquest followed by a later phase of direct colonialism.

Incorporation has everywhere involved two major changes for the zone being incorporated. First, the production structures were reorganized so that they contributed to the overall division of labour in the world economy. Secondly, the political structures were reorganized so that they facilitated the flow of factors of production in the world economy. In the case of Southern Africa, the reorganization of production structures involved the development both of cash crops and of mining operations for export on the world market. The reorganization of political structures meant the creation of colonial states in the region, the eventual boundaries of which were a function primarily of the struggles among the various European imperial and settler forces.

It is this reorganization of production structures which created the new classes and this reorganization of political structures which created the new nations. These classes and nations are institutional consequences of the development of the capitalist world economy. They are, in fact, the principal structural outcome of its hierarchical relations. They are at one and the same time the mode of social imposition of these hierarchies and the mode of social resistance to the inequalities bred by the system.

The object of imperialist expansion is to utilize the labour-power of the peoples of the newly incorporated peripheries at rates of real remuneration as low as possible. Securing such a labour force requires the establishment of a three-part geographical division of peripheral areas: a first zone to produce the export products, within which there is initially often forced labour, later low-paid wage labour; a second zone to produce surplus food to feed the labour force of the first zone, within which there tends to be household production; a third zone to serve as a manpower reserve to produce the labour force for the first zone (and even occasionally for the second), within which there tends to be so-called subsistence production. (The three zones do not necessarily have to fall within a single colonial state.)

It is this three-zone system, with its large component of migrant labour (persons, largely men, leaving the third zone for limited periods, sometimes only once in a lifetime, and returning afterwards to that zone), which permits the super-exploitation of labour in the first (or wage labour) zone. The 'migrant' workers located in such a zone participate in extended households, and over their lifetime the costs of reproduction are disproportionately borne by the work done in non-wage sectors. Thus the employer of wage labour can in effect pay *less than* the minimum necessary wage (that is, the wage assuring the reproduction of the labour force).

It is clear, then, why the conceptual categories which evolved in the context of the core zones of the capitalist world economy — concepts such as proletarian (meaning by that a life-long industrial wage labourer living in an urban area with his whole household) and peasant (meaning a life-long agricultural worker with some kind of hereditary rights to land utilization) — do not seem to fit exactly when we look closely at the peripheral zones of the world economy. The work-force there is not divided into 'traditional' peasants owning the means of production and 'modern' proletarians who have been expropriated from the means of production. Most (or at least many) workers' households are in fact composed of *both* 'proletarians' and 'peasants', the same individuals often being both for part of their lives. It is this combination of roles which defines the relationship of these workers to the world economy and permits the particular extreme form of exploitation they encountered in the colonial era.

The pattern of the creation of the work-force, with its institutionalized interaction between rural 'home' areas and the urban (or mining or cash-crop) areas, favoured the continued recruitment to wage employment through 'family' or 'ethnic' channels, and hence the emergence in the urban and commercialized zones of an 'ethnic' consciousness (called by the colonial overlords 'tribalism'), an ethnic consciousness which was in fact very much the expression of the emerging class position of the various groups integrated into the wage work-force.

The ambiguous relationship of class and ethnic 'membership' is hence a structural reality, indeed a structural creation, of the colonial situation, of colonies located within the capitalist world economy. The initial subjective confusions of large segments of the new work-forces were reinforced deliberately by the colonial authorities with their classic divide-and-rule tactics. It is within this framework and against this definition of the situation that the movements of resistance are born. While awareness of the real inequalities of the colonial situation was central to the demands of these movements from the very beginning, the complexities of the class-ethnic structures were a hindrance to their development. These movements evolved amidst contradictory consciousnesses of class and ethnicity and incorporated these contradictions into their very structures — sometimes in the form of competing movements, more often within a single national liberation movement, and frequently in both ways (as this whole collection of documents illustrates).

The history of each individual political unit (colony) is complex and these histories vary from colony to colony. Generally speaking, however, the story of anti-colonial resistance is the story of the construction of a national liberation movement, more or less unified, more or less representative, which seeks to incarnate the class and national struggles of the majority of the workforce. These histories cannot be appreciated or analysed in isolation. The emergence of such a movement in a particular country is itself the function in part of the political evolution of the world system as a whole.

Beginning in a modest way in the 19th Century, and achieving great force in the 20th, the contradictions of the capitalist world economy have led to the rise of a network of anti-systemic movements. These movements have taken different forms, sometimes emphasizing their class character, sometimes emphasizing their national character, usually doing a bit of both. They have sought to counter the oppressions of the world system and, in their more radical versions, to destroy it.

To build an anti-systemic movement, it is necessary to mobilize popular force, and usually it is politically necessary to mobilize this force initially within the confines of particular states. This narrow geographical definition of anti-systemic movements has been at once their strength and their weakness. It has been their strength because it has forced them to remain close to the concrete grievances of the working classes — urban and rural — they have been mobilizing. It has made it possible for them to achieve political power in some preliminary way — in the case of colonies, to obtain independence. But this narrow geographical focus has also been their weakness. Their enemy, the world bourgeoisie, has seldom hesitated to combine *its* strength on an inter-state level. In the case, for example, of the former Portuguese colonies in Africa, the movements in the separate colonies faced a single colonial power, and one that was in turn widely supported by other imperial powers. Furthermore, when such anti-colonial movements have come to power, they have found that juridical state sovereignty is in part a fiction since they were still bound by the constraints of the inter-state system, the political superstructure of the capitalist world economy.

The movements have not been unaware of these contradictions which have posed dilemmas, both strategic and tactical, for their operations. This book seeks to organize in a coherent manner their reflections on the dilemmas and their perspective on the solutions they might find. These solutions are not facile ones, and it is in the quality of these reflections and the action consequent upon them that we can distinguish those movements which have been truly anti-systemic in their impact and those which have fallen by the wayside, to become open or hidden agents for the maintenance and further development of the capitalist world economy.

The hard thinking of the movements in Southern Africa has been of great consequence for the struggle in that part of the world. But it is of great consequence for movements elsewhere as well. The reinforcement of the worldwide network of movements is in fact the great task of our times, a task in process but far from completed.

1. The Anatomy of Colonialism

Editors' Introduction

The text in this section is a statement addressed to the militants of
FRELIMO. It expresses a point of view shared by all the movements.
Although it was written as early as 1965, in the very beginning of the armed
struggle in Mozambique, it demonstrates that FRELIMO had already at that
time benefited from the experience of the whole series of African states that
had become independent around 1960.

Earlier nationalist movements in Africa had struggled against colonialism
and hence for political independence. But soon thereafter the newly independent states came to be aware that political independence merely marked one
stage in a far more fundamental struggle for national liberation. They came to
realize that 'neo-colonialism' was a reality and in fact a more subtle form of
imperialist control than colonialism.

While most African leaders realized this, only a few stated it publicly.
They were restrained by the very system in which they were involved. But the
liberation movements in areas still under white rule felt no such restraint.
They became the heirs and the spokesmen of a self-critical viewpoint. It is
in this light that the reader should view this warning to militants of the
dangers that lie ahead..

On the cover page of a newspaper published by the Zimbabwe African
National Union in 1967 there appeared this statement in a box: 'Imperialism
is like tick-fever. Animals that suffer from it are never healthy. So are the
nations that are controlled by imperialists. Their economic situation is never
healthy. Remember there is now old and neo-imperialism. Be at guard.'

Colonialism and Neo-Colonialism

FRELIMO

A statement in A Voz da Revolucao, *published by*
FRELIMO in Dar es Salaam in 1965. Translated from

the Portuguese.

Today we fight against Portuguese colonialism. We create, at the same time, the conditions which will prevent neo-colonialism from establishing itself in our country. But we must know exactly what colonialism and neo-colonialism are in order to be able to fight them. Let us begin with colonialism.

The best way to understand the nature of colonialism is to analyse the situation in our country, which is a colony itself. We can see that a foreign country (Portugal) has occupied Mozambique. Portugal has sent out troops to fight the people, they rebel; it has organized an administrative machine — with governors, administrators and policemen spread out all over the country in order to control every region and area of Mozambique. It has created special laws meant to protect the interests of the Portuguese, with absolute disdain for the interests and the rights of the Mozambicans. It has established a system of exploitation of the land and the people, giving out the most fertile areas and the best jobs to the Portuguese, submitting the Mozambicans to forced labour, and creating companies that belong to the Portuguese and others (such as the English, the French, the West Germans, the Swiss and the Belgians) who exploit the industry, the commerce and the agriculture of Mozambique. That is: Portugal dominates and exploits Mozambique *directly*. The government in Mozambique is Portuguese, the laws by which we must abide are made in Portugal, the army comes from Portugal, the profits are sent back either to Portugal or to the imperialist countries which, by agreement with the former also participate in the exploitation of our country; further, if these profits or riches do stay in Mozambique they are shared only by the Portuguese.

This is what colonialism is all about: the exploitation and the direct control of one country over another (in our case, the control and exploitation of Mozambique by Portugal).

Neo-colonialism is a modern form of colonialism. Actually, colonialism and neo-colonialism are the same thing; it is only in their form and in the way they exhibit themselves that they differ. Neo-colonialism is more disguised, more 'modernized'.

It appears as a consequence of the liberation struggle of the colonized peoples. At a certain stage (mainly in Africa) the people rebel against the foreign invaders and enter into an open fight against them. The colonial countries are then forced to spend a great deal of money on the army which they send out to the colonies to fight against the people, with all the necessary war *materiel*, police and administration. In addition, the nationalists seem to threaten the economic structure created by the colonizers, by burning down plantations and warehouses, sabotaging factories, destroying bridges, roads and railway tracks. All this causes a great loss for the colonizing countries. They invent, then, a way of eliminating this difficulty and of exploiting the territory, as before. This they do as follows: the colonialist countries give the colony its independence, but it is only a formal independence, not a real one.

Let's take Mozambique as an example. The Portuguese are spending billions on the war. They may well want to end the war tomorrow without, however, losing the riches of our country. In that case, they will do this: they will declare that they are giving Mozambique its independence. But they choose someone — it may well be an African — who is a friend of theirs, willing to accept and carry out their orders, for the Presidency of Mozambique. Mozambique, in this event, would appear to be independent for it would have its own government, its flag and its anthem. But, in fact, everything would be just as it is today, because its puppet government chosen and controlled by the Portuguese would not do anything for the progress of the people of Mozambique. On the contrary, it would allow the Portuguese full freedom to exploit, as they do today, the commerce, industry, mines and banks of our country. The people of Mozambique would be just as miserable, and the Portuguese would continue to grow rich at our cost. This is what we call neo-colonialism. Its main difference in relation to colonialism is that, in the former, there is no territorial occupation; there is only economic control. The Portuguese would no longer need to have an army or administrators in Mozambique. It would be the puppet government itself which would open all the doors to the Portuguese, forcing us to work for them.

This is the danger of which every Mozambican must beware. We are fighting in order that in Mozambique there may exist a government chosen by the people, representing the will of the people and working for the good of the people of Mozambique.

We fight so that we may destroy colonialism in every one of its forms.

Down with colonialism!

Down with neo-colonialism!

2. The Portuguese Empire

Editors' Introduction

From the very beginning of their struggle, the liberation movements of Portuguese Africa had a very clear analysis of the nature of Portuguese colonialism. One fundamental theme repeats itself throughout: Portuguese colonialism was different from that of other European powers (Britain, France, Belgium) in that Portugal was itself a 'backward' country, itself 'dependent', itself with a largely agricultural and illiterate population.

This was the theme Amilcar Cabral put forward in one of his earliest published analyses in 1960. We begin with this text. It is the theme to which he returned in one of his late important statements in 1971. We end with this statement. This analytical position is filled in by FRELIMO's statement in 1963 and the historical material offered by the MPLA in 1967. They argued that Portugal's role as a 'parasite' country goes back to the 15th Century, goes back, that is, to the very period of Portuguese glory, the very period which is the basis of Portugal's claim to be a principal bearer of world civilization.

Of course, this position of Portuguese 'difference' was not intended to mean that the basic issue was anything other colonial domination. The M.A.C., one of the earliest expressions of the movements of Portuguese Africa took care in its famous Manifesto in 1960 to make clear its distance from all those on the Portuguese left who argued that the issue was fascism rather than colonialism. It was colonialism, M.A.C. said, that bred fascism.

Nonetheless, Portugal was colonial in ways different from the major powers. The implications of this historic fact of Portuguese 'underdevelopment' for the contemporary world economy was spelled out in considerable detail in a discussion document prepared by CONCP (which was the liaison body linking the leading liberation movements in Portugal's African colonies) for the Rome International Conference of Solidarity in 1970. The economic advantages to Portugal of her colonies, the intertwining of Portuguese, South African, and European interests was laid out. And in particular, the document sought to explain why there was a 'change in policy' in 1961 which permitted 'the entry of large amounts of foreign capital into the African colonies and into Portugal itself . . . .'

From this analysis of Portugal's role in the world economy, was derived a the conclusion, stated many times, that Portugal 'cannot permit herself the luxury of decolonization.' The argument was simple. France or Britain decolonized in order to maintain their economic privileges. Remember the argument about neo-colonialism. If Portugal decolonized, neo-colonization would still be a danger. But those who would reap the profit in this case would not be the Portuguese but other, economically stronger European countries. Hence, Portugal could *only* profit from colonialism of the old-fashioned variety.

Nonetheless, from time to time, the Portuguese movements asked themselves whether this 'incapacity to neo-colonize' of Portugal had not been modified by the economic developments since 1961. One example of this self-questioning happens in one of the basic documents prepared for the Second Conference of CONCP in Dar es Salaam in 1965, a document signed by individuals from all the movements. The conclusions drawn from this analysis of the existence of a 'reformist bourgeoisie' were always hesitant. Any thought that Caetano represented in any sense such a reformist group was definitely rejected, as is clear from the article in *Mozambique Revolution* published in 1969.

The coherence of the position of the various movements in CONCP was not reproduced in the documents published by the UPA. This latter organization, less analytic in its approach, tended to stick closely to an analysis of what had occurred in Angola, without seeking to situate Portugal in the framework of the capitalist world economy. However, despite starting from this viewpoint, UPA came up with a pungent description of the Portuguese white settlers which was in fact one we might expect, given the other analyses of the nature of the Portuguese system.

The movements in the Portuguese colonies felt the need to explain to themselves and to the world why they had not achieved independence as early as other states, in the wake of the African independences around 1960. The answer they found was simple and analytically crucial to their whole subsequent strategy of liberation: Portugal's role in the world system was substantially different from other European countries who had colonial domains in Africa. Hence the mode of struggle for independence employed by most African states, the demand for decolonization, was seen as an implausible option. Since Portugal could not afford to decolonize, the leaders of the national liberation movements could not afford to count on such a possibility.

The Facts About Portugal's African Colonies
Abel Djassi (Amilcar Cabral)

> *This extract from a pamphlet published by the Union
> for Democratic Control in London in 1960 was writtenn*

by Amilcar Cabral under the pseudonym of Abel Djassi,
and is probably the first significant publication by the
movements in the English language. Cabral was already
at that time Secretary-General of the PAIGC.

Eleven million Africans suffer under Portuguese colonial domination. The Portuguese colonies cover an area of about two million square kilometres (about 5% of the entire Continent and larger than the combined areas of Spain, France, Germany, Italy and England). The African population of these colonies has been enslaved by a small country, the most backward in Europe.

These two million square kilometres are rich in natural resources. The land supports agriculture and livestock breeding. The sub-soil contains iron, coal, manganese, oil, bauxite, diamonds, gold, precious metals, etc. The variety and beauty of nature offer possibilities for tourists.

Side by side with these natural riches, some of which are exploited by the colonialists, Africans live on a sub-human standard — little or no better than serfs in their own country.

After the slave trade, armed conquest and colonial wars, there came the complete destruction of the economic and social structure of African society. The next phase was European occupation and ever-increasing European immigration into these territories. The lands and possessions of the Africans were looted, the Portuguese 'sovereignty tax' was imposed, and so were compulsory crops for agricultural produce, forced labour, the export of African workers, and total control of the collective and individual life of Africans, either by persuasion or violence.

As the size of the European population grows, so does its contempt for Africans. Africans are excluded from certain types of employment, including some of the most unskilled jobs.

Racial discrimination is either openly or hypocritically practised. Africans have been driven from the remaining fertile regions left to them in order that *colonatos* for Europeans could be built there.* Political, social or trade union organisation is forbidden to the Africans, who do not enjoy even the most elementary human rights. When the United Nations Charter was adopted, giving all countries the right of self-determination, the Portuguese Constitution was hastily changed. The name 'colony' was replaced by 'overseas territory', thus enabling Portugal to claim that she had no colonies and could not therefore make reports on her 'African territories'.

As Africans have awakened and begun moving towards freedom and independence, efforts to control and oppress them have redoubled. A political secret police was created. The colonial army was reinforced. In Portugal, military mobilisation was increased, attended by warlike manoeuvres and demonstrations of force. Air and sea bases were built in the colonies. Military observers were sent to Algeria. Strategic plans were drawn up for a war

---

* *Colonatos* — groups of farms reserved for European settlers.

against the Africans. Political and military agreements were made with other colonial powers. New and increasingly advantageous concessions were given to non-Portuguese enterprises.

The demands of the Africans and the work of their resistance organisations, which are forced to remain underground, have resulted in severe repression. All this was and still is perpetrated in the name of 'Civilisation and Christianity' by the most retrograde kind of colonial system.

Both the human and natural resources of these colonies are exploited and mortgaged at the lowest possible value. The colonialists deny the practice of Christian principles in their lack of reverence for the human being, and they do everything they can to hide the true effects of their 'civilising influence'.

While humanity discovers its unity and strives for community of interest based on peace and the recognition of the Rights of Man, of freedom and equality among all peoples, the Portuguese colonialists prepare to launch new colonial wars.

Portuguese colonialism can offer only flimsy arguments, devoid of human or scientific content, to justify its existence and conceal its crimes. These arguments are negated by the very facts which the Portuguese colonialists attempt to conceal. The salient arguments are as follows:

(a) 'Historical rights.'
   Answer:
   This concept, so far as 'Portuguese Africa' is concerned, was buried at the Berlin Conference in 1885 by the colonial powers, and has, in any case, never been accepted by Africans.
(b) The process of 'civilising' — the real means and results of which are carefully concealed by Portugal.
   Answer:
   This process is being carried out by an underdeveloped country with a lower national income than, for example, Ghana, and which has not as yet been able to solve its own problems.
(c) The colonialist 'theory' of so-called 'assimilation'.
   Answer:
   This is unacceptable not only in theory but even more in practice. It is based on the racist idea of the 'incompetence or lack of dignity' of African people, and implies that African cultures and civilisations have no value.
(d) The idea of creating a 'multi-racial society' within the colonies, legally based on the Native Statute — Portuguese *apartheid.*
   Answer:
   This prevents any social contact with the so-called 'civilised' population, and reduces 99% of the African population to sub-human conditions.
(e) 'National unity' with the colonies, a concept which was hastily brought into the Portuguese Constitution as a means of avoiding the responsibilities set out in the United Nations Charter.
   Answer:
   This disgraceful subterfuge totally contradicts all the geographic, historic,

ethnic, social and cultural facts, and it even comes into conflict with the
laws prevailing in the colonies concerning their practical relationship with
Portugal.

(f) The 'state of peace' that is claimed by Salazar to exist.

Answer:

In these colonies Africans have no political rights and cannot form trade
unions. Africans do not enjoy even the most elementary human rights.
Despite a vicious secret police, an inhuman colonial administration, and
brutal soldiers and settlers' militia, African nationalist organisations are
offering active resistance to Portuguese colonialism.

It might be asked whether Portuguese colonialism has not done a certain
amount of good in Africa. Justice is always relative. For the Africans who for
five centuries have lived under Portuguese domination, Portuguese
colonialism represents a reign of evil, and where evil reigns there is no place
for good. As for other people, particularly those who fortunately have not
known colonial domination, they will first have to acquaint themselves with
all the facts before passing judgment.

Those people who really love truth and justice must overcome the barriers
that Portugal sets up against visitors to these colonies. They must go there
without allowing themselves to be deceived in any way and they must carefully study the real situation of the people. They must observe the whole
truth of what is happening there, and then they will be able to judge the
'civilising influence' of Portugal. When they know the truth these people
cannot but realise the desperate situation of Africans in the Portuguese
territories. This colonialism is in process of systematically depriving Africans
of the most essential requirements for living, and has taken a heavy toll in
African lives, suffering and humiliation.

Portugal is an underdeveloped country with 40% illiteracy and with one
of the lowest standards of living in Europe. If she could have a 'civilising
influence' on any people, she would be accomplishing a kind of miracle.
Colonialism, a historical phenomenon which is now disappearing, has never
depended on miracles to keep it alive. Portugal is exercising the only kind
of 'civilising influence' she can — one that corresponds to the type of colonialism she has adopted and to her position as a colonial power whose
economy, culture and civilisation are backward.

Colonial Assimilation in Left Vocabulary
M.A.C.

*This extract is from the Manifesto of the Movimento
Anti-Colonialista (M.A.C.), an early movement which
grouped together many of the persons who later became*

leaders in the various movements of the CONCP.

The thesis that the liberty and progress of our peoples is dependent upon a prior progressive politico-social revolution in Portugal is none other than the theory of colonial assimilation dressed up in a vocabulary that claims to be revolutionary. This thesis consecrates the pretension that Portugal ought to constitute for all time, or at least for some period of time, a nation-model for the peoples she dominates.

'Salazarism', the Portuguese variant of Fascism, is not our principal enemy. 'Salazarism' is a virulent instrument, but inevitably a temporary one, of ancient and hateful Portuguese colonialism. Portuguese colonialists and colonial exploitation underlay, truly and unquestionably, the creation and reinforcement of 'Salazarism' over thirty years of sad history.

The long-term factors which have determined the lives of our peoples, the specific conditions of our communities in practice, the concrete content of the present-day situation of our peoples, the need to mobilize all Africans for the anti-colonial struggle, the unfolding prospect of our liberating and progressive struggle — all this means that it is impossible to allow the assimilation of Africans into Portuguese politico-social movements. The 'deportugalization' of the interests and preoccupations (often egotistic), of the acts and psychology of a small minority of Africans, can and must be useful to the 'process' of de-alienation of our peoples, to our struggle against Portuguese colonialism.

Our peoples and the Portuguese people have different destinies which we shall fulfil in peace, amity, co-operation and equality of rights and duties. We are African peoples and it is to Africa that our destinies have been and always will be linked.

But to struggle against Portuguese colonialism, our peoples must assist as much as possible the people of Portugal in their struggle against fascism. Because as long as the Portuguese colonial structure endures, it is certain that the Portuguese people will run the risk of being the victim of fascist dictatorships. Therefore, the Portuguese Opposition, which struggles for the liberation of the Portuguese people from the fascist regime, can, by means of an effective alliance with our movements of national liberation taking the form of a united front against fascism and colonialism, give concrete proof that it defends the fundamental interests of the Portuguese people and that it does indeed respect the fundamental Rights of Man.

M.A.C., interpreting the sentiments of our peoples, who desire a frank and loyal collaboration with the Portuguese people, on the basis of mutual respect and the right to self-determination and independence, is ready to enter an effective alliance with the democratic and progressive forces of Portugal, at whatever level the Portuguese Opposition is disposed to do it, for the common struggle to liquidate totally Portuguese colonialism and fascism.

Why We Fight
FRELIMO

A statement by FRELIMO published in the Boletim de
Informacao *(Dar es Salaam) in September 1963.*

A large part of the Black population is unemployed. Do they not need to
feed themselves adequately? Do they not also need to educate their children?
   There is a great difference between a White and a Black. The White,
because he is white, finds a job easily, earns a good living, can support his
family and cover his expenses including the education of his children. While
the African obtains work with difficulty, and as a result earns miserably little,
not being able to satisfy even his minimum needs.
   When there is a competition, 300—400 persons enter, but systematically
only Whites win even if there are Africans with greater knowledge.
   Why is it that the African, owner of the land, must suffer and the White
enrich himself at the cost of the African?
   Do the people of Mozambique wish to continue to suffer? We are certain
they do not.
   Almost all the commerce of Mozambique is in the hands of Whites and
Indians. There are very few Blacks in commerce, and those who are are poor.
   It is rare to see a bar or a shop belonging to a Black because it is difficult
to get a licence. When they can, they construct a shed and use it to earn their
daily bread; but when it's discovered by the police, the poor man's bar is
seized and closed. The Black woman who sells peanuts in the streets, does it
furtively, fearing that 'Papa Policeman' will say to her: 'Come now, mama,
you can't sell peanuts here, do you hear? Go home and hurry up.'
   We Mozambicans cannot continue to accept such humiliations. The White
man cannot abuse our Black mothers. She is a Mozambican lady. She has a
right to life.
   In industry the same things happen as in commerce. There are many
African workers who are quite skilled in their jobs, but badly paid. Where
then is the equality between Whites and Blacks?
   The large majority of Mozambican Blacks live from agriculture. Everything that the Black has achieved or won, he has done with great effort. The
White man has seized everything and the Black must be satisfied with a
capulana (sarong) in exchange for maize, catfish, peanuts, or even cotton.
   Cotton is one of the sources of wealth for the Portuguese in Mozambique,
and they have accumulated many fortunes.
   It is very sure that the African is suffering, working only for the White
man. Thus, for example, in the province of Cabo Delgado the Portuguese
use a method to buy cotton cheap. They create many categories in terms
of which payment to the Black man is made. Thus even the highest quality
of cotton is placed in a lower category; and the African can never protest.
   The modern methods the Portuguese have introduced into agriculture in
Mozambique have as their object perfecting the exploitation of the land

and the workers. The new technical methods serve only to develop those crops that interest Portuguese companies without any consideration for the interests of the Africans. Furthermore, the new methods the Portuguese use tend to favour and legitimize the swindle that occurs when products are bought from African growers.

The education and training of Mozambican youngsters require money. But if Africans earn very little, where can they get this money? It's almost impossible. This is why the number of educated Africans is still rather small. There is only one barrier to their mental development — MONEY. When the White man educates his children, the Black man is perturbed, because he wishes to do the same but cannot for lack of money.

Faced with all these obstacles in trade, in industry, in agriculture, and in education, what do the people of Mozambique say? Do they wish to continue under the yoke of the colonialist fascist Salazar?

No, we have all had enough of so much oppression. The torture is coming to an end. It is time to demand our rights. But if the Portuguese do not wish to leave, what are we going to do? ONLY FIGHT. It is only through struggle that they will be convinced we want freedom, that we want to take back our land.

Mozambique is only for Mozambicans and we do not accept the intervention of any outsider. Many promise us their assistance but it is we who must take the initiative. We are going to expel the Portuguese!

Let us shout at the top of our lungs: FREEDOM! FREEDOM! FREEDOM!

Portuguese Settlement in Angola
UPA

Extract from a Declaration of the Steering Committee of the Uniao das Populacoes de Angola (UPA), issued in Leopoldville in 1960 under the title 'The Struggle of Angola'.

For years the Portuguese colonialist policy has been to send to Angola all the poverty stricken, the failures from the metropolitan areas, and the poor and illiterate peasant families of Portugal in order to establish them as colonists on this land wrested from the native peoples. As a result, the natives, to whom the land rightfully belongs, know only the blackest misery.

The influx of peasants has brought competition between Portuguese and African workers. To reduce the number of unemployed Portuguese, the colonial administration grants them a monopoly over all kinds of labour; taxi drivers, waiters in hotels and restaurants, street sweepers, clerks in shops — all such occupations are reserved for Portuguese workers. In construction work, the foremen and artisans are all Portuguese, while only the unskilled labour is left to the Africans. Because of this gross discrimination, the Portuguese labourers are better paid and enjoy all the social advantages that are denied to their African colleagues.

All the Africans who fail to find work, either in the cities or in the country, are recruited with or without their consent as *contratados*. Thus, it is that today, in spite of the abolition of forced labour by the International Labour Conference held at Geneva in 1931, Portuguese colonialism upholds a slave economy, of which Angola is an outstanding example.

The forced labour market supports and, at the same time, undermines the economy of the country. Continued recourse to slavery is determined by an essential factor — the present-day state of agrarian and pre-industrial economy of Portugal and thus the shortage and lack of Portuguese capital in the control of colonial resources. All sectors of Angolan activity are supported by a labour market based on contracts furnished by the official authorities.

Forced recruitment in itself constitutes a soul-searing sight, which recalls that of the days of trade in black slaves inaugurated on the coasts of West Africa by these same Portuguese people, following the example of the Carthaginians. No selection is made; no social position is taken into consideration; households with children are recruited and separated and assigned to different regions. At the end of a term of forced labour, the length of which is never defined because it is left to the discretion of the colonist, the members of a family may be unable to reunite because death, assassination, and often deportation — in cases of disobedience — have been perpetrated by the feudal masters, that is, the colonial administration and the colonist . . . .

The Political Situation in Portugal and the Liberation Struggle in the Portuguese Colonies
L. de Almeida et al.

*This was one of the 'basic documents' prepared for the
Second Conference of CONCP 3—8 October 1965, held
in Dar es Salaam. The authors were L. de Almeida (MPLA),
A. Braganca (then of the Secretariat of CONCP), A.
Duarte (PAIGC), P. Mocumbi (FRELIMO), and E.
Rocha (MPLA).*

Neo-colonialism is undoubtedly the main obstacle to be overcome by the African masses, if they are to fulfil their aspirations of complete independence.

Although Portugal is a colonial country, its economy exhibits those characteristics peculiar to underdevelopment: an agriculture essentially directed at the satisfaction of internal needs, an unimportant industrial sector, an extremely limited consumption sector and an export sector based on a fairly large number of processed primary products.* The imperialist powers (Great Britain, France, Germany and the USA) share among each other the continued economic control over this country.

Because of this, Portugal could not shield itself from the impact of the offensive of the financial circles of the neo-capitalist states, West Germany and France in particular, nor was it able to ignore the changes occurring in Europe and Africa.

It is the existence of the vast 'Portuguese' socio-economic domain represented essentially by the colonies, which has permitted the Portuguese bourgeoisie to close the breaches in the structure of the 'New State' by resorting to the type of solutions that might be termed 'flight forward'. The massive emigration of the working masses, together with the systematic pillage which took place in the colonies, have contributed — by leading to the stagnation of the economy and the survival of a parasitic bourgeoisie — to hampering the advent of the industrial revolution in Portugal.

The internal contradictions of the regime, the retrograde position of Portugal and its increasing isolation internationally, the threat which the liberation movements of the peoples of the Third World constitute, and the pressure stemming from international finance nevertheless alarmed certain sectors of the Portuguese bourgeoisie, even before the outbreak of the wars of liberation.

It is the national liberation struggles in Angola, Guinea, and Mozambique that account for the alterations which one may presently observe in the political and economic structures of Portugal, changes that have occasioned internal disputes within the regime.

European imperialism, in compliance with the new neo-colonialist strategy, had decided to launch an economic offensive with the aim of acquiring new markets in the underdeveloped areas of the old continent. Portugal is thus invited to participate in the economic and political construction of Europe.

In the last decade, Portugal has been increasingly penetrated by capital from external sources, bringing in its wake the development of more modern economic methods as contrasted to the traditional sector. Even in the colonies, there is occurring a transformation, albeit to a lesser degree, of the classical exploitative schema by the establishment of associated capitalist interests that take the form of large commercial and mining firms.

Within the Portuguese bourgeoisie, there exists an increasing split of economic and political interests. Without question, the interests of the conservative element, the owners of the latifundia, the textile and cork manufacturers, those of the poor and moderate income settlers diverge more and more from the interests of that fraction of the Portuguese bourgeoisie allied

---

* This backwardness in the economy is aggravated by the feudal and para-feudal systems of land tenure.

to European high finance. These differences appear concretely as a political struggle within the structure which until now has served as the guarantee of the compromise between the various elements of the Fascist Portuguese bourgeoisie: the *'Uniao Nacional'*.

The commencement of the wars of liberation gave new ammunition to the reformist wing of the bourgeoisie, whose political representatives are former collaborators of the Fascist regime. This group, while expressing scepticism about the possibility of Portugal being able to remain in the colonies by means of the army, need a transition period in order to attain political power, to readjust the country's fragile economic and financial structures in a European direction, and eventually to create neo-colonialist apparatuses in our countries.

The penetration of capital into Portugal and the colonies since 1961, the issuing of new basic laws, the effort to promote new African elites, constitute various attempts to mystify the peoples of our countries, as well as African and international public opinion. It is important to notice that these attempts were made at a time when certain political figures, belonging to the reformist section of the bourgeoisie, held portfolios in the government. They are part of the efforts towards the gradual creation of such neo-colonialist apparatuses. If the reformist bourgeoisie were to start a process of 'decoloni-zation' the exact forms it would take after they took power would depend, in each of our countries, on the comparative strength of popular forces as mobilized in the liberation movement versus that of the repressive armies.

The African social instruments of this neo-colonialist policy might be located principally in the strata of the petty bourgeoisie and the traditional chiefs.

However, Salazarism, the viewpoint of the ultra-colonialist elements of the bourgeoisie, has succeeded in the short run in postponing the disaster that the loss of the colonies would represent to the Portuguese bourgeoisie by preventing the increasing conflicts between the opposing elements within the Portuguese ruling classes from exploding.

The unstable equilibrium of the Portuguese bourgeoisie rests at one and the same time on the intensification of repression in the colonies and on the appeal to foreign capital. But the financial burdens of maintaining repressive armies in three zones of combat, as well as a police apparatus, surpasses the economic possibilities of an underdeveloped country such as Portugal.

Discontent increases among the popular strata, the youth, the middle bourgeoisie and even in certain Catholic circles. Once the fragile economic structures of Portugal and the sacrifices imposed upon the working classes were no longer sufficient to sustain the costs of the colonial war, it became necessary to appeal for international military and financial assistance. The first countries which lent their aid to Portuguese colonialism were Spain and South Africa, but later there came the various NATO countries, in particular West Germany, Great Britain and the USA. The present regime is thus able to continue to wage its colonial wars by a combination of past accumulation of financial reserves, extraordinary taxes and foreign loans.

But neither the doctrine of the *Estado Novo* nor the moral support of the

Church provides ideological or moral justification for this genocidal enterprise.

As the struggle of our peoples becomes deeper and more extensive, military costs go up, and the Fascist bourgeoisie ties Portuguese monopoly capital ever more closely to imperialism. The contradictions within the bourgeoisie itself become sharper, which will speed up the pauperization of the petty and middle bourgeoisie, and the intensification of the anti-Fascist struggle.

The ultra-colonialist segment of the bourgeoisie must face up to the historical impossibility in political, economic and even intellectual terms of its perceiving the national liberation movement intelligently in the new spirit of our times. The bourgeoisie pursues the logic of its options: it will die as its world disappears. The independence of our countries will bring about its destruction. It has no choice but to continue the war *at any cost*.

The armed insurrection of the Angolan people, in February 1961, aroused at first a homogeneous reaction in Portugal: the propaganda apparatus of the regime, counting on patriotic sentiments with racist overtones, and taking advantage of the absence of an anti-colonialist political consciousness, was able to bring the Portuguese people to approve of 'killing Blacks'.

The violent reaction of the ruling groups in Lisbon to the position taken at the UN by the United States demonstrates the extent to which a climate of national exaltation reigned in Portugal at that time. Chauvinistic mobilization created a base for the 'depolarization' of the anti-Fascist resistance.

Then, in what constituted a second stage, the contradictions became sharpened between, on the one hand, an intermediate bourgeoisie allied to international capitalism, which supported a certain political liberalization, and on the other hand, a national monopolist bourgeoisie. This phase, having begun in early 1963, saw the development of two parallel movements: the first, an evolution in the economic policy of the Portuguese state; and the second, a psychological change in the Portuguese people itself.

We can state that the first round of the struggle within the Portuguese bourgeoisie was won by the lobby of the monopolist bourgeoisie. They were able to ensure that the regime continued along the same lines of ultra-colonialist exploitation based on traditional administrative and political patterns.

But the wind of change that now blows in Portugal is in part the consequence of political pressure exerted by the imperialist powers. Granted access by the new administrative regulations to investment in the colonies and drawing on their experience elsewhere in Africa, those powers backed the regime in Lisbon financially, economically and militarily.

As for the level of the popular masses, here we witness a tangible movement of political reaction against the pursuit of colonial wars.

In the beginning of 1961, the fact of a colonial war constituted a source of economic profit for all those involved in the Portuguese army: the General Staff and the various military commands, the majority of the junior officers and the draftees. There has been little change in this position since.

The movements of protest and the ever increasing number of deserters still result from individual attitudes. They tend to be found primarily among the junior officers who have come from the universities where they had taken part in campaigns of political clarification on the question of colonialism.

The three categories of factors which exert an influence on the anti-colonialist attitudes of the Portuguese people are as follows:

a) the action taken by progressive political movements which feel the need to attack Fascism on its home ground;

b) the increase in the cost of living, aggravated by wartime sales taxes;

c) the increasingly important action taken by the advanced sectors of the Portuguese students.

It is obvious that a complete evaluation of the impact of the colonial war must consider the qualitative differences that have emerged within Portuguese society, as a result of the fighting on three fronts which are taking their toll in increasing casualty rates and exhaustion. In the last analysis, it will only be in the reaction of the population to these realities that we can expect a mobilization against the colonial war in Portugal.

Conclusions

1) The impact of the European neo-capitalist offensive upon the fragile socio-economic structures of Portugal has brought about a split in the economic interests of the Portuguese bourgeoisie. This split has repercussions on the regime. The contradictions within the Portuguese social strata have become sharper due to the national liberation struggles.

2) Economic, political and psychological motives explain why the most retrograde sector of the ruling bourgeoisie fights to keep the political and economic status quo and pursue the colonial wars.

3) Taking into account the present state of relations of internal and international forces, some changes in the Portuguese political scene may well occur shortly. In this case, the reformist bourgeoisie would play a decisive role on the basis of a compromise with international finance.

4) This sector of the bourgeoisie would attempt to apply neo-colonialist solutions which might nonetheless differ from country to country, depending on the strength of the local forces and also on the political position of the neighbouring states.

5) Despite the serious differences of orientation among the various trends of the Portuguese opposition, we must take their struggle against the Salazar regime and colonialism to be a political fact favourable to our cause of national liberation.

6) While recommending increasing cooperation between the Portuguese democratic opposition and the liberation movements within the CONCP on the basis of mutual advantage, we must bear in mind that the objective of our struggle is a form of national independence that excludes any neo-

colonialist solution.

A Parasite Country Par Excellence
MPLA

*This article, under the rubric 'Facts from the History
of Colonialist Portugal', appeared in* Angola in Arms,
*an MPLA publication issued in Dar es Salaam, in Year I,
No. 5, July/Aug./Sept. 1967. Slight editing has been
necessary to render parts of it intelligible in English.*

During the second half of the 15th Century and the first half of the 16th,
the Portuguese pirates, incited by an unchecked greed, arrived in Angola,
Mozambique, India and Brazil. Attacked by cholera, they threw themselves
into the practice of genocide and pillage, savagely and sadistically murdering
the people they found with the objective of accumulating wealth.

Ships arrived in Lisbon fully loaded with gold, precious stones, spices and
ivory and even with elephants and rhinoceroses! All that they found they
robbed! But especially slaves, African slaves, to toil and manure with their
sweat the lands of Alentejo; others they brought simply to be used as
servants or as symbols of 'exoticism' in the houses of the wealthiest families.

From 1500 on, incalculable fortunes began to pour into Lisbon; the
Portuguese people, until then poor and repressed, abandoned their previously
pursued occupations – some to dedicate themselves to this bewildering new
life, others to flattery of the wealthy and still others to the mendacity.

The avarice was in such a high degree that the caravels carried loads double
or triple their normal capacity, and the more they carried the faster they were
shipwrecked! This is the real reason for the so-called 'tragic maritime history'
which has been the source of many crocodile tears on the part of the fascist
historians'.

The great German bankers of the time, those associated with the famous
Fugger and Weser Houses, came to establish their main branches in Lisbon.
The Italian cities of Florence, Venice and Genoa, citadels of the famous
Medici, Bardi and Caponi, became totally bankrupted as they stopped being
the centres of the commerce with the East, their 'glorious' place was now
taken over by Portugal.

Lisbon, as the Salazarist 'historians' presumptively write, became a 'cosmo-
politan city'; from all points in Europe the great traders flew to Lisbon; and
bankers too, from the best representatives of the German banks to those of
the prominent Hanseatic League, and from England and France. On the other
hand, the Portuguese set up commercial representation in Flanders and in
England.

All looked as if it would never end. The owners of Portugal were living

totally wrapped up in a golden dream of Alice in Wonderland, and the king
of this epoch, Manuel the First, was given the epithet, the *Fortunate* . . .

It is only this idyllic aspect which is narrated to us by the history manuals
of the Salazarists. However, the sordid side of the history of Portugal —
together with the good — is presented by several historians, including J.B.
Trend in his book *Portugal* (published in 1957 in London). We quote:

> They [the Portuguese] did not produce anything in their
> country; neither in agriculture nor in industry. Although, on the
> surface, all looked like a perpetual carnival, the nation was in its
> entirety begging for bread.

And he continues:

> The king had to order from Flanders many shiploads of wheat.
> After 1503—1504 a famine plague invaded the nation (in 1505).
> The tremendous wealth present in Lisbon was not usefully
> applied to the nation. In 1521 the hunger reached alarming pro-
> portions such that the poor who wandered through the streets of
> Lisbon often died and remained, for a long time, without being
> buried, lying on the streets. Cereals continued to be imported
> from abroad; Portugal began to import wheat and barley from
> France and North Africa as well as from Flanders.

Food products from salted meat to wheat and fish all came from abroad.
All the elementary manufactured goods, from textiles to furniture, were
imported. *Portugal was the Parasite Country par excellence*. This was and
continues to be the preponderant feature of the Portugal of yesterday and
today.

But all this is natural, some will probably say. This also happened in
England during the period of primitive capital formation, when the poor
wandered through the streets and were decapitated by the 'very Christian'
King Henry the VIIth. But it isn't! The essential thing to keep in mind is the
fact that, while Holland, England, France and the other countries took
advantage of the exploitation of the wealth of their colonies to industrialize
their economies — to jump from the Middle Ages to Capitalism — Portugal,
on the contrary, became more and more economically retarded. Instead of
industrializing their country, by building up first agriculture and then small
industry, the Portuguese abandoned both, and with the wealth they
plundered from the African, Asian and American people of their colonies,
they imported those commodities essential to the life of any nation.

All Angolans know very well that the small Portuguese shopkeeper — the
one who spends his life selling all the petty things, including the
five cents of manioc flour and dry beans — is a clever but insidious robber.
But what is less well known by many Angolans is that these Portuguese
reveal themselves incapable of understanding the most elementary mechanics

of commerce on a large scale, because for this it is necessary to have an open mind and . . . to know some accounting!

Therefore the foreigners, particularly the Dutch, were the ones who took advantage of the incapacity of the Portuguese merchants, buying the spices in Lisbon and reselling them, at a price four or more times higher than the purchase price, in several markets across Central and Northern Europe. In their dealings the Dutch took advantage, among other things, of the repeated plagues and famines which constantly invaded Portugal and which forced her to buy food abroad at extraordinarily high prices.

Thus Portugal, the then wealthiest country in Europe, found herself deeply in debt. And, as the writer Perry Anderson in his book *Portugal et la Fin de l'Ultra-Colonialisme* states 'The debts of Portugal vis-a-vis Flanders reached such a high amount that in 1543 the interest rate in Antwerp was 50%. In 1544 the real debt was 2 million *cruzados* and in 1552 3 million; in 1560 the debt was so high that the creditors refused to charge any interest.'

In all this a unique phenomenon is clearly apparent: the wealth stolen by Portugal, rather than assisting its modernization, was used in the industrialization of other European countries.

The Portuguese pirates came to the colonies to rob the spices, the gold, the ivory from India and Angola for the Dutch to industrialize their country!

And later, during the Kingdom of John III, faced with constant pressure from the numerous creditors, the pirate king decided to entrust the Jewish bankers with the mission of settling the debts of the nation; with great stupefaction the bankers arrived at the conclusion that, in order to pay for the deficit in the balance of payments, an amount was needed more than four times the annual revenue of the nation itself.

Alarmed at such a 'brilliant' record, and trying desperately to solve the situation, the 'most Christian' king of the bandits took the measure he deemed appropriate; he launched the pogroms against the Jews and set up the Holy Office Tribunal run by that most saintly man — Saint Ignatius of Loyola (the sadly famous Inquisition).

From then on, under the accusation of practising sorcery, thousands upon thousands of Jews were burnt alive, while many others were expelled from Portugal. And . . . since the money and goods belonging to them were affected' by fetish, they were all, naturally, confiscated by the 'Christian' state so that the debts could be paid.

In a sign of gratitude for the services rendered to the Church and the nation the 'great' King John III of Portugal was given the epithet *Piedoso* (Pious).

Following the commercial bankruptcy which resulted from the tremendous slowdown of the spice trade with India, another golden period occurred with the sugar trade, this time with the 'exploration' of the sugar companies in Brazil during the 17th Century. But by the end of the century new competitors came into the picture, the Britons and the French, with their own colonies in West Indies. Thus, once again, Portugal's economy fell into the lethargic state from which it only came out in the 18th Century with the 'discovery' of the gold and diamond mines in *Minas Gerais*, also in Brazil. However, this golden epoch was of a rather short duration for in 1822 Brazil became independent from Portugal and the 'mother country' continued its normal course as an indebted, poor, and stagnated country.

But one may ask oneself again: What did all this money get spent on? Most of it was wasted on several commercial ventures which only benefited the other European countries, while the rest was lavishly spent on many luxurious objects to satisfy an infernal and offensive but . . . simple-minded love of luxury.

For example, the Salazarist 'historians' themselves, very delighted, narrate that King John V, without knowing what to do with so much gold brought in from Brazil, ordered that the *Mafra Convent* be built for him and that a huge carillon from England, made of solid gold, be used on the structure. The British industrialists, having considered this an absurd expenditure, decided to ask whether the Portuguese monarch was really ordering from England a solid-gold-made carillon. Simpleminded, the King of pirates, with the intention of boasting his wealth, ordered in reply two similar solid-gold-made carillons!

Finally, by the end of the 19th Century and during the first 67 years of the 20th, Portugal enjoyed a new period of national grandeur, thanks to the exploitation of the peoples and wealth of her African colonies, more particularly Angola.

But, as in the past, Portugal did not industrialize itself. Most of the tremendous profits made in the colonies are and continue to be sucked up by the international monopolies, while the relatively small but still big portion which accrues to the small Portuguese oligarchy is lavishly wasted in the Estoril casinos as well as at the expensive cabarets in Paris.

Therefore we are, in reality, faced by a factual demonstration of the incapacity on the part of the Portuguese leaders to bring their country out of its secular retardation. This fact is so entrenched in the mentality of the present leaders of the fascist regime of Portugal that they don't even hesitate to boast publicly that 'Portugal is and will always be an agricultural country!'

But no wonder. Why will this not be the case if this country has already accustomed itself to live as a parasite of other peoples?! . . .

Caetano: No Essential Change
FRELIMO

> *This extract is from* Mozambique Revolution, *the principal publication of FRELIMO which appeared in Dar es Salaam. It is found in No. 40, 25 September 1969, under the title 'Caetano, Capitalism, and Cabora Bassa*'.

Cold hard economic facts lie behind all the myths and nonsense which Caetano and others within the Fascist Portuguese government have put forward for maintaining their colonial rule in Africa. They are determined to hold on to their colonial possessions in Africa because these are the greatest source of their wealth, and they help to maintain the Fascist domination over Portuguese workers and peasants. That is why virtually half of Portugal's budget is devoted to the war in Africa.

At the same time, other capitalist countries also have taken a keen interest in the wealth which Portugal robs from Africa. To some extent Portugal fears the competition of countries like the USA and West Germany which have entered the economy of Mozambique and Angola, but Portugal needs the help of these capitalist nations both at home and abroad. Consequently, Caetano has inherited from Salazar the policy of selling the riches of Mozambique, Angola and Guinea to the allies of NATO, with the specific intention of using them as a shield against the ever expanding action of FRELIMO, MPLA and PAIGC. Franco Nogueira, Portugal's Foreign Minister, has openly stated that: '*The Portuguese government is in a position to demand the co-operation of Western powers in the defence of Portuguese possessions in Southern Africa.*'

However, the propaganda of the Liberation Movements and their progressive allies forced Portugal to pay lip-service to some liberal tendencies in the capitalist countries. Her NATO allies have always been willing to help Portugal deceive public opinion in the West. E.g. Britain, being a major investor in Portugal and in the Portuguese colonies, has always helped to whitewash Portuguese Fascism and protect Portugal from its critics. Since Caetano came to power, the British press have engaged in a campaign to present him as a 'liberal', claiming that he is carrying out reforms within Portugal. *The deliberate lie that Caetano is a 'liberal' is intended to prepare the way for increasingly close relations between Portugal and the Western capitalist nations, especially with regard to Portugal's colonial policies.*

One of the many contradictions of colonialism is that, although the colonialists wanted quick profits, they were not even competent enough to discover how rich Africa really was. This was particularly true of the Portuguese who always hoped that in Africa they would find gold lying around on the ground ready to be picked up. In Mozambique this was not the case, so the Portuguese said that Mozambique was poor. In recent years, it has been becoming more and more obvious that Mozambique has tremendous mineral potential, apart from its agricultural wealth.

Western powers have looked with greedy eyes at the signs of the riches which lie under the soil of Mozambique, and by sharing out the whole of Mozambique in huge concessions to Western capitalist companies, the Portuguese government is gaining revenues to carry out its war of oppression, as well as giving other capitalist nations a direct stake in maintaining Portuguese colonialism. This is the way that Caetano is strengthening Portugal's alliances with all capitalists, racists and imperialists.

Mozambique has been appearing quite frequently in the last year or two

in the financial and commercial journals of the capitalist world. They have
been discussing the possibilities of coal, petroleum, natural gas, asbestos,
bauxite, iron, titanium, beryl, colombo-tantalite, lepidolite, crome, nickel,
bismuth, gold, silver, uranium, diamonds, microlite, tourmaline and mica.

Ever since the discovery in 1965 of natural gas in Pande (not far from
Beira) all the Western powers have been eager to prospect for oil and
natural gas in Mozambique, for the geological signs are all favourable. The
Portuguese government has granted concessions to over one dozen companies,
coming from the USA, West Germany, France and South Africa. Most of
these companies, such as Gulf Oil and the IPC, are already notorious for their
exploitation of the Middle East, Latin America and other parts of Africa.
Their presence in Mozambique represents a further threat to the peoples of
Mozambique. In fact, *the policy of encouraging these companies is part of
the Portuguese war against the people of Mozambique.*

Portuguese Colonialism in the Age of Imperialism
CONCP

> *Extract from a pre-conference discussion document
> prepared by CONCP for the International Conference
> of Solidarity held in Rome in June 1970.*

Portugal, the least advanced of the imperialist powers, has held on to its
colonies in Africa — Angola, Guinea Bissau and Mozambique — longer and
more desperately than any other. In the process its subordinate role in the
world imperialist system has deepened: the last of the colonial powers is now
little more than a neo-colony itself. Pressed from above and below — by
international business and political interests abroad; by the working class and
peasantry at home; and by the rising force of the liberation movements in
the overseas territories — the Portuguese ruling class finds itself left with little
time and little space . . . .

Relative to Portuguese, foreign investment has always played a dominating role in the overseas territories although in absolute terms, and compared
with recent developments, it has not been so very large. As a businessman in
Mozambique put it: 'When you judge the Government's attitude to foreign
capital today, you'll do well to remember that when Salazar took over in
Portugal just about forty years ago Mozambique was virtually owned by
foreigners — many of them British.' This situation can be traced back to the
beginning of the century when the chartered company was established as
the instrument of control — like the Cia da Mocambique which had sovereign
rights over the province of Manica e Sofala and was financed by British,
French and Belgian capital. This branch of foreign involvement is manifested
today in some of the large plantation and transporting companies like Sena

Sugar Estates, the Benguela Railway and DIAMANG. In 1926, however, with the accession to power of Antonio Salazar, there was immediate firm government control over the activities of these companies and the beginning of more than thirty years of a very introverted economic policy in the colonies that is too easily termed 'economic nationalism'. It was more than this and had all its roots in Salazar's philosophy of the 'New State'.

The economic developments in the colonies were, and still are, to a large extent a function of developments in the Portuguese economy − both in terms of the raw materials required and the availability of capital to invest in obtaining them. Thus, during the thirties and forties period of economic crisis and war, there was relatively little new investment by Portugal. This by no means meant that the colonies were disregarded; on the contrary, the idea of Portugal as an imperial power and the closer integration of the colonies and the metropole was a pillar of Salazar's theory of the New State. Portuguese colonial policy has been defined by one writer as falling into three distinct phases: the period of discoveries, the period of pacification and 'the period of exaggerated misconceptions of Portuguese colonial destiny as manifested since 1926'.

The New State, incorporated in the 1930 Colonial Act and the 1933 Organic Law centralised administration (thereby countering the early twenties trend towards administrative and political autonomy) and by presenting a united imperial front showed the world that Portugal was still a force to be reckoned with. The Colonial Act affirmed the unity and solidarity of a Portugal consisting of peoples ethnically, economically and administratively varied, but united in goals and interests. This 'colonial mystique from the values of the past and the promises of the future' was probably far more an objective creation in the face of disunity and political crisis at home and the sense of insecurity generated by previous Anglo-German plots to carve up the territories, followed by League of Nations proposals to control finances and hence also the colonies, than a reflection of average Portuguese sentiment, but there can be no doubt as to its success. The idea of the Lusitanian community centred on Lisbon soon established itself in the international arena and made its influence felt on all subsequent colonial legislation.

But the most important point to be borne in mind when considering this phenomenon is that in fact we are dealing with just another colonialist and imperialist set-up in which political power is directed towards economic gain by the 'mother country'. Nowhere is this better illustrated than in the case of cotton and the textile industry. In 1925 it was officially estimated that Portugal's annual requirement of raw cotton was approximately 17,000 tons, of which only 800 tons came from Mozambique and Angola. In 1926 the Portuguese Government decided to establish cotton as an African peasant crop − by a regime of forced cultivation. This was done by granting purchasing monopolies to concessionary companies who were made responsible for developing cotton growing by Africans within the area of their concessions and had the right to acquire and process all cotton produced. Cotton thus became an obligatory crop for Africans living in areas designated as cotton producing — a regulation harshly enforced by local administration officials, much to the detriment of the peasant's own subsistence crops.

A system of price control, compulsory quotas for supplies to Portugal and restrictions on local textile production ensured Portugal a supply of raw cotton at prices which gave her textile industry an advantage in the world market. At the same time the colonies provided a secure market for a large part of the industry's output. For Portugal the scheme was highly successful: in 1960 she received 87% of her raw cotton requirements from the colonies and ranked twelfth among European producers of cotton thread and cloth, with an industry comprising 419 factories employing a total of 70,000 workers. In 1963 cotton goods provided an export revenue of 1,500 million escudos ($52,5 million), about one eighth of visible exports. The growth of one of Portugal's most important industries can thus be traced directly to a conscious policy of colonial exploitation in which forced cultivation was an essential part . . . .

Portugal reaps other, more complex benefits from the possession of the colonies. They have a perpetual trade deficit with Portugal which buys many of its imports from them at prices below the world level. This surplus for Portugal is an important contribution to its own trade position as it has a chronically unfavourable balance with the rest of the world. Despite this, the fact that there is always a balance of payments surplus is due partly to invisible revenue from tourism and migrants' remittances but also to the surplus balances of the territories. In 1968 the overall balance of international payments of the escudo zone showed a surplus of 4,115 million escudos ($144 million approx.); the overseas territories together contributed 2,241 million escudos ($78 million approx.), more than half. These are derived mainly from mineral exports and from the earnings of the transit trade. The plans for complete integration of the overseas territories envisaged the establishment by 1972 of an area of free trade between Portugal and the overseas territories, and the free movement of capital and persons. Although some tariff barriers have been removed this still operates to the advantage of Portugal whose goods have a free market in the territories, often to the disadvantage of local industries. There has been no move to free the currency exchange controls that restrict the territories' trade. There is no free movement of capital — the escudo in the territories is not freely convertible to that of the metropole even though the territories are considered part of the escudo zone for balance of payments. Moreover, although the territories' surpluses are with foreign countries and thus in valuable foreign exchange (and in hard currency at that — Angola coffee goes to America, iron ore to Japan and West Germany, Mozambican and Angolan oil to America, South African payments for migrant labour are in gold), the territories do not have control over their own foreign exchange earnings.

Inter-territorial payments within the escudo zone are cleared through a central exchange which is the Bank of Portugal in Lisbon, where the exchange holdings of each territory are kept in separate reserve funds. All accounts are cleared in escudos and thus the net gold and foreign exchange earned by the territories benefit Portugal's account. The Portuguese concept of "economic integration" therefore means that diamonds produced in Angola are sold by Diamang to Portugal, who sells them on the international market and earns the foreign exchange. Deprived of these foreign exchange earnings and the profits, the territory in turn has to borrow from Diamang and receives a loan in escudos. In 1967 Mozambique had a balance of payments surplus with foreign countries of 923 million escudos ($32 million approx.), a balance of payments deficit of 333 million escudos ($12 million approx.) with Portugal, and yet it had to obtain a 150 million escudos ($5¼ million) loan from the Escudo Zone Monetary Fund to facilitate its payments to Portugal.

With the flood of foreign investment into the colonies in the past few years, mainly concentrated in the profitable export sectors of oil, minerals and a few crops, the economic raison d'etre for Portugal's policies is not hard to find. Indeed, Portugal is now going out of her way to do everything possible to encourage as much foreign capital as possible. In September 1969 the Portuguese Finance Corporation was created to promote financial operations and investments, especially those that involve relations with foreign countries. Its initial capital of $300 million has been subscribed by the Portuguese government and the overseas territories as well as by 'various banking and credit institutions' in Portugal, the latter being so completely tied up with international monopoly capital as to be merely a subsidiary of Western European and American financial combines.

A glance at the so-called Third National Development Plan reveals a similar trend. It was originally envisaged that 'national' sources would provide 64% of the total, including 15% from the Portuguese Government and almost 20% from the territorial governments. In the 1969 programme, however, financing from the central government has dropped to 6.5% and that of the territorial governments to less than 10% of the total. Compared with 1968, external financing was expected to rise from 2,768.7 million escudos ($97 million approx.) to 4,170 million escudos ($146 million approx.) Moreover, if the transitional Development Plan is anything to go by, actual government expenditure will not even reach this target. In Mozambique, for example, only 29.3% of the estimates were actually spent. Of this more than half went on transport and communications (presumably for the war effort), 49% of its original target, while only 25% of the original target was spent on health, education and welfare.

The Metropole Today
All these developments are hardly surprising when one considers that the same thing has been happening in Portugal itself, which is now virtually a colony of Western capital.

Foreign control permeates all major sectors of the economy except agriculture (and even this is now under pressure with the encouragement being given to the settlement of northern European farmers and the sale of large tracts of land). The most important banks — such as the Banco Nacional Ultramarino, la Banco Portugues do Atlantico, la Banco Burnay, la Banco Espirito Santo, la Banco Borges e Irmao- are dominated by foreign capital which through them control the most important national economic activities.

The Moncorvo iron mines, the most important in the country, belong to the German steel trust, Vereinigte Stahlwerke. The sixty most important uranian mines are British and American-owned — and Portugal is one of the world's most important suppliers of uranium. Wolfram production is controlled by British capital. Other less important minerals such as tin, molybdenum, coal, copper and manganese are all dominated by foreign interests. In other words, almost the entire natural resources of the country are controlled by foreign capital. And so are the service industries: production and distribution of electricity is dominated by SOFINA (USA), urban transport and water distribution are run by British companies, as is international radio-telephone communications.

Thus, the financial invasion of the colonies is a natural extension of the situation in Portugal, but South Africa also provides a route through which monopoly capital, already deeply entrenched there, can find access to the Portuguese colonies. The labour requirements of the South African mines early on led to the formation of important economic links between South Africa and Mozambique. Since the 1903 Witwatersrand Agreement South Africa has regularly been supplied with cheap migrant labour from Mozambique in return for agreements involving increased South African use of the port of Lourenco Marques and hard currency cash payments, which have made a significant contribution to the income of the Portuguese government of Mozambique. Until comparatively recently, though, the interdependence of the two countries was played down by their respective governments; old colonial rivalries and the theoretical differences between their racial policies coupled with the traditional South African disdain for the Portuguese, discouraged the extension of these links into other sectors of the economy.

The expansion of the activities of international capital in South Africa has probably been an important influence behind the recent increase in South African economic involvement in Angola and Mozambique, but the threat posed by the liberation wars has been largely responsible for the change in diplomatic attitudes. Faced with this danger the South Africans soon 'came to discover that their policies were not so very different after all from those of the Portuguese, and the discovery that they all shared a concept of white supremacy, whether called assimilation or apartheid, drew the countries of southern Africa into closer rapport'. This 'rapport' has since been considerably strengthened. As the South African Foreign Minister put it in April 1969, 'We are two very friendly countries and we are perfectly identified with each other as defenders of civilisation in Africa. We have a common mission to fulfil and we are fulfilling it. We South Africans, government and people, respect and admire the Portuguese, and we are fully aware that, in confronting and defeating terrorism, the Portuguese, are rendering a noteworthy service to the West and humanity itself.' On the military level, extensive assistance by South Africa — financial, material and in manpower, is well known. Financial involvement in mining in Angola and agriculture and transport in Mozambique have been outlined above. To foster closer trade relations between Angola, Mozambique and South Africa the Bank of Lisbon and South Africa was formed in 1965, resulting within a few years in South Africa replacing Britain as Mozambique's most important trading partner after Portugal. However, the ultimate in collaboration between the racist regimes and international capital will be achieved in the two major hydro-electric projects for Angola and Mozambique — the Cunene and Cabora Bassa.

Portuguese — S.A. Collaboration

The strategic advantages of Portuguese–South   African collaboration are by no means one-sided. Apart from her vast army Portugal has one very import-ant contribution to make to the alliance — oil. Despite extensive efforts no significant deposits of oil have yet been found in South Africa itself but in Cabinda alone Portugal is now producing 7.5 million tons of oil per year. Since her own requirements are only 3.75 million tons, this leaves a signi-ficant surplus which could be exported to South Africa. As the *Financial Times* has pointed out: 'The fact that Cabinda could, in the event of U.N. sanctions and blockades, supply the needs of most of Southern Africa . . . is an important new factor in the international equation.'

Strategic considerations have also played their part in the rapproche-ment between Portugal and the rest of Western Europe. Over the past few years almost every major foreign policy statement by the Portuguese Government has stressed the importance of Angola and Mozambique in securing Western control over the Atlantic from the West Coast of Africa, and over the Indian Ocean from the East Coast. Such pronouncements have inevitably been accompanied by demands for the extension of the NATO area to cover the colonies, a demand which in practice has long since been met. Portugal's relative success with this line of argument is closely linked with the 'open door' economic policy. It can hardly be coincidental that, 'the oldest ally' apart, the two countries with the heaviest financial involvement in Portugal and the colonies are those that have proved the staunchest allies in the colonial wars — USA and West Germany.

The war has not only created a political need for Portugal to search for allies but has also caused a drain on her financial resources which has made it imperative for her to find foreign credits to offset military expenditures. In 1967 Portugal's balance of payments surplus of 3,641 million escudos ($127 million) was due partly to its surplus on capital account with medium and long-term capital movements, mainly to credits for imports and financial loans. To give a few examples of this recent flow of foreign capital to Portugal: in the three years 1965–1967 loans to the public sector alone totalled $4,120 million including:
$345 million from U.S. banks

$984 millions for the bridge over the Tagus
$1,044 million external loans in U.S. dollars
$135 from Siemens/Kreditanstalt for the postal and telegraph service
$851 credits for shipbuilding.

In 1969 Marcelo Caetano admitted the close connection between the colonial wars and international financing: 'All the military effort overseas has been and will go on being supported from the ordinary income which before was largely used to cover development expenses. Now we have to face many of these expenses with money obtained by loans.' Hence Decree Law 47296 of 31 October 1966 which authorised the Minister of Finance to contract internal and external loans to finance the development plans.

The nature of the Portuguese governing elite itself and its relations with international capital helps to explain the speed with which the 1961 change of policy was able to take effect. The ownership of both land and industry in Portugal is concentrated in the hands of a few families who, protected by the Roman Catholic Church and the army, have been allowed free reign over the economy. The lack of domestic capital has always made members of this group receptive to links with foreign companies, but the fear that foreign capital could swamp them and usurp their control over the economy has also won widespread support for the pre-1961 restrictive policy. This conflict was disguised during the height of the Salazarist period but the influence of the 'outward-looking' capitalists within the government can be demonstrated by the fact that even in 1958 more than 48 former ministers and Salazarists, four governors of Angola and four ambassadors held directorships in the largest companies, most of which were foreign. The economic and political contacts already existed through which foreign firms could immediately take advantage of the relaxation of official controls.

Recently the Portuguese have been announcing plans involving the large-scale immigration of the whites into the colonies, associated with the Cabora Bassa and Cunene dam projects. This suggests that they intend to create a white power on the model of South Africa and Rhodesia.

In terms of Portugal's immediate national interests this plan must represent a certain sacrifice in favour of South Africa, for Portugal would be unable to supply more than a fraction of these immigrants herself. Total emigration to Africa in 1965 was only 14,012 and with her present labour shortage Portugal could not afford to step this up significantly even if she could provide the necessary incentives. The immigrants must clearly be collected from all poorer countries of Europe, with a probable contribution from South Africa and Rhodesia. As such their loyalties would be local and, rather than looking towards the Portuguese Empire, they would naturally turn to South Africa as the main protector of their interests.

Recent relations between Portugal and South Africa, culminating in Vorster's unprecedented visit to Lisbon, indicate that despite these drawbacks Portugal is intending to opt for the South African solution. This is not incompatible with her other recent tendency to seek closer relations with Europe. Both moves indicate that the Portuguese Government is being forced to recognise the reality of its subordinate role in the capitalist world.

The apparent conflict between 'Europe' and 'South Africa' is largely spurious. Much of the capital in South Africa is European and many of the big companies interested in the Portuguese territories operate from both Europe and South Africa. Portugal is not in the position of trying to decide whether to hand over control to South Africa or to Europe; the situation is rather that international capital, represented by both South African and European companies, is already taking control in the Portuguese colonies and is seeking the South African political solution as the best means of furthering its interests.

Portugal is not an Imperialist Country
Amilcar Cabral

Extract of a speech by Amilcar Cabral given at a solidarity rally in Helsinki (Finland) on 20 October 1971.

You know that in our fight we do not try to explain to our militants, our people, our populations, how deep and complex is the fight against imperialism. Our people's situation was such, prior to the beginning of the fight, our political experience so slight, that it would have been difficult for us to pose the question of this fight on the basis of one directly aimed against colonialism and imperialism. We were forced to conduct our people's mobilization and organization for the struggle, at first, on the basis of concrete everyday problems of their life, moving later to larger concepts, to generalized views of colonialism and imperialism. Today people understand very well what is meant by colonialism, and Portuguese colonialism in particular, and are beginning to develop in their minds a clear notion of the phenomenon of imperialism. But last year, during a meeting with the members of our party's local units, I was discussing with them problems concerning Portuguese colonialism, and I said that Portugal is not an imperialist country; it is a colonialist country in the imperialist chain, but that its own nature is not that of an imperialist country.

Anyone familiar with Portugal's economy throughout its history quickly realizes that the Portuguese economic substructure has never attained a level which we may term imperialist. After the Treaty of Methuen of 1701, Portugal became a semi-colony of England, and at the level of Africa's exploitation it has been and still is nothing but an intermediate agent of our people's imperialist exploitation. It is the policeman of this exploitation, but it is not the real imperialist power which exploits our people. We have but to be reminded that most Portuguese industries, including that of the famous Porto wine, railways, telephones, etc. belong, just as do Portuguese mines, to foreign enterprises. We have but to be reminded that more than 60% of its exports from Angola and Mozambique go to the U.S., England, Belgium, France, West Germany, but not to Portugal.

But my peasant comrade, from a village party unit, who knew nothing of such things, when he heard me say that Portugal is not imperialist, told me; 'Cabral, everyone tells us that we fight against imperialism, that we fight against the Portuguese, but now you're telling us that they are not imperialists; so, tell me: who is Mr. Imperialism that everyone speaks about but no one sees?.' We see thus posed, in the language of a peasant, the main question of the fight against imperialism, that is, the distinction between imperialism and imperialist domination. Sometimes we hear people cry out 'Down with imperialism' in their own country, but in reality they are fighting against imperialist domination. It appears to be of vital importance to distinguish imperialism from imperialist domination, to situate both in their historical perspective and to define their geographical locations.

As you well know, a new system of production and its distribution, called capitalism, emerged historically out of the Middle Ages. In certain countries capitalism developed with all the contradictions inherent in the development known as imperialism. Imperialism — as you know better than myself — is the result of the gigantic concentration of financial capital in capitalist countries through the creation of monopolies, and firstly of the monopolies of capitalist enterprises. This monopoly domination is essentially and characteristically an économic phenomenon. Then there follow implications of a political, social, cultural, moral character. We must thus distinguish the economic fact of these implications on the one hand, and characterize the relationship of capitalism with the rest of the world, on the other. It is not an overstatement to assert that, from the moment that the economic and financial (thus monopolistic) domination attained a certain level and thus was consolidated, a relentless struggle began between free enterprise capital and financial capital, the latter represented by monopolies and banks. Even a superficial analysis of contemporary and present-day economic history, shows that, in general, financial capital, i.e. imperialism, is the victorious element in this fight. This is to say that capitalism has given birth to imperialism, and has created the conditions necessary for the destruction of the former. You know that this new situation is characterized by complex contradictions that lead to a permanent confrontation, be it an open and peaceful one or not, between the imperialist countries themselves, in search of a new equilibrium in the relationship of forces, and in function of the need to obtain raw materials and markets. Imperialism appears, when analysed in this fashion, with its real face, situated where it really belongs, that is, in the capitalist countries which have become imperialist ones. Thus, imperialism exists in capitalist countries and not in our countries.

It was the steadily increasing need for new markets and raw materials, the insatiable thirst for surplus value, which determined the imperialist domination of the world. By the time imperialism had attained a very high level, it had already made a first division of the world; it is at the beginning of this century that it proceeded, as you know, to make a new partition, particularly of Africa, by means of the Berlin Conference. That is to say that the internal concentration of financial capital in capitalist countries goes hand in hand with the monopolization of colonies, their conquest by imperialist countries.

It is in the framework of this colonial monopoly that the sharpest contradictions among capitalist countries themselves have been revealed, leading to two world wars. It is also in this framework that it is interesting to consider how Portugal, a non-imperialist country, an underdeveloped country, succeeded in preserving its colonies, despite the fierce jealousy of the imperialist countries. We can say clearly that England is responsible for this success. At the time of the Berlin Conference, Portugal was really a semi-colony of England. England pursued the tactic of defending Portuguese interests vigorously because it knew that, if Portugal could preserve its colonies, England would be able to exploit them as if they were its own. England prevented Angola and Mozambique in particular, but also Guinea, the Cape Verde Islands, etc., from becoming prey for the other imperialist countries. In the course of the partition, they were preserved by Portugal but exploited by England as well.

Thus, imperialist domination is the economic and political domination of non-capitalist countries or peoples by imperialism or imperialist powers. This is to say that we consider imperialist countries as a core in the general framework of the world economy. They have created on their periphery countries dominated by imperialism. If a country was still at a non-capitalist stage of development, the domination was purely colonialist. If such a country had already certain beginnings of capitalism, the domination was neo-colonialist, or semi-colonial. Thus imperialism, or rather the domination of people by financial capital, operates in colonialist, neo-colonialist, or semi-colonialist forms. It is this domination which is found in our countries, from Vietnam or China, to Cuba, or Tierra del Fuego, or Chile, as well as for a time in certain European countries, such as Portugal and others. It is this imperialist-dominated area which is generally called today the poor South in contrast with the rich North.

But it is important to distinguish the various situations found in both the poor South and the rich North. It is not all homogeneous. We lack the time necessary to analyse this distinction. We would simply like to emphasize its existence. Countries such as Sweden, Finland and others, even though they belong to the rich North, have never been imperialist countries.

What is important is to conclude by saying that the fight against imperialism must be fought within the imperialist countries, and the struggle against imperialist domination must be fought in our own countries. In this fight against imperialist domination in our countries, we consider that the most important struggle today is the one directed against neo-colonialism. In its classical form colonialism exists no longer, even if we are fighting an archaic Portuguese colonialism, whereas neo-colonialism continues to establish its roots everywhere in the world by means of puppets in order to deceive the people in their struggle for real liberation. Cuba fought against a neo-colonialism practically as old as its fictitious independence, and was able to win. Vietnam presently fights courageously against an also quite neo-neo-colonialism, and will undoubtedly win in South Vietnam just as it has won in North Vietnam.

What is important is to recognize the obvious character of the intimate link between the fight against imperialism in imperialist countries, and that against the imperialist domination in our countries. The eventual destruction of financial capital within the capitalist world necessarily implies the destruction of imperialist domination. If, by some miracle, monopoly financial capital in the United States were to be destroyed, and if this country were to become a progressive one the Vietnamese people's fight would cease to make sense. What is important is to realize that the progressive destruction of imperialist domination of our countries is a decisive factor in the destruction of financial capital in imperialist countries. In this intimate and dynamic connection between these struggles, is located the decisive importance of the unity and solidarity of all anti-imperialist forces in the world. Unity and solidarity are decisive factors for the overall success of the fight against imperialism.

The Coup d'Etat of April 25
FRELIMO

A statement of FRELIMO issued on April 27, 1974.

On 25 April 1974, we learned from radio broadcasts about the coup d'etat in Portugal by the armed forces which resulted in the ousting of the Government of Marcello Caetano and its replacement by a 'Junta of National Salvation'. This movement, according to its promoters, is intended to provide a solution to the present crisis which the Portuguese regime and society are going through after 13 years of colonial war.

The coup d'etat which has just taken place cannot be seen in isolation. It is a result of the new awareness of growing sectors of the Portuguese people that the purpose of the colonial war launched by the Fascist regime is to suppress the colonized peoples' aspiration to independence and freedom and is against the desire for well-being and political and social democracy of the Portuguese people themselves.

At this time we hail, in the first place, the Portuguese democratic forces which for many years have been actively and courageously opposing the colonial wars. This growing awareness is closely bound up with the affirmation of the unshakable will of the Mozambican people, and of the peoples of Angola, Guinea-Bissau and Cape Verde islands, to achieve independence and freedom. This will has taken on material form in the armed struggle for national liberation, which has been steadily growing and has already reached vital regions of our country. The coincidence between the crisis of the regime in Portugal and the great advances of the national liberation struggle in Mozambique over the past two years is no accident, but additional proof of the impact of our struggle on the situation in Portugal. The determinant factor of the situation in Portugal and the colonies has been and still is the struggle of our peoples. And the fundamental issue upon which the solution of all other problems depends is the independence of the peoples of Mozambique, Angola and Guinea-Bissau and Cape Verde Islands, as well as that of the remaining Portuguese colonies.

As far as the Portuguese people are concerned, to the extent that the principles contained in the proclamations that the leaders of the coup d'etat have made up to now are put into force, this will doubtless be a step forward towards the establishment of democracy in Portugal. The young people who engaged in action aimed at putting an end to 48 years of uninterrupted dictatorship in Portugal, acting in line with the aspirations of the Portuguese people to realize their legitimate right to democracy, liberty and real independence, are the same young people who, when they were made to fight against our people, understood the unjust nature of the war in which they were engaged and the character of the regime which forced them to give up their lives for the defence of interests contrary to the interests of their people. The establishment of democracy in Portugal would be a victory for the Portuguese people, a victory at which we would rejoice.

For the Mozambican people, under the leadership of FRELIMO, the correct definition of who is the enemy has always been an essential point of principle. The enemy of the Mozambican people is not the Portuguese people, themselves victims of fascism, but the Portuguese colonial system. And an important section of the Portuguese army itself was made to understand that it was not defending the interests of its people in the colonial wars when it felt the growing disaffection of Portuguese opinion with regard to the war it is waging in the colonies. If our struggle thus contributed to the Portuguese people's struggle against fascism and to win their right to democracy, FRELIMO cannot but congratulate itself for having contributed to this. But just as the Portuguese people have the right to independence and democracy, this same right cannot be denied the Mozambican people. It is for this elementary but essential right that we are fighting. The objectives of FRELIMO are very clear, the total and complete independence of the Mozambican people and the liquidation of Portuguese colonialism. The Mozambican people are an entity quite distinct from the Portuguese people, and they have their own political, cultural and social personality which can only be realized through the independence of Mozambique.

We are not fighting to become Portuguese with black skins. We are fighting to affirm ourselves as Mozambicans, without this meaning contempt for the Portuguese people or any other people. In this respect, FRELIMO reaffirms its wish to fully co-operate with all peoples in the world on a basis of independence, equality, respect and mutual interest, FRELIMO also reaffirms that the definition of a Mozambican has nothing to do with skin colour or racial, ethnic, religious or any other origin. Members of FRELIMO are all Mozambicans who adhere to its programme of struggle against Portuguese colonialism, for the independence of Mozambique. FRELIMO is not a racialist organization and it is not waging a racialist war. We reaffirm here what we declared in July 1972 when we opened a new front: 'On starting the struggle in Manica e Sofala where an important section of the Portuguese community in our country is established, we reaffirm that our struggle is not against them, that our victory can only benefit those who live from honest labour, those who suffer from colonial and Fascist exploitations. The Mozambican people fraternally call upon the Portuguese soldiers, the Protuguese people to join the common effort of liberation. At the same time as hailing the growing support from white Mozambicans for the struggle for national liberation, we wish to warn certain sectors of the European population of Mozambique against the attempts of the ultra-racist forces, encouraged by the neighbouring racist countries, to transform our armed struggle for liberation into a total war between whites and blacks. This manoeuvre has as its purpose to make the white settlers participate actively in suppressing our people. That attitude makes them instruments of other forces and does not serve their own interests or the interests of the Mozambican people.'

Freedom and independence, the affirmation of our own personality — these then are the objectives of our struggle, FRELIMO fighters are not professional soldiers. They are the Mozambican people in arms. They are, before all else, political militants who have taken up arms to put an end to the daily violence of colonial domination, exploitation and repression. It is up to the Portuguese Government to learn from past experience and understand that only through recognition of the right to independence. If, Mozambican people, led by FRELIMO, their authentic and legitimate representative, will the war end. Any attempt to elude the real problem will only lead to new and equally avoidable sacrifices. The way to solve the problem is clear recognition of the Mozambican people's right to the independence. If, however, the objective of the coup d'etat is to find new formulae to perpetuate the oppression of our people, then the Portuguese leaders are warned that they will face our firm determination. The Mozambican people, over 10 years of heroic armed struggle, have endured heavy sacrifices and shed the blood of their finest sons and daughters to defend the inalienable principle of their sovereignty as a free and independent nation. Politically and militarily tempered, encouraged by the growing successes of the armed struggle for national liberation, more united than ever under the leadership of FRELIMO, the Mozambican people will not retreat before any sacrifice in ensuring that their rights and fundamental aspirations triumph. We cannot accept that democracy for the Portuguese people should serve as a cover to prevent the independence of our people. Just as Caetano's era clearly demonstrated that liberal fascism does not exist, it must also be understood that there is no such thing as democratic colonialism.

At this moment it is important that all the forces in solidarity with the people of Mozambique and with the peoples of Angola, Guinea-Bissau, Cape Verde and Sao Tome e Principe continue their action for the recognition of our right to complete independence. They must remain vigilant in the face of any manoeuvres aimed at blocking the process of our total liberation coming not only from the Portuguese Government, but from the regimes in South Africa and racist Rhodesia. It is also essential that the forces which support our struggle step up their assistance of every kind to the liberation movements, so that with the end of Portuguese colonialism, the aspirations of our peoples, which are those of all mankind, may be fulfilled.

Independence or Death!
We shall win!
The struggle continues!

3. The Rule of White Settlers

Editors' Introduction

The history of South Africa, Namibia and Zimbabwe is different from that of Portuguese Africa in two fundamental respects. They have been part at one time or another of the British Empire and are marked by its traditions – a certain parliamentary style, the use (at least partially) of the English language, the predominance of Protestant Christianity – and are still today linked more closely in economic terms to the United Kingdom than to any other outside country.

A second difference, however, has been at least as important. Partly because of different cultural and political traditions, and partly for ecological reasons, the ratio of white settlers to black Africans was higher in these three territories than in Portuguese Africa. And even more importantly, the white settlers had a long tradition of autonomous government. The whites have had substantial political rights in South Africa since the 19th Century and full self-government since 1910. The whites in Namibia acquired these rights more or less when South Africa assumed political control in the wake of the First World War. The whites in Zimbabwe obtained substantial autonomy as the Crown Colony of Southern Rhodesia in 1923 and declared a 'unilateral declaration of independence' (UDI) in 1965.

In Portuguese Africa, whites were in power but in political terms the white *settlers* were not, whereas in the three anglophone countries the rule of white settlers did prevail.

As a direct consequence, a particularly sharp and explicit form of racial discrimination developed, known in South Africa as *apartheid*. It was in theory a system of 'separate development', and one which applied to both South Africa and Namibia. While the government in power in Rhodesia made some theoretical distinctions between its own laws and those of South Africa, the position of the national liberation movements was that these distinctions were paper ones, the reality being substantially the same.

There is very little difference in views among the movements about the merits of white settler rule. It was seen as vicious, exploitative and based on lies. In choosing the texts from various movements, therefore, we do so less to underline different perspectives than to develop specific sub-themes elaborated in one or another paper.

We start with an analysis of the system of apartheid power by the African National Congress (S.A.) which explained the land and labour policy of the government and the apparatus of terror and discrimination which supports it. The analysis by the small Unity Movement developed the familiar theme of the economic roots of the conflict between Boer and Briton in South Africa, as well as their cooperation. The policy statement of the South African Communist Party argued its premise of 'two South Africas', the white one which is an 'advanced capitalist state' and the second one which has 'all the features of a colony'. The statement by SWAPO of Namibia concentrated on attacking a central myth of the South African regime, that apartheid results in 'multi-national development'. Rather they see it as 'developing underdevelopment'.

While there runs through this material an assertion about the unusual, perhaps unique, feature of the South African system — the combination of a colonial state within an independent capitalist state — the movements writing about Zimbabwe were at some pains to show that they, too, lived under apartheid. Certain differences of emphasis can be seen however. The ZAPU statement asserted that land was the key issue in Zimbabwe, whereas the ANC statement had made it only one of several for South Africa. The statement by Frolizi, a short-lived organization formed by some former leaders of ZAPU and ZANU in 1971, emphasized the *evolution* of a 'settler-colonial bourgeois society' wherein the economic forces had developed to a point such that 'they are no longer compatible with classical colonial relations of property'.

The ZANU paper and the statement of the African National Council (Zimbabwe) both agreed with the idea that the mode of government in Rhodesia had been evolving — towards a system of apartheid copied from South Africa. The ZANU statement denounced the settlers for their 'Nazi' crimes. The ANC (Zimbabwe) condemned the settlers for arrogantly seeking to swindle the Africans, and also condemned the British Government for its naivete in believing otherwise. [This statement was of course written at a time when ANC (Zimbabwe) was still strongly opposed to the Smith regime.]

To point up the unbridgeable gap in perspective between the movements and the white settlers, we include two paragraphs of an information booklet put out by the then Rhodesian Government the year before UDI.

Race and Apartheid Power
ANC (South Africa)

Extract from an article in Sechaba, *III, 4, April 1969.*
Sechaba *is the official organ of the African National Congress (South Africa).*

Apartheid racism is a system of intense colonial-type exploitation. The difference between South Africa and other systems of colonialism is that in South Africa coloniser and colonised are present in the same country. The colony is not a distinct territory, separated by distance from the empire. Rulers and ruled live side by side within the same geographical boundaries. But colour and race are used as the dividing line between the resident army of occupation of the whites and their subject populations, Africans in the vast majority, and Indians and Coloured people. The White group dominates in every sphere and all political and economic power is concentrated in the hands of the so-called 'master' race. Insurmountable barriers are built by law and force, to seal off the spheres preserved for the White minority, and to exclude Africans from it except where they are needed to produce the wealth of the country and man the economy, at prescribed levels of employment and rates of pay. Theories of race supremacy are used to buttress this rigid system of colour stratification. Where the race theorising does not work – as it has not worked because nothing in 300 years of the history of White domination has convinced Africans of their own inferiority – then there is rule by terror. The shooting at Sharpeville. Government by emergency proclamation. Banishments, trials and detentions. The torture of political activists, the execution of political prisoners.

Apartheid is the official policy of the Nationalist Party which came to power – in all-white elections – in 1948. But the roots of the apartheid system go much farther back than 1948, through successive minority white governments and three centuries of white rule in South Africa.

The occupation of the country was achieved by military conquest of the African people, and the steady dispossession of their land and cattle and the forced use of their labour. Early conflicts between Afrikaner (Boer) and English-speaking settlers led to the division of South Africa into British possessions and 'Boer' Republics, culminating in the Boer War at the beginning of this century, in which the Boer Republics were defeated. But by 1910 and the adoption of the South African Constitution, the disputing sides of white supremacy had already closed their ranks against the challenge of African demands. Between them, two parties, the United Party led by General Smuts and the Nationalist Party, led successively by Malan, Strijdom, Verwoerd and now Vorster, monopolised state power and the country's economic resources and devised a system of race rule to make this minority power impregnable. Smuts said of his policy, in 1945: 'There are certain things about which all South Africans are agreed, all parties and all sections except those who are quite mad. This is . . . that it is fixed policy to maintain white supremacy . . .' In 1936 Dr. Malan said: 'Reduced to its simplest form, the problem is nothing else than this: We want to keep South Africa white. Keeping it white can only mean one thing, namely White domination, not 'leadership' or guidance, but control, supremacy.' Two minority white parties, but a single policy of white domination.

The early pattern of the economy was one of mining and industry dominated by British capital and representative in the main, of United Party political interests; with Afrikaner economic interests entrenched in agriculture and the white farming community. Before World War 2 the Afrikaner share of economic power was relatively insignificant. That pattern has changed. The rise to political power of the Nationalist Party was accompanied by a sustained campaign for the acquisition of Afrikaner Nationalist economic capital. Nationalist power today has an economic base of the bulk of the farming capital of the country, an expanding sector of private industrial and commercial capital, and a complete monopoly of State capital. By 1960 the amount of foreign capital invested in South Africa was about the same as the total of State capital, and the direction being taken by the economy was calculated to further strengthen the hold of State capital under the direction of the Nationalist Party and its supporters. In recent years there has also been a convergence between the two sectors of White economic power. Leading representatives of Afrikaner Nationalist and State capital have joined the boards of directors of the old mining and finance houses, the banks and insurance companies; and the mining-finance houses have themselves acquired industrial assets and interests.

South Africa is extremely rich in resources. She produces 43 per cent of the mineral output of the entire continent, and two-thirds of the world's gold. She uses twice as much steel and electricity as the rest of Africa combined. 40 per cent of the continent's industrial products and 80 per cent of its coal come from South Africa. 30 per cent of the continent's income is generated in South Africa. Since the end of World War 2 South Africa has maintained an above average rate of growth. Between 1960 and 1965 it was an average figure of more than 6 per cent, one of the fastest in the capitalist world. This exceptional rate of growth is possible because of the special nature of apartheid. On the one hand, the economy has reached a high level of industrial expansion, and on the other hand, it is guaranteed, through the workings of apartheid laws and controls, an exceptionally high degree of exploitation of cheap African labour. How does apartheid work?

Cornerstone of the apartheid system is its land and labour policy. Africans are prohibited by law from owning or occupying more than 13 per cent of the total land area of the country. These areas reserved for Africans were known first as reserves, latterly as the Bantu homelands, or Bantustans. 'What they (the white police-makers) desire is to force into reserves as many Africans as possible under conditions which will compel them to come out and work for the Whites,' said a liberal judge in 1931. Years of forcing too large populations into these areas together with a continuous history of neglect and a minimal, almost total lack of capital expenditure on improvements have turned these reserved areas into labour reserves with a debilitated African agriculture that cannot support its population. This poverty, together with the policy of compulsory taxation — a poll tax per head of male population regardless of income or whether the taxpayer is in employment or not — is the flywheel of the system of migrant labour. African labour is channelled into the mines, into the white farming areas, into industry and the cities, but it is regarded as temporary labour. The pass laws and other controls keep this labour market but place obstacles in the way of growth of secure and stable African urban communities and the development of an organised labour force, with trade union rights.

The economy cannot function without African labour, and each year demands an ever-increasing supply of it. Without African labour South Africa could not have reached, nor could it maintain, its present level of industrial production. The mining industry and agriculture are totally dependent on African labour. Africans, together with the other non-white groups, constitute 99 per cent of the unskilled workers in industry, 66 per cent of the semi-skilled and 17 per cent of the skilled labour (mostly Indian and Coloured skilled workers, for Africans are prohibited by law from doing skilled work.) Whatever the theorists of apartheid say about separate development of the races, this is impossible under South Africa's highly industrialised and integrated economy. Of the total African population, approximately 4½ million live in the reserves. (Of these more than 40 per cent of the men between the ages of 15 and 64 are migrant workers.) The rest are distributed in approximately even proportions as labour for the white farming areas and industry. By 1950, 28 per cent of South Africa's non-whites lived in the towns; by 1960 the figure had risen to 37 per cent; and by 1970 it is expected to rise to 45 per cent.

When the Nationalist Party came to power in 1948 it advocated apartheid as official policy, instead of the previous system of segregation of the United Party, though, as pointed out, one was a development from the basis laid already by the other. The election manifesto of the Nationalist Party described apartheid as follows: 'In general terms our policy envisages segregating the most important ethnic groups and sub-groups in their own areas, where every group will be enabled to develop into a self-sufficient unit. We endorse the general principle of territorial segregation of Bantu (Africans) and Whites. *The Bantu (African) in the urban area as a whole should be regarded as migratory citizens not entitled to political or social rights equal to those of the Whites.'* The African people were expected to abandon their claim to rights and equality in the whole country, and to confine their aspirations to Bantustans or homelands. These Bantustans were to be built out of over 200 reserved areas (in which only 40 per cent of the total African population lives, remember) to which not an additional acre of land was to be added to help make them economically viable. The first Bantustan was set up in the Transkei, others are to follow, making up eight in all. These areas contain less than two-fifths of the African population of the country. The scheme is a device to try to stop the thrust of a united non-tribal liberation struggle of the African people, and to dissipate their unity in scores of societies thrust back into tribalism. White supremacy, it is calculated, will be strengthened by using tribal chiefs and reinforced tribal authority to focus attention not on the concentration of power in White hands but on a number of small tribal states. Above all the Bantustan scheme is used to rationalise the tragedies and hardships created by apartheid — the economic pressures, the break-up of families, the ceaseless houndings by the police, the heavy burden of discriminatory laws — on the grounds that Africans may 'develop in their own areas'.

But the experience of the Transkei, the first Bantustan, shows that this is simply not the case. The Transkei's independence is fictional. It has no real power, and no possibilities for economic development. On the Legislative Council or so-called Transkei Parliament there are 109 members, but 64 are chiefs, virtually government civil servants and liable to summary dismissal for anti-government acts or sentiments. The Council may legislate only in certain proscribed fields, like justice, education and internal affairs, but its laws are promulgated subject to the approval of the South African Cabinet. As for development, this is impossible without heavy capital outlay, and though plans were laid on paper, they have not come to anything. It was, for instance, proclaimed government policy to establish industries in the Transkei to provide economic opportunities and development possibilities denied to Africans in the rest of the country. From 1948 to 1965 nine industries only were opened, employing in all 1389 Africans. In 17 years a programme of so-called industrialisation created only 82 new jobs a year.

Whatever propaganda boost the Bantustans may be given as part of the new look of apartheid, they remain backward impoverished areas from which Africans have to commute to work in white enterprises, leaving their families behind them. All the major industries, all the mineral wealth, all the important harbour facilities and the best arable land are in those parts of the country earmarked for white ownership and control. White prosperity and the present rate of industrial and other production are not possible without the steady supply of African labour. Apartheid as a scheme for so-called separate development is thus a deception.

But as a system of the intense exploitation of the South African majority it is unparalleled. The overwhelming bulk of the wealth of South Africa is enjoyed by a white population whose standard of living (based on the national income per head) is the highest of any major country in the world except the United States of America. But South Africa's dramatic rate of growth and this white minority prosperity has been achieved at tragic cost to the conditions of life of the majority of the people. On the gold mines African cash wages are, in real buying power, no higher today than they were in 1911. National income figures for South Africa tell the facts of the division by colour of the prosperity and poverty:

National Income per Head

Net National Income in South Africa	£2,535 m.
National Income Per capita (all races)	148.5 m.
National Income per capita for Whites	624 m.
National Income per capita for Non-Whites	36.7 m.

This means that the per capita income for Whites is 17 times that for Non-Whites.

Even in the years of South Africa's economic boom, after World War 2, the Non-White population shared hardly at all in the growing wealth of the country:

Growth in National Income per head of Non-Whites since the War:

1950	£28.7
1960	27.0
1961	27.6
1962	28.3
1963	29.95

In manufacturing industry, where half a million Africans are employed, the average wage is £21 a month. In industry the wage gap between Whites and Africans is 5 to 1; in mining it is 12 to 1. In 1960 the Whites, who constituted 19.3 per cent of the population accounted for 67 per cent of the national income; the Africans who constituted 68.4 per cent of the population received 26.5 per cent. The reservation of skilled jobs to whites only, started for the mining industry in 1911, has steadily been extended to other occupations. Trade unions are segregated by race and African trade unions are refused registration. African strikes are illegal, with threats of heavy penalties (a fine of £500 or three years' imprisonment or both). The earnings of African workers are determined not by collective bargaining but by decree of the white minority government.

The key to the technique of race rule is the total absolute exclusion of Non-Whites from participation in any aspect of government, whether legislative or executive. Only Whites may be nominated or elected as members of Parliament, Provincial Councils or Town Councils. Even the wretched provision under earlier laws whereby a small group of African voters could elect three White members to represent their interests in Parliament was abolished. No African may sit as judge, magistrate or prosecutor, nor may he serve on a jury. No Africans can become officers in the army or the police force. No African may serve in the civil service except at the most menial rank in a clerical department serving Africans only. Discrimination in education is designed to keep Africans at the most menial levels in society. Under the Bantu Education Act it is illegal for African children to receive any but state-controlled education, and this is specially conducted to ensure that there will be no place for Africans 'above certain forms of labour' (the words of the former Prime Minister Dr. Verwoerd). When it comes to expenditure on education the same discrimination operates: about £63 is spent on the education of a white child and £9 on an African child.

The statute book is heavy with discriminatory laws amended to make them progressively more burdensome and oppressive. Under the Population Registration Act of 1960 the entire population is classified by race and sub-group. Humiliating 'race' tests have been inflicted on people, and families torn asunder in the registration of different members as different races or sub-groups. Under the Group Areas Act, different group areas have been declared for different population groups, and settled communities have been uprooted and arbitrarily transported to different areas totally undeveloped and barely provided with by social services and education. Under the Prohibition of Mixed Marriages Act, marriages between Whites and Africans were made illegal. Under the Immorality Act, sexual relations between the races are punishable by heavy penalties. The pass laws and influx control measures, which restrict the movement of Africans out of the reserves have been made more stringent and applied to African women. A thousand Africans a day are arrested under the pass laws and hauled before court for prosecution and imprisonment. Africans in the cities must live compulsorily in segregated areas, may not enter such areas without previous permission, and, if they are arrested at any time of night or day, must prove before court that they have not been in the area without permission for longer than 72 hours. Curfews operate at night and breaking the curfew is a criminal offence. When it comes to social services, the Unemployment Insurance Act has been amended to exclude Africans from its benefits. Health services for Africans are slender, and in one of the most flourishing societies of this century, the infant mortality rate for Africans in some cities is as high as 400 per 1,000.

Boer vs. Briton
Unity Movement

> *Excerpt from a pamphlet issued by the Unity Movement in Cape Town on 1 September 1960, entitled 'The Pan-Africanist Venture in Perspective'.*

It is pertinent to remember that the Boers and the British were rivals in the conquest and exploitation of Southern Africa. These represented two different economies, feudalistic and capitalist respectively. With the discovery of gold and diamonds in the latter part of the 19th Century, industrialisation was on the order of the day and the tempo of development was speeded up. British imperialism dropped all pretences of respecting small Boer Republics and independent African tribes. Capitalist development necessitated a unified economy in South Africa. The Boers and the Africans had to be vanquished and British rule firmly established. The Boer War was an incident in this process.

As soon as the Boers were defeated, however, the British found it expedient to rehabilitate them and paid reparations to the vanquished. They needed the Boers to act as supervisors over the millions of potential Black workers and as guardians over the investments of British imperialism. With the Act of Union in 1910 the Boers were placed on a footing of political equality as co-rulers of the country. As a further sop to ensure that the Boers supported the Union, the constituencies were weighted in their favour, i.e. of the farmers. In fact, the Dutch farmers were granted political representation far in excess of their economic power. But imperialism took the precaution of counter-balancing this by granting a limited vote to African and Coloured males in the Cape. At this stage the real and unchallenged rulers of the country were the Chamber of Mines; for the whole economy of the Union hung upon the mining industry and the employment of cheap Black labour.

Then came the First World War. A section of the Boers seized the opportunity to revolt and were crushed. This was the section that nursed the passions of the Boer War and identified themselves with a strong nationalism, whipping up antagonism against the English section, the foreigners and invaders. After the war, however, the impetus to the development of industry made an increasing number of Afrikaners realise the benefits of belonging to an economy that was attached to world capitalism. The rich farmers invested their surplus capital in industrial concerns and thus, from now on, cast in their lot with that of the industrialists. A clear class distinction is now discernible in the Boer camp.

The interlocking of Boer and British capital found political expression in the coalition between Hertzog and Smuts. And this political marriage between the Chamber of Mines and the rich farmers sounded the death knell of the African vote in the Cape. British imperialism no longer required the African as a safeguard against the Boers of the north. At this stage the Chamber of Mines was still dominant both economically and politically. Secondly, industry did not have an independent political voice, but its interests were catered for by the same party that represented the Chamber of Mines. Its spokesmen attached themselves to this party.

Now Dr. Malan, who had refused to be drawn into the Hertzog-Smuts deal, broke away and sought support from the small farmers, railway workers, government employees, small businessmen and intellectuals: in a word, the Afrikaner petit-bourgeois. This section belongs to that class which, wedged in between the two fundamental classes in society, the bourgeoisie and the working class, is unstable and susceptible to spurious propaganda. They are all the more prone to fall for catch-phrases because of their precarious position in society. Malan, then, appealed to the racial passions of a fanatic group dedicated to the salvation of the Boers. It was a racialism that fed itself on hatred of all other sections. They saw the English as usurpers and exploiters; and towards the Africans and other Non-Whites they maintained the attitude of the old Boer Republics, regarding them as created by God to minister to the chosen people. It was a narrow, rabid racialism that was given the grandiloquent name of Afrikaner Nationalism.

In this atmosphere secret societies flourished and chief among them was the Broederbond, whose devotees were dedicated to the advancement and ultimate triumph of the Afrikaner Volk. They set themselves the task of penetrating into every sphere of public life and every department of State. Their avowed aim was the advancement of Afrikanerdom, but in actual practice this meant the promotion of the individual. The Broederbond organised boycotts of Non-Afrikaner shops and 'Buy Afrikaner' campaigns were pushed with tremendous zeal. In this way insurance companies and other business ventures of the Afrikaners grew by leaps and bounds. Afrikaner businessmen utilised this so-called Nationalism for their own ends. For them, Afrikanerdom became synonymous with their particular interest.

With the outbreak of the Second World War, the Afrikaner die-hards saw an opportunity of welding the Volk together. In full anticipation of a victory for Hitler, they stood out against British imperialism. The end of the war found the Afrikaner businessmen with ready cash and the post-war boom in industry swept them to the crest of the wave. It was they who made funds available for the party machine. The highly organised Broederbond, with its key men strategically placed in every sphere, every department, could now go all out in preparing for elections. It was the Nationalist Party, controlled by the Broederbond, that won the elections in 1948. The Malan victory was the victory of a party controlled by the petit-bourgeois. For the first time in the history of South Africa, the big financial interests found themselves ousted from the Government. Here, then, we have the phenomenon where the big bourgeoisie is represented by a minority in its own parliament.

Since then South Africa has been under the rule of the petit-bourgeois, and they have used their new-won power like men intoxicated with it. But it itself is ruled by a Junta within, namely, the Broederbond. At first, the bourgeoisie, not realising the extent to which the Nationalist Party was under the influence of the Broederbond, gave their support to the new government. Dr Malan, after all, had been trained in the traditions of orthodox parliamentarism. And in any event, they reckoned, the responsibility of being in power usually has the effect of mellowing or taming those invested with it. The next step, however, was the supplanting of Dr. Malan, who was not a member of the Broederbond, by Strijdom, its representative. By this time the positions in the Nationalist Party itself were filled by the Broeders and it was they who packed the enlarged Senate. Then, on the death of Strijdom, it was natural that the Broederbond should elect their chief, Dr. Verwoerd. Thus we have the spectacle that the party functionary is the Government in South Africa.

Dr. Verwoerd was elected to the premiership in a strictly constitutional manner. And yet in the eyes of the various parties in and out of Parliament he is still regarded in the nature of an interloper. And neither is he the voice of his own party as a whole. Once more we see 'Afrikanerdom' split by class interests. That section within the Nationalist Party which had supplied the funds, and whose financial interests have become bound up with international capital, find themselves prisoners, in their own party.

Under normal conditions in a capitalist country, the cabinet of the party in power serves as the executive for the financiers and industrialists. But the present government in South Africa is the executive of the junta, the Broederbond. And it is this ruling Afrikaner section of the petit-bourgeoisie that considers itself at war with the big financier; it is still fighting the Boer War.

This Broederbond government can think and behave only as a petit-bourgeois. It cannot comprehend the complex functioning of finance capital and the inter-relationships that result from its operations. Myopic in its vision, it legislates for the individual. There is altogether a devastating preoccupation with pettifogging legislation. Job reservation, industries in the bushes, Bantu-stans, etc., are a sop to party supporters. But all these are an irritant to big business. They have the cumulative effect of seriously interfering with the natural flow of capital and clogging the economic development of the country. To the petit-bourgeois, the fact that the rate of economic develop-ment in South Africa has today become the lowest in Africa has no meaning. He seems impervious to their impact. He is even impervious to the rapid loss of confidence on the part of overseas investors, the heavy slump in the stock exchange, which can have such a serious effect on the South African economy. With the mentality of a Trek Boer, he would seem to consider that all that is necessary is to pull in his belt a bit, while droughts and other such like divine visitations are sent to try him. What is one to think of a cabinet minister who blandly remarks that there is far too much made of loses on the stock exchange? Here speaks clearly, not the voice of capital, but that of a representative of functionaries.

This pettifogging legislation, then, which is made in the interests of a petit-bourgeois utopia and a racial myth, produces tensions which in turn make it necessary to employ strong-arm methods. The State of Emergency, where the rule of law is replaced with rule by edict, is a step towards a permanent state of fascism, not only for the Blacks as hitherto, but applied to all.

Now, fascism is a form of rule which the bourgeoisie falls back upon as a last resort. As a general rule, finance capital flourished best in a bourgeois democracy which guarantees the maximum freedom possible under capital-ism. The bourgeoisie avoids the imposition of fascism as long as possible. For fascism implies the open use of force and the maintenance of a huge unpro-ductive army. It is a confession that capitalism can no longer maintain itself; it can no longer afford to rule by the ordinary bourgeois democratic means. It involves the exacerbation of class tensions, all of which tend to frighten away the free flow of capital.

The situation as it is now, under the Nationalist petit-bourgeois govern-ment, is intolerable to finance capital. It must get rid of the stranglehold of the Broederbond. This was the state of affairs — a state of conflict between the bourgeoisie and the petit-bourgeoisie — when the P.A.C. adventurers burst upon the South African scene.

A New Type of Colonialism
SACP

Excerpt from 'The Road to South African Freedom',

—

published in 1962 by the South African Communist Party.

South Africa is not a colony but an independent state. Yet masses of our people enjoy neither independence nor freedom. The conceding of independence to South Africa by Britain, in 1910, was not a victory over the forces of colonialism and imperialism. It was designed in the interests of imperialism. Power was transferred not into the hands of the masses of people of South Africa, but into the hands of the White minority alone. The evils of colonialism, in so far as the non-White majority was concerned, were perpetuated and reinforced. A new type of colonialism was developed, in which the oppressing White nation occupied the same territory as the oppressed people themselves and lived side by side with them.

A rapid process of industrialisation was set in train, especially during the two world wars. South African heavy industry and secondary industry grew to occupy first place on the Continent. This process had profound effects on the country's social structure. It concentrated great wealth and profits in the hands of the upper strata of the White population. It revolutionised the economy, transforming it from a predominantly agricultural into an industrial-agricultural economy, with an urban working class, mainly non-White, which is the largest in Africa. But no commensurate benefits of this industrialisation have been enjoyed by the masses of non-White people.

On one level, that of 'White South Africa', there are all the features of an advanced capitalist state in its final stage of imperialism. There are highly developed industrial monopolies, and the merging of industrial and finance capital. The land is farmed along capitalist lines, employing wage labour, and producing cash crops for the local and export markets. The South African monopoly capitalists, who are closely linked with British, United States and other foreign imperialist interests, export capital abroad, especially in Africa. Greedy for expansion, South African imperialism reaches out to incorporate other territories — South West Africa and the Protectorates.

But on another level, that of 'Non-White South Africa', there are all the features of a colony. The indigenous population is subjected to extreme national oppression, poverty and exploitation, lack of all democratic rights and political domination by a group which does everything it can to emphasise and perpetuate its alien 'European' character. The African Reserves show the complete lack of industry, communications, transport and power resources which are characteristic of African territories under colonial rule throughout the Continent. Typical, too, of imperialist rule, is the reliance by the state upon brute force and terror, and upon the most backward tribal elements and institutions which are deliberately and artificially preserved. Non-White South Africa is the colony of White South Africa itself.

It is this combination of the worst features both of imperialism and of colonialism, within a single national frontier, which determines the special nature of the South African system, and has brought upon its rulers the justified hatred and contempt of progressive and democratic people throughout the world.

All Whites enjoy privileges in South Africa. They alone can vote and be elected to parliament and local government bodies. They have used this privilege to monopolise nearly all economic, educational, cultural and social opportunities. This gives the impression that the ruling class is composed of the entire White population. In fact, however, real power is in the hands of the monpolists who own and control the mines, the banks and finance houses, and most of the farms and major industries. The gold and diamond mines are owned by seven mining-financial corporations and controlled by a handful of powerful financiers. These seven corporations are closely linked with British and American imperialist interests. They control capital investment in mining alone of R490 million, and employ almost 500,000 workers. In addition, they dominate large sections of manufacturing industries. They are linked with the main banks, two of which control assets of over R2,000 million, mainly in the forms of loans to industry, commerce and the state. They own vast tracts of arable land and mining rights in almost every part of the country. In agriculture too monopoly dominates. Four per cent of the farms make up an area amounting to almost four-tenths of the total White-owned farmland. Thus, in mining, industry, commerce and farming, monopolists dominate the country's economy. They are also closely linked with *state monopoly capital* ventures, such as Iscor (Iron and Steel), Escom (Electricity) and Sasol (Petrol).

These monopolists are the real power in South Africa. The special type of colonialism in South Africa serves, in the first place, their interests. Low non-White wages; the reserves of poverty; the compound labour system and the importation of hundreds of thousands of contract labourers from beyond our borders; the pass laws and poll tax and rigid police control of labour and of movement — all are designed to keep their profits high. In 1961 these seven mining corporations and their subsidiaries made a working profit of nearly R212 million and paid out dividends of R101 million to shareholders.

The South African monopolists act as allies and agents of foreign imperialist interests. One-quarter of the capital of the seven mining-financial groups is owned abroad, mainly by British and American investors. In 1958, dividends of R43 million were paid out abroad. The two biggest banks are largely controlled from Britain, and in recent years United States capital investment in South Africa has grown rapidly, exceeding all other American investments in the rest of Africa put together.

Effective economic domination in South Africa is thus exercised by an alliance of local White monopoly interests in mining, industry and agriculture, together with foreign imperialists and representatives of state monopoly capitalism. These interests have conflicts among themselves, which are reflected in the main White political parties and groupings. But they find common ground in the perpetuation of the colonial-type subjugation of the non-White population.

The system of colonial domination over and robbery of the non-White masses is not in the genuine, long-term interest of the workers, small farmers, middle-class and professional elements who make up the bulk of the White population. White domination means more and more police and military expenditure to burden the taxpayer and divert men and resources from useful production. It means that the poverty-stricken masses are unable to form an adequate market for South African industry and agriculture. It means more and more dictatorial police-state measures, the extinguishing of civil liberties for Whites as well as non-Whites. It means a South Africa despised and shunned by the whole world, subjected to economic, diplomatic, cultural and other forms of isolation, boycott and sanctions. It means a future of uncertainty and fear. The maintenance of White supremacy involves ever-increasing repression and violence by the government, resistance by the oppressed people and the steady drift to civil war. Only the complete emancipation of the non-White peoples can create conditions of equality and friendship among the nationalities of South Africa and eliminate the roots of race hatred and antagonism which are the greatest threat to the continued security and existence of the White population itself. The national liberation of the non-Whites which will break the power of monopoly capitalism is thus in the deepest long-term interest of the bulk of the Whites. Progressive and far-seeing Whites ally themselves unconditionally with the struggle of the masses of the people for freedom and equality.

On the whole, the White workers represent an 'aristocracy of labour'. The monopolists have extended numerous concessions to them. They receive relatively high wages. Non-White miners receive an average of R144 a year plus food and compound housing; White miners R2470. African male farm workers average R68 a year; Whites R1050. Whites have a monopoly of the best paid jobs, and of entry into skilled trades. They are invariably given positions of authority over non-Whites. The relatively high standards of life and wages enjoyed by White workers represent, in reality, a share in the super profits made by the capitalists out of the gross exploitation of the non-Whites. Systematically indoctrinated with the creed of White superiority, the White worker imagines himself to be a part of the ruling class and willingly acts as a tool and an accomplice in the maintenance of colonialism and capitalism. However, in reality, the White worker, like the non-White worker at his side, is subjected to exploitation by the same capitalist owners of the means of production. White workers' wages in general are high in comparison with those of non-Whites. But many categories of White workers are paid little more than non-Whites, and also struggle to support their families. The White worker is subjected to the insecurity of the capitalist system, with its constant threats of depression, short-time and unemployment. The division of trade unions on racial lines weakens all sections of workers in their constant struggle with the bosses for better pay and conditions and shorter hours of work. The fundamental interests of all South African workers, like those of workers everywhere, lie in unity: unity in the struggle for the day-to-day interests of the working class, for the ending of race

discrimination and division, for a free, democratic South Africa as the only
possible basis for the winning of socialism, the overthrow of the capitalist
class and the ending of human exploitation.

The Multi-National Development Myth
SWAPO

*Extract from a statement on 'Namibia's African
"Homelands"', printed in* Namibia News, *a publication
of SWAPO, in Vol. 5, Nos. 9 & 10, Sept./Oct. 1972.*

South Africa's policy of establishing ethnically based partially independent
'homelands', with a panoply of executive and legislative powers, was first
set out in detail by the official report published in 1964 by the Odendaal
Commission. This recommended the establishment of ten 'homelands' for
the indigenous inhabitants of the country, classified as Bantu, Bushmen,
Coloureds and Rehoboth Basters, and a five-year development plan, financed
by the SA Government. The proposals of Odendaal, accepted in their entirety
by the SA Government represent the application to Namibia of full-scale
'separate development' — the setting aside of specified land for the exclusive
use of one population group.
   The 'homelands' policy began to be implemented after the verdict of the
International Court of Justice in 1966, interpreted as favourable to South
Africa. Since the visit to Dr Waldheim, UN Secretary-General, to Namibia
in March, and the diplomatic initiative which ensued, the process has been
speeded up. As opposed to self-determination for the Namibian people as
a whole, which Dr Waldheim stated in his report 'Report by the Secretary-
General on the implementation of Security Council Resolution 30g (1972)
concerning the question of Namibia — S/10738 of 17/7/72' as the only outcome acceptable to the UN, South African strategy is currently to put
forward its concept of 'multinational development' as an alternative to the
multi-racial self-determination envisaged by Namibians and the UN.
   'Constitutional evolution' is currently the highest priority of the South
African cabinet, which envisages the use of constitutional rights granted
to the 'homelands' as a bargaining counter in any negotiated settlement.
If no deal with the UN can be agreed, by these tactics, no time will have been
lost. Since March the South Africans have taken the following steps: the
opening of the 1st session of the East Caprivi Legislative Assembly (23/3),
acceptance of the requests of the Ovambo and Kavango Legislative
Assemblies for 'self-government' (June, July), and the setting aside of land
in the south for Namaland. These limited measures of decentralisation
contrast with the overall incorporation of Namibia as a fifth province. The
SWA Affairs Act of 1969 removed from the Administration at Windhoek,

powers over taxation, finance and African affairs, re-allocating them to the appropriate government departments in Pretoria – the development of the 'homelands' is master-minded by the SA Department of Bantu Administration and Development.

'Multi-national development' as envisaged by the South African regime in Namibia involves not only the institutionalisation of apartheid in the form of the separation of different 'ethnic' groups, into areas for exclusive occupation, but also the myth that the areas so designated are the areas of traditional occupation by the respective population group. This distortion of history means in practice the enforced removal of almost 100,000 people from the parts of the country in which they are actually living. The effect of the 'homelands' policy, if carried out entirely, would be to perpetuate the division of Namibia into two separate areas: a European area, containing the developed economic resources, mining, fishing and stock-rearing; and an African area of 10 units, lacking any of the means necessary for economic self-sufficiency . . . .

The official development proposals offer no hope of self-sustaining economic development for the 'homelands'. Despite apparent devolution of power, Pretoria has intensified its control over the natural and human resources of Namibia. In so doing it is seeking to internalise discontent within the homelands. This is why Ovambo and Kavango bantustans have been made responsible for labour recruiting for the south. Ownership of minerals remains outside African hands, and the discovery of new resources in Kaokoveld, Damaraland, and Ovamboland emphasises the basic economic unity of Namibia. SA and foreign companies are now prospecting in the Kaokoveld plateau, at Etosha in Ovamboland, in Trekkopje (Damaraland) for fluospar, oil, and uranium. The infrastructure of the south is now being extended north to Angola as part of the Kunene scheme, funded by the SA Government. In reality much of the necessary capital comes from the taxation of the major mining companies operating in Namibia. For the three financial years of 1968, 1969, and 1970, the State received an average of £22 million in direct taxes, and a further £6 million from the diamond export duty. Between 1948 and 1969, the Tsumeb Corporation alone paid out £60 million in taxes; and the manager I.A. Ratledge claimed that this had enabled the construction of the Cape Town – Luanda road. Since 1969 taxation is paid directly into the SA Treasury.

The economic resources provided by mining operations are crucial to the ability of SA to erect the 'homeland' structure and perpetuate the present colonial economy. For this reason, genuine economic self-sufficiency and agricultural process cannot be the product of isolated 'development' schemes by officials and government agencies, but only of the redirection of the available economic resources on a nation-wide level.

Migratory labour will continue as the only significant economic function for the African population, with the 'homelands' acting as enforced tribal social bases for the provision of temporary labour under contract.

In the 19th Century, Africans were living in all the habitable areas of

Namibia, with three main areas of settlement. Nama and related groups occupied the south and central plateau area, Herero the central and western regions, Damara the central region, Ovambo groups a region stretching north into Angola, eastwards into the Okavango delta. The predominant mode of economic activity was pastoral, and although crops such as maize and vegetables were grown there was no pattern of settled agriculture. This meant considerable overlap and mixing between the different groups. Under German administration, Namibia was divided by the 'Red Line' with the 'Police Zone' as the area of effective German control and European settlement. The Nama, Herero and Damara were dispossessed of their lands and dispersed after the uprisings of 1904–1906. With the northern people, the Germans were content to sign treaties with the tribal chiefs to ensure a supply of men for the developing mines and railways inside the 'Police Zone'. There were no civil or political rights for Africans in the areas of European influence.

After 1919, and the granting of the Mandate by the League of Nations to South Africa, this administrative structure was extended. The new regime initiated a crash settlement programme which led to immigration of 1,500 farmers from South Africa between 1920 and 1929. They were provided with land which had been taken from the Africans by the Germans; in order to provide a labour supply for the sheep and cattle farms, areas inside the 'Police Zone' were set aside as 'Native Reserves' for the Damara, Herero, Nama groups. But in practice many Africans preferred to reside in the areas of European industry and commerce, such as Windhoek, Walvis Bay, Okahandja, Swakopmund, or on the farms in the districts of Gobabis, Keetmanshoep, Marienthal and Omaruru. The reserves came under the control of the appropriate magistrate for the district, and the main blocs were in the north-east on the edge of the Kalahari, north-west, and south.

The northern sector, which included the Kaokoveld, Ovamboland and Okavango was administered only indirectly, through a 'native commissioner', since it was 'recognised as unsuitable land for whites' (Odendaal). At any one time, 10% of the adult males were under contract as 'extra-territorial and northern natives' in the southern sector formed by the 'Police Zone'. The Caprivi Strip, like the Walvis Bay enclave, was administered by the South African Government. Reserves and controlled migrant labour (since 1943 via Swanla) together formed a system of internal colonialism, officially termed 'segregation'.

By 1960, the structure initiated by the Germans was established. Of the total area of 318,261 square miles, 48% comprised European farms, 26% African reserves, the remainder being government land, towns, prohibited diamond areas and game reserves. Out of this total, the northern sector comprised 97,798 square miles, of which 56,185 square miles was African land. In the southern sector 23,523 square miles had been set aside as African reserves. Apart from the Rehoboth Gebiet, occupied almost exclusively by Rehoboth Basters, these southern reserves contained populations comprising several ethnic communities.

Of the total population of 526,000 estimated in that year's census, 287,000 lived in the northern, 239,000 in the southern sector. Of these, 73,000 were European, with 73% in the towns and 27% in the rural areas. There were 5,000 farmers. Africans in the south were distributed as follows: 39,000 in the 'home areas', 59,000 in 'urban areas' (shanties and compounds on the outskirts of the towns), 68,000 on the farms as labourers and shepherds. Less than 30% of the Africans actually resided in the land set aside by the authorities. The great expansion in mining activities since 1945, the establishment of fish canning factories at Walvis Bay and Luderitz, and small scale manufacturing concerns in Windhoek, increased the needs for unskilled and semi-skilled Africans for work in the urban centres, where tribal allegiances had little practical meaning. This is the human reality which the SA Government set out to rectify by the application of the Nationalist principle of 'separate development' to Namibia, where it assumes the character of a fantastic myth.

The 'Commission of Enquiry into SWA Affairs', 1962–1963, produced a blueprint for the creation of Bantustans in Namibia, together with a rationale to justify it. The population was classified into 12 ethnic groups (9 African, Coloured, Rehoboth, White) each with an area for exclusive occupation in the 'homeland'. While the white 'homeland' would integrate with South Africa, the indigenous 'homelands' were to develop into 'Native nations' with the option of eventual 'independence'. These were to be formed out of the existing reserves, and additional land was to be set aside to form a 'consolidated' area. Odendaal listed 423 European farms which were to be acquired – but most of the additions were to come from government lands and game reserves. While the proposed expansion of African lands is considerable (increasing the proportion of the total to 39%), the allocation of land is designed to effect the permanent fragmentation of the country into apparently homogenous areas, and the 'homelands' do not contain the human and natural resources to sustain the promised 'independence'. This is partly due to the type of land allocated, and partly to the geographical location. The whole exercise is funded under a five-year development plan by SA, costing R 115 million, of which R 49 million is for the Kunene hydro-electric project, and R 17 million compensation for farmers.

The Odendaal scheme for ten 'native nations' is currently being realised by legislation setting aside land and granting limited powers, and the enforced removal of Africans living outside their ethnically demarcated areas. Approximately 20%, mainly in the 'Police Zone', are required to move to different areas. The Coloured group have no 'homeland' but instead must live in separate townships, such as Khomasdal outside Windhoek, where 5,000 people now live. Demographically, only the homelands of Kaokoveld, Ovamboland, Kavangoland, East Caprivi in the north, and Rehoboth in the south are located in traditional living areas. Damaraland, Hereroland, Bushmanland, Namaland, and Tswanaland require the shift of 95%, 74%, 66%, 93%, and 100% of the population. This involves the abolition of seven reserves.

An examination of the 'homelands' with regard to potential economic viability shows equally that the elementary foundations for any genuine form of self-determination are lacking. The African economy of the reserves is a bare subsistence one, with desert dryness and poor soil setting severe limits. Rainfall increases from the south to the northeast from less than four inches to between twelve and twenty in the northeast. In good years the northern area can be self-sufficient in grains — but this is the sole favourable aspect of the allocated land. The central plateau extending the length of Namibia comprises two climatic areas: the Kalahari 'sandveld', and the 'hardveld' with no sand covering. The hardveld is where the pasture is nutritionally satisfactory, and each farm has proved groundwater. The sandveld areas have been avoided by white farmers, as here the water content of the deep-lying rocks are not replenishable from local rainfall, and the grasses are deficient in protein and phosphorous. This makes for endemic stock disease. This sandveld covers all the northern area, except terrace land flooded by the Okavango and parts of Caprivi. Hereroland is entirely sandveld and 80% waterless: Aminuis, the only hardveld area, is taken over by the government. Kaokoveld is the driest area in the north with less than two inches of rain. Apart from an area in the east, Damaraland is mainly Namib desert. Bushman-land, Tswanaland, and Namaland are semi-desert areas, with Namaland supporting small stock of karakul sheep. The Rehoboth Gebiet has a number of poor stock-farms, but is dependent on outside supplies of food and water.

The poor quality of this land is the key to the economics of the apartheid system, which requires the 'Integration' of African subsistence farmers into the commercial economic sector, without the responsibility of housing and social services. Social infrastructure must be provided by the traditional social system in the 'homelands'.

This aim, rather than the announced aim of 'development' consonant with political 'independence', emerges clearly from the absence of the means for economic self-sufficiency in the homelands, either separately, or in some form of 'federation', as proposed by Dr Muller, the South African Foreign Minister. Odendaal contained only scant proposals for improving or diversify-ing the subsistence economies; as with the earlier Tomlinson Commission in SA there is no attempt to trace the elements of an agricultural revolution, partly because this would mean large holdings and heavy capital investment, involving competition with the vested interest of white farmers, whose whole economic experience has been based on the denial of equal opportunities to the Africans. According to the SWA Survey of 1967, the northern reserves had 665,000 cattle, southern reserves 139,000 cattle (total 2,346,000), 492,000 and 274,000 goats respectively (total 1,539,000), while the southern reserves had 97,000 karakul (total 3,097,000) . . .

The South African bantustan scheme is an obvious attempt to ensure the continued dependence of the Namibian people on the South African economic system and its resources. As demonstrated above, the so-called 'Homelands', planned by the South African Government, are not viable units but are dependent upon the possibility of obtaining limited cash incomes by working in the so-called 'White Areas'.

The bantustan policy is therefore totally fallacious, and is merely a crafty device not only to keep the occupied Namibian people in continued sub-serviance but also to deceive the international community.

Land: Rhodesia's Powder Keg
ZAPU

Statement of ZAPU published in Zimbabwe Review *(Lusaka), No. 9, 24 October 1966.*

At the 1961 Constitutional Conference, our leader Joshua Nkomo made it categorically clear that any constitutional settlement in Rhodesia should solve the land issue. Five years later, Britain is still toying around Rhodesia's constitutional aspects without any consideration of this key issue. This impels us to restate the position over this vital issue.

In 1923, when the white settlers negotiated internal self-government, they demanded from the British Government that land in Rhodesia should be divided among the racial communities, with settlers holding exclusive ownership rights to part of the country. The British Government turned down their demands but blessed them with internal self-government. Armed with this new weapon, the settlers proceeded to take measures to achieve their objective. To bluff British public opinion, they appointed a commission, the 'Land Commission of 1925' to find possibilities of such an apportionment of land. Africans were not consulted and those interviewed rejected the idea. The Commission headed by Morris Carter, a servant of settler interests, recommended land apportionment on a racial basis, giving the white settlers exclusive rights over large tracts of land. After a detailed survey of which land to grab, the settler Parliament passed the Land Apportionment Act 1931: This law empowered the settler government, or commissions and agencies set up by it, to divide the land into European and African areas. In the European areas, the white settlers have exclusive ownership rights over such designated areas. The African can reside in such an area as a worker (for the white man) but can neither own land there nor use it for productive purposes. His residence in such areas is by permit of the settler authority and the permit is given only on condition that the applicant has written proof that he is employed. On termination of his services, his employer notifies the local authority and the African loses his right of residence in such an area.

But the kernel of land apportionment is economic privilege. In a country with a population of over four million Africans and 220,000 white settlers, the land is apportioned as follows:—

European			African Reserves:	21,020,000 acres
Area	:	47,897,000 acres	Special African	
Forest Area	:	3,190,000 acres	Area :	12,878,000 acres
Game reserves,			African Purchase	
Parks, etc.	:	4,057,000 acres	Area :	8,052,000 acres
Total area			Total (African	
(European)		55,134,000 acres	area)	41,950,000 acres

Thus four million are allocated less than 42% of the land whilst 6% of the population has exclusive rights over 58% of Rhodesian soil. It should be noted that Special African areas represent African residential areas or townships in the urban areas. In these areas, Africans are prohibited from using the land for productive purposes. Thus in fact, the bulk of the African population lives in and cultivates 21 million acres or 22% of the land surface. To consolidate their devilish schemes, the settler Parliament passes the Land Husbandry Act 1951. The Land Husbandry act was designed to be an administrative instrument for the implementation of the Land Apportionment Act under the new conditions that had arisen. Population increase from 1931 had resulted in serious overcrowding in the African reserves, the land formally allocated to every family had further to be subdivided into yet smaller plots. Every household was allocated a maximum of 6 acres, and livestock had to be drastically reduced since grazing land had become scarce. The Land Husbandry Act empowered the regime to remove families and groups of families or entire villages from their residence if the land was required by a white farmer. Tens of thousands of families were removed from lands which they had owned and cultivated for decades. The regime had to use armed troops to effect such measures since it met with stiff opposition from the African population. Under the guise of land consolidation, the African people were systematically dispossessed of rich land and driven to arid areas to give room to the new overlords — the white settlers.

The 21 million acres of land allocated to the African population consisted of (i) dry, arid regions where cultivation of any crops is impossible and rearing livestock impracticable due to lack of water; (ii) swampy areas infested by tsetse flies and unsuitable for human habitation; (iii) arable regions but with low rainfall and poor soils. It is in this belt where the African lives. On the other hand, European areas consist of rich land with good rainfall. Industrial and commercial centres are in this belt, thus making farm products near consumption markets. We must further note that, in the whole of Rhodesia, all European land was occupied by only 4,630 farmers in 1961 (I.L.O. statistics). In 1966, there are less than 6,000 white farmers.

Land policy in Rhodesia is a deliberate device to ensure a constant reservoir of cheap labour for industry and commerce. Deprived of his land and incapable of subsisting on anything else, the African is driven to industry as a wage slave. The exodus of the population from rural areas to urban areas is out of proportion with industry's ability to absorb all the available manpower. Unemployment is the logical result and this provides the industrialists with the necessary artillery to flout the rights of the workers — aware that any 'dissidents' could be dismissed and replaced instantly. It further creates a situation in which the labour supply is higher than the demand for labour, and wages can thus be kept low. The stability of such a supply/demand curve ensures stagnant wage bills.

Exclusive ownership of farm land leads to monopoly production. Cash crops are thus controlled by a handful of people throughout the various stages — production and distribution. The interests of industrial, finance and agricultural capital are closely interwoven. Farmers get loans from finance houses, their products are raw materials for industry in Rhodesia and abroad, and industrial concerns are in turn shareholders in the finance houses, and so the vicious circle goes on. Many farms are owned by absentee landlords (British) and vast tracts of land are owned by certain companies (British). It is necessary to note that, of the vast tracts owned by the white settlers, a very small percentage is under cultivation. In other words, they do not own these acres in order to use every one of them. Exclusive ownership has a deeper philosophy: the dispossession of the African people of any means of production so as to compel them to be dependent on a certain class and thus become tools for use by the white settlers and their financial bosses.

The land issue thus emerges as a key point since land is the basic interest of the white minority. The expropriation of African land by the white settlers constitutes a major bone of contention. The resistance of the white minority to majority rule is based, among other things, on the fear of losing exclusive rights over land. Whilst the white settlers are hirelings for the protection of British interests, they too have a stake to preserve; exclusive land ownership is the price they demand for their role in preserving British interests.

The Zimbabwe African People's Union has made it perfectly clear that the land in Zimbabwe belongs to all people and there can be no question of exclusive ownership of the land by any class or group of persons. The struggle for liberation, therefore, envisages the recovery of the land into the hands of the legitimate owners: *The People of Zimbabwe*. Land is a great economic potential and the wealth thereof must be shared fairly by all. Our policy remains the same: reclamation of the land and redistribution in the interests of the people.

The white settlers in Rhodesia have an unshaken determination to maintain the status quo in agriculture, for it ensures their continued domination of the African people and is a means to perpetuate a position of economic privilege. On the other hand, the readjustment of the land policy is a prime consideration for the African people. The Policy of ZAPU has been made clear several times and it will be sufficient here to quote a recent statement by ZAPU's Deputy President, J.R. Dambadza Chikerema; 'Therefore in fairness to Zimbabwe and its people the basic principle that the land belongs to the *People* of Zimbabwe must be conceded, and this must be the guiding principle for any readjustment of land.'

Manifesto

FROLIZI

*The Manifesto of the Front for the Liberation of
Zimbabwe (Frolizi) adopted at their inaugural congress
held from 21 August to 5 September 1972.*

(1) The national liberation and democratic revolution of the broad masses of
the colonial and neo-colonial peoples of Africa, Asia and America against
colonialism, neo-colonialism and imperialism in general is one of the major
historical features of our epoch. This anti-colonialist, anti-imperialist revolution is a powerful force recognised as such by all, and against which imperialists have entered a common front. A continuous struggle that starts here
and ends in a constitutional or revolutionary change has been and is going
on, inflicting heavy blows on a crumbling and decaying imperialism.

(2) Modern imperialism sprouted from capitalism. Capitalism's need for
higher profits, raw materials, and constantly expanding markets forced
it to settle and establish links everywhere. By settling and setting up connect-
ions everywhere, imperialist capitalism was effecting colonialism.

(3) The rounding of the Cape of Good Hope, the conquest of American,
Asian and African markets opened the ground for colonialism. And, as time
went by, each step in the development of imperialism was accompanied by
a corresponding economic and political advance of colonial settlers. In certain
areas like Zimbabwe and Southern Africa as a whole, there developed settler-
colonialism — a state in which an assortment of misfits from the colonising
countries are settled in a colony, granted political power over the heads of
the indigenous people, for the purpose of defending and protecting colonial
capitalism in particular, and imperialism in general.

(4) The forces of economic activity in settler-colonial bourgeois society
in Zimbabwe have developed to a stage when they are no longer compatible
with classical colonial relations of property. These relations have become a
stumbling block to the development of colonial capitalism. This is in the
sense that, with the growth of economic activity, there must be a corresponding growth of investment in such fields as education, health, etc., and
there must be land reform and more and more capital formation. Labour,
both indigenous and settler-colonial, must compete freely on the job market;
and the social and political set-up must shift along with changes in the
economic structure.

(5) Thus, settler-colonialism cannot develop optimally without revolution-
ising economic relations; and with them the whole relations of society. Con-
servation of the old features inevitably leads to revolution. But at the same
time, constant changes in economic and social life, uncertainty and agitation
also lead to revolution. It is quite clear from this that the settler-colonial
power structure in our country, Zimbabwe, is in a fix; and that the inevita-
bility of victory by the revolutionary forces cannot be questionable. The
people's demand for political power shall win.

(6) The forms of economic activity in Zimbabwe are at this stage incompatible with its content. The people need and deserve better economic remuneration and living standards. But if this is met, the settler-colonial racist bourgeois supremacy will collapse since the people's economic power creates demands for political control of the state. On the other hand, if the people's demands for both political and economic power are not met, the people must and will fight to achieve this. Thus, independently of anybody's will, there is bound to be violent revolutionary change in Zimbabwe, organised and effected by the people.

(7) The people of Zimbabwe have gone through various stages of political development. The struggle against colonialism and imperialism began with the colonisation of our country some eighty years ago. The invasion of Zimbabwe by imperialist Britain was spearheaded by advance parties of hunters, prospectors and missionaries, paving the way for the British South Africa Company organised by the greatest of imperialists in Africa, Cecil John Rhodes. The colonial settlers claim that the African chiefs granted him mining and other concessions, following which he occupied the country by force of arms. After the occupation, the colonial settlers introduced the system of poll tax and forced labour in farms, mines, and road and railway projects in which thousands and thousands of Zimbabweans working as slaves lost their lives. The people of Zimbabwe replied to this rape with fierce and resolute armed resistance which culminated in the so-called rebellions of the 1890s.

(8) In the resistance war of that time, the struggle was led by traditional authorities using the force of the village people, that is, the peasants. This struggle aimed at restoring and defending the people's land by force of arms. Later, the emerging nationalists started a struggle of a new kind, using the force of the workers and the peasants. The fight was against the evils of the system and for better living conditions under the same system. At these early stages, the people of Zimbabwe were more or less incoherent masses. If there were united actions, it was not the result of their own solidarity but that of a union of traditional authorities and the emerging nationalists.

(9) But with the development of the settler-colonial bourgeois system the people of Zimbabwe became concentrated in greater masses of uprooted peasants, urban and rural wage labourers, and middle sector elements. The people's unity developed. Their organisation into a political party appeared and went into operation under the leadership of the nationalists. The programme of the movement was national independence through constitutional struggle. Unfortunately, the movement and unity of the people was upset by the extensive and intensive enemy machine of repression as well as by power competition within the nationalist leadership. But the people's national movement always comes back to life, stronger and more militant in revolutionary struggle against oppression and exploitation.

(10) The national liberation and democratic revolutionary movement arises from the interests of the people as a whole. It is distinguishable by that:

(i) in the national liberation struggle of the people, it brings to the forefront the common interest of the entire people.

(ii) in the various stages of development which the revolutionary struggle must go through, it always stands for the interests of the movement and people as a whole.

(11) The national liberation and democratic movement, therefore, is practically the most advanced and resolute force of the people against colonialism and neo-colonialism. Moreover, it has, ideologically, the advantage of clearly grasping the line of march, the conditions and general results of the people's action, in the light of historical necessity, that is:—

(i) life is primary to ideas and political consciousness; and all political activity by the people is a reflection of differences in modes of life within society.

(ii) the revolution is bound to win, as the world is a complex of processes and not a fixed state of affairs.

(iii) there is bound to be struggle between the oppressed and exploited on the one hand, and the oppressors and exploiters on the other, which ends in a revolutionary reconstitution of society.

(12) Such conclusions are not just arbitrary ideas or invented principles; they express in general terms actual relations emanating from concrete conditions. The complete overthrow of the settler-colonial state, the abolition of existing settler-colonial bourgeois property relations and all forms and kinds of exploitation as well as links with imperialism are therefore the focus of the Zimbabwe national liberation and democratic revolutionary movement. The mission of the Front for the Liberation of Zimbabwe is to create, through armed struggle, a state of affairs which widened, enriched and promoted the interests of the broad masses of the oppressed and exploited people of Zimbabwe.

Crime Against Humanity
ZANU

This paper was submitted by ZANU to a UN-sponsored international seminar on apartheid, held in Kitwe (Zambia) in August 1967.

Man's memory may be short, even the memories of those that had the misfortune only two decades ago of being directly subjected to the practical and systematic implementation of the doctrines of racial superiority of the Nazi regime in Germany and all over Europe. The present victims of apartheid, of racial discrimination and of the remnants of colonialism, the subject matter of this seminar, cannot fail to read the signs and draw parallels between that doctrine in Nazi Germany that brought catastrophe on the world and its present manifestations in Southern Africa. While the world, particularly the Western world, watches with studied complacency and pious condemnation, apartheid, that twin sister of Nazism, has reared its ugly head and, with similarly calculated defiance of humanity, is spreading its tentacles over the whole of Southern Africa.

Apartheid, racial discrimination and colonialism constitute a problem affecting the whole of Southern Africa. They are component parts of an inhuman system that not only merits the moral condemnation of the whole civilized world but should be fought and destroyed by and through the unqualified and active participation of every country signatory to the United Nations Declaration on Human Rights if the world is to be spared the horrid spectacle of another Nazi-type holocaust in this part of the world.

In examining this problem we would like to confine our remarks in this paper particularly to Southern Rhodesia, which in fact is an integral part of the same problem and illustrates in remarkable detail the vicious application of this system all over the area of Southern Africa. While the rest of the world has condemned and tried to ostracise the Ian Smith regime diplomatically, economically and politically, South Africa and Portugal have flown in the face of world opinion and flouted international decisions by giving succour and help to bolster this regime and frustrate United Nations action against it. Nor was this flagrant defiance a matter of accident. The cornerstone of Rhodesian apartheid and racial discrimination is the Land Apportionment Act enacted in 1930—31. A comparative historical analysis will illustrate the point we wish to make:

(1) The Rhodesian settlers came from South Africa. Up to 1923, Rhodesia was governed by the British South Africa Company and Royal Charter.

(2) When in 1923 they got internal self-government, their first act was to introduce Land Apportionment.

(3) South Africa had introduced the Land Acts in 1912.

In 1948 South Africa intensified apartheid by introducing the Group Areas Acts and Rhodesia today is introducing similar measures for the total implementation of apartheid in respect to all races in the country.

The Group Areas Act in South Africa has relegated to an inferior position the African majority of the land. This same philosophy, that the African is an inferior race, that forever he must be isolated and never allowed to develop beyond limits defined by the ruling minority 'superior' race, has taken root in Southern Rhodesia. To allay the outraged conscience of the world, the apartheid fascist Nationalist Government of South Africa has developed the so-called Bantu homelands (Bantustan) system; similarly, the rebel Rhodesia Front Government has started implementing the so-called 'Community Development' system whose tenets derive much inspiration from the Bantustan regime of South Africa. Under these regimes, as is now well known internationally, the African majority has no rights in the areas designated as white preserves, which in both countries are the richest, most fertile parts of the land; he must content himself with scratching a bare subsistence from the most barren and infertile areas of the land. Both operate under the guise of a doctrine purporting to preserve the so-called *separate cultural identity* of each race; meanwhile he (the African) supplies the labour and manpower on which white industries, mines and farms run and he must look to himself and to the proceeds of his scratchings on the bare land to supply his own education and funds for all the other facilities he may need.

It is significant that, while the white minority Government of Vorster appeals to all whites to produce a baby for South Africa and the Ian Smith regime of Rhodesia appeals for more white immigration to Rhodesia, both talk of an African population explosion and have introduced under the guise of birth control the Nazi sterilization campaign aimed at the reduction of the African population by scientific diminution. The world will never know, any more than in Nazi Germany's time, the extent of this crime against humanity because the present perpetrators thereof wrap these measures in scientific terms. But let not the world be deceived twice. We have in this area as vicious, inhuman and calculated regimes as that which practised the mass killings of the Jews and 'in the name of science' practised human sterilization as one of the final solutions to the so-called Jewish problem.

Rhodesia: Apartheid Is Already Here
ANC (Zimbabwe)

*Excerpt from a speech by Bishop Abel Muzorewa,
chairman of the African National Council (Zimbabwe)
at a mass rally held in London by the Rhodesia
Emergency Campaign Committee in February 1972.*

Mr Smith became the leader of the Rhodesia Front because he was prepared to stop at nothing to ensure that Rhodesia would remain a country ruled *by* the whites and *for* the whites, for as long as the rule of the gun permits. The Principles of the Rhodesia Front are Apartheid principles. There is no question of Apartheid drifting to Rhodesia. *It is already there.* Does this British Government really think that the Africans of Rhodesia are so naive, are so stupid as to believe that Mr Smith will ever allow the Africans the basic human right to rule themselves? Does this government think that we are children who can be fooled by such a blatant lie? I assure you we are not children, we are not fooled — we are grown men and, by God, we have dignity!

When a black baby is born in Rhodesia it learns very quickly that to be black in Rhodesia is more important than to be human. He sees his father treated as a child. If he is lucky this black child might go to school and then he will be told he has no culture, no history, no honour. If he is lucky enough to go on to secondary school he is told that he is a kaffir and not a person. If he goes for a job he will be told he is either not educated enough or too well educated. If he can't get a job he is told he is a lazy useless African.

If he then asks why this should be so, he is condemned as a subversive and a trouble maker. Every day of his life he is insulted and when he asks why, he is told it is because he is not a person, because persons are white and because God is not only white but also a settler. Mr Smith and Sir Alec Douglas Home call themselves Christians. I wonder what Christ would say if he were an African in Rhodesia. He would probably have no chance to say anything. Rather he would probably be rotting in a dirty little prison cell in some fly-infested part of Rhodesia.

I have already told you that we reject these proposals not because anyone has threatened or intimidated us into rejection. We reject them *in spite of* a system of intimidation which surrounds the life of every African from the cradle to the grave — and tells him that the white people are superior to him, and nothing they propose for him can be rejected. The right to decide how and where and why one should live is surely basic to this problem. Rhodesian whites believe that they alone are competent to govern us, and if we don't agree to this we must be intimidated into agreement. Today, once again, *we reject the myth of our inferiority, we reject this intimidation.*

Whether that intimidation comes from the District Commissioner, who in our intimidatory system is free to take away a man's land or cattle at his own discretion; whether it is from the policeman who has the power to stop any African on the street and demand his pass — *We reject it.*

Whether that intimidation is by a cabinet minister, who without explanation or reason can take away a man's or a woman's freedom for any length of time from one hour to fifteen years — *we reject it.*

Whether it is the intimidation of municipal authorities in the townships, who can take away a man's home and throw him and his family on to the street, without explanation — *we reject it.*

Whether it is the intimidation of the employer, who can sack his workers without reason, knowing that that man and his family will starve — *we reject it.*

Whether it is the intimidation of whites by such measures as the deprivation of a person's citizenship, as in the case of Clutton-Brock, simply for his opposition to racialism, or the detention in solitary confinement of the Todds because they have the courage of their convictions — *we reject it.*

We reject a policy and a regime that can justify the murder of 31 unarmed human beings on the streets of Gwelo, Salisbury and Umtali and the arrest of the Todds and the Chinamanos, and over 250 people whose only crime is to stand up for their dignity and to ask the world simply to treat them as human beings.

We reject the intimidation of a government of thugs. Above all, my brothers and sisters, *We Reject Injustice and Demand Our Freedom.*

Achievement of the Pioneers
Southern Rhodesian Government

> *The opening of the historical section of 'Southern*
> *Rhodesia — Advance to Maturity', a publication of the*
> *office of the High Commissioner for Southern*
> *Rhodesia in London in December 1964.*

When the Pioneers arrived shortly before the turn of the century they found an inhospitable country sparsely settled by tribes that had driven out the Bushmen and Hottentots whose original hunting grounds this had been. The last invaders to impose their will on the numerically superior Mashona and other tribes were the Matabele who had made the countryside within raiding distance of Bulawayo their domain, only 37 years before the Pioneers occupied Mashonaland in accordance with the mandate granted by the British Government.

The African population in what is now Southern Rhodesia amounted at that time to some 400,000. With the advent of the European, inter-tribal warfare ceased, the threat of famine receded and Western medicine began to make ever-increasing inroads into the incidence of disease. By 1923, when Southern Rhodesia was formally annexed to the Crown and granted responsible government, African numbers had risen to some 900,000. On the outbreak of the 1939 War, when conscription was introduced to control the number of white Rhodesians flocking to the Colours, black Rhodesians numbered approximately 1½ million. Today there are 3,850,000 Africans and their numbers are increasing by some 134,000 per year.

4. Roles of Various Classes and Groups in Colonial Society

Editor's Introduction

The relationship of class and nation, of the class struggle and the struggle for national liberation is an old and thorny question. Most writers have argued over priority of importance. A few have argued a hypothesis of alternating importance. The leader of the PAIGC, Amilcar Cabral, wrestled seriously with this intellectual problem, not as an academic exercise, but as a concrete problem for the national liberation movements to resolve, in order to determine their strategy. His approach was in many ways original, and his speech to the Havana Conference of 1966, reproduced in part below, rapidly became famous for its clarity and vigour. We also reproduce a more obscure but very important late (1971) statement of his key concept, the 'nation-class'.

History Before and After the Class Struggle
Amilcar Cabral

> *Excerpt of a speech given by Amilcar Cabral to the First Tricontinental Congress in Havana, 3–12 January 1966.*

Those who affirm — and rightly so as far as we are concerned — that the motor force of history is the class struggle, will give it greater application by becoming more profoundly familiar with the essential characteristics of specific colonized peoples (dominated by imperialism). In fact, in the general evolution of humanity and of each people or human group that are a part of it, classes appear neither as a generalized and simultaneous phenomenon in all these groups, nor as one finished, perfect, uniform, and spontaneous totality. The definition of classes in the core of a group or groups of human beings is fundamentally the result of the progressive development of productive forces and of the characteristics of distribution of the wealth produced by that group or usurped by other groups. That is to say, the socio-economic phenomenon of *class* comes out of and develops from at least two essential and interdependent variables: the level of the productive forces and the system of ownership of the means of production. This development occurs slowly, unequally, and gradually, by quantitative leaps which are generally imperceptible, with essential variants which lead at a certain point of accumulation, to qualitative transformations which are translated into the appearance of classes and the conflict among classes.

Factors outside a given socio-economic union in movement can influence more or less significantly the process of the class development, accelerating it, retarding it, or even provoking regressions. When the influence of these factors ceases for whatever reason, the process returns to its own independent course and its rhythm comes to be determined not only by its own internally related characteristics, but also by the results of the effect that the temporal action of external factors has had on it. On the strictly internal level, the rhythm of the process can change but remains continuous and progressive, sharp advances being possible only in case of an increase in sudden alterations — mutations — at the level of productive forces or within the system of ownership. These sharp transformations in the internal process of the development of classes as a result of mutations at the level of productive forces or in the system of ownership, have come to be called in economic and political language, *revolutions.*

On the other hand, it is evident that the possibilities of this process are influenced significantly by external factors, in particular by the interaction of human groups which is gradually augmented by the progress of the means of transportation and communication that the world and humanity have created, eliminating the isolation among human groups in the same region, among regions on the same continent, and among continents. The progress that characterizes a long phase of history that began with the invention of the first methods of transportation, had already become evident in the Punic voyages and in Greek colonization, and was accentuated by maritime discoveries, the invention of steam engines, and the discovery of electricity. And which promises, in our times with the peaceful development of atomic energy, to send men to the stars, or at least to humanize the universe.

What has been said allows us to raise the following questions: Does history begin only at the moment when the *class* phenomenon, and consequently, the class struggle appears? An affirmative reply would mean placing outside history the whole period of the life of human groups, beginning with the discovery of hunting, followed by nomad and sedentary agriculture, up to the beginning of cattle breeding and the private ownership of land. But it would also mean — which we refuse to accept — considering that various human groups of Africa, Asia, and Latin America lived without a history or outside of history at the time they were brought under the yoke of imperialism. It would be to consider that peoples of our countries, like the Balantas of Guinea, the Cuanhamas of Angola, and the Macondes of Mozambique, still live — if we leave aside the very small influences of colonialism to which they were subjected — outside history or that they have no history at all.

This rejection based on the concrete knowledge of the socio-economic reality of our countries and on the analyses of the developmental process of the *class phenomenon,* as was made before, leads us to the admission that, if the class struggle is the moving force of history, it is so for a certain historical period. This means that *before* the class struggle (and necessarily *after* the class struggle, because in this world there is no before without an after), some factor (or some factors), was and will be the motor of history. We are not reluctant to admit that this factor in the history of each human group is the *method of production* (the level of productive forces and the regime of ownership) which characterizes that group. Besides, as we have seen, the definition of class and class struggle are themselves a result of the development of the productive forces combined with the regime of ownership of the means of production. It therefore seems to us correct to conclude that the level of productive forces, the essential determinant of the character and form of the class struggle, is the real and permanent moving force of history.

If we accept this conclusion, the doubts which disturb our mind will be eliminated. Because, if on the one hand we see the existence of history before the class struggle guaranteed, and avoid for some of the human groups of our countries (and perhaps of our continents) the sad condition of people without history, on the other hand we see the continuity of history secured, even after the disappearance of the class struggle or of classes themselves. And while it was not we who postulated on scientific bases, the disappearance of *classes* as an historical fatality, we agree with this conclusion, that in a certain way establishes coherence and, at the same time, grants nations such as Cuba, that are building socialism, the pleasant certainty that they will not lack a history when they finish the process of the liquidation of the *class phenomenon* and the class struggle in the midst of their social and economic system. Eternity is not something of this world, but man will outlive classes, and will continue producing and making history, because he cannot get rid of the burden of his necessities, his hands, and his brains, that are at the base of the development of the productive forces.

The Nation-Class
Amilcar Cabral

> *Response to an interview question by Amilcar Cabral on 28 October 1971. The interview was conducted on behalf of two journals of the Portuguese underground opposition and is reproduced from* Anticolonialismo, *No. 2, February 1972. Translated from Portuguese.*

Question: Amilcar Cabral, in 1964 you stated that it was not the class struggle but rather the colonial situation which was of prime historical importance at that time. What exactly must we understand by this, and what are the political consequences of such a view?

Answer: This statement is the result of an appreciation of our own reality. We are not unaware that, in the course of the history of our people, there have emerged class phenomena, varying in definition and state of development. We have on the one hand the Balantas, for example, a horizontal society, and on the other we have a society such as the Fulas already built up in the form of a pyramid and thus with classes fairly well defined. Meanwhile, we know that colonial domination in our country, just as in others, but we are here referring to our own case, creates an identical situation for everyone. And when the fight against colonial domination begins, it is not the product of one class even though the idea may have sprung up from the class which has become aware more rapidly or earlier of colonial domination and of the necessity of combatting it. But this revolt is not the product of a class as such. Rather it is a whole society acting as a nation-class that carries it out. This nation-class, which may be more or less clearly structured, is dominated not by people from the colonized country but rather by the ruling class of the colonized country. This is our view, and hence our struggle is essentially based not on a class struggle but rather on the struggle led by our nation-class against the Portuguese ruling class. It is precisely here that we find the link between our struggle and that of the Portuguese people for the social, economic and cultural transformation of their lives; because the Portuguese people is also conducting a struggle, utilizing progressively more developed forms, against the same ruling class.

Naturally, the consequences are: firstly, through this fight we are shaping our African Nation which, as you know, was not yet very well defined, with all the problems of many ethnic groups, of the divisions created by the colonialist power itself (distinctions between natives and *assimilados*, between city dwellers and peasants, etc.). We are building our African Nation which is becoming more and more conscious of itself. But at the same time we must be alert to the development of classes within this new nation. In the meanwhile, the struggle gives us experience based exactly on this postulate. In this way, not only do we strengthen our political and moral unity as a nation, but we also strengthen our vigilance so as to keep the class struggle from taking on aspects which could be detrimental to the progress of our own people. This is all I can say in a brief form on this vast and very complex problem.

5. The Bourgeoisie

Editors' Introduction

The national liberation movements, seeking to analyse the class situation of their countries, profited from, yet were also burdened by, a long heritage of analyses by European Marxists who utilized terms like 'bourgeoisie' in a specific historical context.

In terms of the history of Modern Europe, the word 'bourgeois' means two quite different things. It means the class of merchants (and free professionals) who emerged as the protagonists of the capitalist system and who, in social terms, are a *middle* group, between the upper group, the aristocracy, and the lower group without rights, the plebs, mostly in fact peasants. But once the Industrial Revolution was in full swing, beginning in the Nineteenth Century, the socio-political role of the aristocracy declined sharply. The bourgeoisie came to power, economically, politically and socially. They were now an *upper* class polarized against a lower class increasingly taking the form of an urban proletariat.

If this were not confusion enough, the world process of colonization of the Nineteenth Century added a further element. In a colony, the ruling group was perhaps a 'bourgeoisie', but one of a distinctive ethnic group different from the indigenous population. For Cabral, as we have seen, this group stood in opposition to the *lower* class, the indigenous 'nation-class'.

But if we come to the latter conclusion, then can we say there exists at all in the colonial situation a local bourgeoisie? To say yes is to undermine the concept of 'nation-class'. To say no is to ignore patent differences of wealth, occupation, education, style of life between a small 'privileged' group and the majority of the population. By ignoring this distinction, a movement might find itself unable to explain the political reality of its inner life.

It is no accident, then, that the leaders of the movements approached this definitional problem with some prudence and that their statements sometimes lacked total internal coherence. There are statements that accentuate the absence of an African bourgeoisie in the true sense. The statements by Marcellino Dos Santos, Vice-President of FRELIMO, and George Nyandoro, at the time Secretary-General of ZAPU, were of this variety.

By contrast, two statements of the MPLA, one anonymous and one by Paulo Jorge, discuss the problem of the urban petty bourgeoisie, especially the *assimilados*. These statements indicated some doubt as to whether these elements wished to subsume themselves in the Angolan 'nation-class'. In part, the position of the MPLA reflected the social reality of Angola. In part, it reflected a particular *political* problem wherein the MPLA had long found itself under attack by the UPA and others for being 'dominated' by these *assimilados*.

The implications become clear in the article by Viriato da Cruz. It is a famous article written in *Revolution*, published in Paris. The article distinguished two groups of *assimilados*, those likely to be 'patriotic' and those likely to support the Portuguese. It was written by da Cruz shortly after he had been expelled from the MPLA and just before he joined forces with Holden Roberto's UPA. The target of his implicit attack was clearly the MPLA.

One attempt to place the whole question in sober perspective was made by Mario de Andrade in the basic document he submitted to the Second Conference of CONCP in 1965. Andrade sought to describe the anatomy of the class structure as it had concretely emerged in the Portuguese colonies, concluding that, although privileged strata could be distinguished, the key fact was the absence of 'proprietary classes'.

It should be noted that there are no analyses from South Africa included in this section. It is not because the question is simpler there, but because it is more complex. The existence there, alone in Southern Africa, of a significant urban proletariat means that the issue herein discussed cannot be sensibly approached without talking simultaneously about the role of the 'working classes'. This is to be found in the section that follows this one.

A Bourgeoisie?

Marcellino dos Santos

Excerpt from 'Marcellino Dos Santos Talks to Sechaba'
in Sechaba, *IV, 11/12, Nov./Dec. 1970.*

Concretely, what is the position of the bourgeoisie in Mozambique? There are at present two systems: the colonial capitalist system and also the traditional communal economic system. At the level of the communal economy we will have to face the traditional chiefs who have certain interests which they will attempt to maintain. We feel that in a limited way they would be opposed to the struggle for national liberation. In Mozambique today we find that almost 90% of the traditional chiefs have not been elected to their posts in the normal tribal fashion, but have been appointed by the Portuguese. Usually at a certain point the traditional chief was unable to follow government directives for moral reasons, and then the Portuguese replaced him. In this manner the traditional chiefs have been humiliated, they have a grudge against colonialism. But they have nevertheless kept certain benefits in terms of the tribal system. We therefore feel that at the tribal level there is a general tendency to oppose a liberation leading to emancipation.

If we examine the capitalist economy, we find that the Mozambicans are not really represented in the capitalist structure and do not belong to the bourgeois class, except in agriculture where we find a limited number of Mozambican landowners, but their economic power is small and they do not represent a social force. Therefore the majority of the population would be favourable to a system without the exploitation of man by man.

On the African scene, we find today that there is a new political consciousness developing. In the countries which have become independent, people who have tasted independence have realised that this was not enough. Movements have developed, a certain political consciousness has appeared, which calls for more than a hymn and a flag. Taking these new developments into consideration we feel that we must devise a system which will benefit our people. On the practical level we are simply using methods which respect this orientation.

When we look at Portuguese colonialism, a fascist colonialism which does not accept the principle of independence, we must realise that it is a fight until death — either them or us. When we look at the material strength of Portugal compared to our strength we have to look for our strength not only in technical terms but in man himself. We must obtain the dedication of all those who are prepared to fight for liberation. We have to find slogans to build our unity. We cannot be tribalists, nor racists because we have to show that it is exploitation we want to destroy. If we had tackled the problem as a racial one we would be forced to condone the exploiters with black skins!

We in South Africa find that the form of the political contradiction is very sharply between black and white. In what way is this different in Mozambique and how does this fit in with your concept of Mozambique nationalism?

I think that the conditions in South Africa are quite different than in Mozambique where fascism affects both Whites and Blacks — the Portuguese Government does not only oppress the blacks, it also oppresses the Whites. Under these circumstances unity does not exist among the white population. Under this oppressive system, the material conditions of the 200,000 Whites in Mozambique are not always brilliant. There is a large section of the population which has a low standard of living; this is very important.

There is also the class of the liberal professions who have this urge for freedom. The relations existing between the Blacks and Whites are not that distant. There is still apparent racial discrimination in cinemas, buses etc., but there are Blacks who maintain contact with the white population.

The Only Real Exploiters Are Foreigners
George Nyandoro

> *Excerpt from interview by the Liberation Support*
> *Movement (USA and Canada) with George Nyandoro,*
> *then Secretary-General of ZAPU, which appeared in 1970.*

Traditionally we had no capitalism in Zimbabwe and the social fabric
contained many collective aspects and principles of mutual responsibility
and aid. I can't say there was no personal property by individuals. There
were some people with more cattle than others, and so on. But normally, if
a person had no cattle, someone would give him a cow and out of the
progeny of that cow he could build up his own stock. If you were willing to
work hard, society gave you the means of making a living. If you didn't
work hard, or were lazy, you were the laughing stock of the community.
So you were forced by society to work hard. Much of this remains even
today, particularly in the countryside, where most of our people have not yet
been drawn into capitalist relations of production. So in terms of socialist
ideological training, what needs to be done is to sharpen our people's awareness of certain fundamental tenets of socialism which were practised traditionally. Then it will not be very difficult to introduce and teach scientific
socialism – for it will not be an entirely new thing for the masses to
comprehend. It must also be said that the only real exploiters known by the
present generation of people in Zimbabwe have been foreigners – white
settlers from Britain and South Africa. These are the people who have
established capitalist industry and farming in our country, who have sucked
the wealth out of our land and labour, and who have been oppressing us. So
the struggle is seen by the masses as being between the whites and the blacks.
Very few Africans have acquired any real wealth in Zimbabwe and they are
merely agents of the capitalists who may own a small shop, engage in petty
trade, etc., and who get some of the crumbs which fall from the master's
table. The settlers think they are creating a middle class with these people.
But such Africans are not really capitalists, not really rich – though psycho-
logically they are made to believe that they are capitalists. As for the broad
masses of the people, they accept ZAPU's socialist policies without question.
For them black is synonymous with the oppressed class and white with the
rich capitalist class.

The Problem of the *Assimilados*
MPLA

> *Excerpt from a pamphlet entitled* Angola *published by*
> *Information CONCP on behalf of MPLA in Algiers in*
> *1969. Translated from French.*

The Portuguese have artificially divided the Angolan population into 'natives' (99% of the total) and *assimilados* (1%). From these figures it is evident that the 'assimilation' phenomenon has been quite limited.

The 'assimilation' policy, which is not the invention of Portuguese colonialism, was pursued by other colonizers, who favoured the creation of a restricted privileged class able to serve as an intermediary between them and the popular masses.

This policy was bound to fail, in Angola and elsewhere, because the 'assimilated' were the first ones to lay down the theoretical and practical basis of the fight for national independence.

The problem of the *assimilados* must be seen in terms of social classes. It is the problem of the participation of the petty bourgeoisie, including the relatively important sector of intellectuals, and of the middle bourgeoisie where it exists. Naturally, all social classes and strata should participate in the fight for national liberation. The problem is to know whose interests must have priority, those of the masses or those of a small minority which would like to replace the colonizers.

The MPLA, as has been stated in its programme, has taken upon itself the task of 'constantly defending essentially the interests of the peasant and working masses'.

The Indifference of the Urban Petty Bourgeoisie
Paulo Jorge

> *Excerpt from an interview by the Liberation Support Movement (USA and Canada) with Paulo Jorge, head of the Department of Information & Propaganda of the MPLA. The interview appeared in 1973.*

I would say that up to this point most of our urban 'sympathizers', especially the educated elements, remain more or less indifferent to the armed struggle and are afraid to get involved with MPLA activities. Of course, some have already escaped the persecution of PIDE or the police and come to join us in the liberated areas; a few have even been sent abroad for military and/or technical training. At present, however, the number is not great. But, as your question suggests, at a certain stage of our military activity in the towns and cities we are confident that many more of these petty-bourgeois elements will become insecure and come over to the revolution, thus helping the MPLA to solve its problem of shortages of middle cadre personnel.

Two Groups of *Assimilados*
Viriato da Cruz

From the article, 'Angola: Quelle Independance' by
Viriato da Cruz, in Revolution, *No. 6, February 1964.*
Translated from French.

The socio-political and cultural consequences of Portuguese 'assimilation' have played and still play an important role in the development of Angolan nationalism, since its principal leaders belong to the category of the *assimilados*.

To understand the relation between the parties and their leaders in Angola, we must start by emphasizing that the *assimilado* sector does not have, on the whole, a homogenous socio-economic and ethnic content. By way of simple observation, one may divide this sector into two groups: the 'assimilated-object' group, and the assimilated group destined in the colonial context to attain social and economic success. Among the first group there are the civil servants and employees in commerce and industry. In the second group are found those *assimilados* who, thanks to scholarships of the government or the missions, or because of the privileged situation of their families, were able to acquire a specialization in different professional fields in Portugal. Because of their social condition, their education, their psychology, and the social functions to which they aspire, the majority of the members of this group display behaviour similar to that of the petty bourgeoisie.

Whereas the majority of the *assimilados* of the first group, because they suffered exploitation in the colony, rejected colonialism in their innermost behaviour, it was not the same with the second group of *assimilados*. These, often sheltered from direct exploitation, and more integrated into Portuguese society than any other African group, opposed colonialism on the basis of patriotism, self-interest, or even solidarity.

Each one of these groups of *assimilados* has tended towards different solutions of the colonial problem, depending on their respective interests and social conditions. It is for the first group as opposed to the second that Portuguese culture has been the prime reference group.

Hierarchy of Privilege in Portuguese Colonial Society
Mario de Andrade

A section of the basic document entitled 'La Lutte de
Liberation Nationale dans les Colonies Portugaises'
submitted by Mario de Andrade to the Second
Conference of CONCP in Dar es Salaam, 3–8 October
1965. Translated from French.

Colonization always affects the physiognomy of African societies by the conjunction of three inseparable mechanisms of domination which are utilized in the spheres of the economy, the administration and the missions.

The destruction of the social frameworks of our countries is the direct result of the outdatedness and underdevelopment of the socio-economic structures of Portuguese colonialism.

The progression of Lusitanian expansion since the 15th Century has not been based on a coherent policy towards the peoples of the occupied or controlled territories. The original motives of evangelization and commerce developed into an attempt to integrate parts of Africa into the economic orbit of the Portuguese crown.

With the onset of administrative occupation, which dates from the beginning of this century, the various social communities now located under colonial rule underwent very profound changes.

One fact is undeniable. Despite regional differences, the Portuguese intrusion into the Atlantic islands and on the mainland created colonized societies. Hence the conflict between those attempting to integrate them in a system of dependence and those rejecting Portuguese sovereignty.

The principal agents of change affecting the physiognomy of our societies are: the maintenance of forced labour, successor to the slave trade, which in certain cases had lasted as long as three centuries; depopulation and detribalization; economic relations based upon colonial trade and the consequent strangulation of the autochthonous sectors of production; the manipulation and forced integration of the traditional chiefs into the administrative system; missionary attacks on traditional culture and the psychological foundations of these cultures.

The domination involved in the economic realm, by clarifying most brutally the situation of societies under Portuguese colonial rule, brings to light which social strata are most affected by foreign exploitation, and thus explains in the last analysis, the programmatic orientation of our national liberation movement.

The Atlantic Islands
The plan which changed the population of the Atlantic islands (Cape Verde and Sao Tome) so fundamentally rested on a common basis: the settlement of Portuguese residents (*moradores*) under a system of *donatorios*; the introduction of first cotton and then sugar cane; and the importation of slaves right from the start. Production relations revolved around these two products, which thus shaped a social structure based on slavery. With the decline of sugar and cotton production in the second half of the 17th Century, the islands were reduced to mere slave trade way stations. There exists a close connection between economic development, the creation of peoples, and social stratification. The introduction of new profitable crops (coffee and cocoa) in Sao Tome in the 19th Century, and the abolition of slavery, opened a period of severe competition for the appropriation of land. This 'agrarian revolution' in Sao Tome and Principe created two distinct

forms of farming: one which was directly associated with the exploitation of cash crops, and the other almost exclusively dependent on subsistence agriculture. The great landowners (descendants of Portuguese settlers) having lost their privileges by this time in an unequal struggle against the Portuguese occupier, ceased to play the role of dominant group, and their fate became in practice linked to that of the *forros* or *libertos*.[1] In Cape Verde, this led in turn to agricultural crises and the total dependency of agriculture on Portuguese finance. The social conflicts of the beginning of the 19th Century thus created a pattern of stratification which has remained the same up to the present day.

In general terms, it was a Creole society made up of the 'children', plus the *Tongas* and *Angolares*,[2] as well as contract workers on the plantations (Cape Verdians, Angolans, Mozambicans). The colonial high society, the sole holder of the islands' wealth, was made up exclusively of Portuguese colonists.

The agrarian structure which characterizes the present economy of the Cape Verde Islands also derives from the time of the abolition of slavery. The descendants of the landowners were able to gain control of the large latifundias, while the slaves and their descendants were reduced to the condition of tenant-farmers. This peasant majority, dependent solely on the product of their labour, was the most affected by the disastrous consequences of agricultural crises. Finally, it should be noted, concerning the social landscape of the rural milieu, that it includes nearly 100 large landowners, and large numbers of medium-sized and small ones.

The erosion of the soil due to exploitation and plundering of the land, the worsening of climatic conditions, and — most of all — the crises resulting from starvation, have bled the islands demographically, as can be seen in the rate of emigration, which is the highest of all areas under Portuguese colonial rule.

The civil servants, a privileged stratum, are primarily concentrated in urban areas.

The middle stratum of bureaucrats, the wage workers, the petty merchants and the artisans, constitute part, in terms of their psychology, of the local bourgeoisie.

Guinea
The economic activity of the Portuguese in Guinea was almost exclusively commercial. After the initial phase of the slave trade monopoly, reserved to the European and Cape Verdian *donatorios*, there followed the settlement of merchants. The appearance of companies engaging in the Atlantic slave

1. *Forros* or *libertos:* those who were considered free after the abolition of slavery.
2. *Tongas:* the children of slaves and of workers on the agricultural plantations; *Angolares:* a social group probably originating from Angola. The first contingent dates from the 16th Century, following the shipwreck of a slave ship on the island. They are largely fishermen.

trade dates from this time. Such companies gradually disappeared in a third stage, as we witness the development of local products (peanuts). The fourth stage is marked by the return of commercial monopolies into the hands of the Portuguese.

A mono-mercantile repurchase type of economy is the constant feature of these economic stages: slaves in the past, and peanuts in the present.

The development of the peanut crop since the early part of this century opened the path to soil erosion, and deeply shook up the life of the African populations, by introducing them to the beginnings of the economic, political and social change that characterizes contemporary Portuguese rule. Peanut cultivation which became compulsory for the autochthonous populations, modified the physiognomy of Guinea. The Portuguese occupation shaped it as a trading-post colony.

Rural social stratification is largely identical with tribal stratification: great customary chiefs imposed by the colonial administration; an aristocracy among the Fula, Mandingos and Madjaques; a small group of peasant landowners; dioulas, merchants, and transporters; rural artisans; the peasants.

In the urban African milieu the following social distinctions may be observed: middle and lower civil servants, clerks in banking, commercial and other officers, small merchants — the whole forming a group we might call the 'petty bourgeoisie' (estimated to be nearly 10,000 people, of 1.5% of the total population); nearly 23 to 30,000 wage workers; the 'lumpenproletariat', an element stemming from the combined effects of detribalization and the rural exodus.

The Europeans, almost exclusively located in the urban areas, form colonial high society.

Angola and Mozambique

Certain particularities of the geographical situation and ecological conditions of Angola and Mozambique made possible a broader exploitation of these countries by the colonial state, Portuguese firms, and international capitalism. These two African territories not only offer an important variety of agricultural, mineral and energy resources, but also provide the possibility for white settlement in the most fertile climatic areas.

It therefore became part of the logic of the Portuguese colonists to seek the dual goal of economic exploitation and settlement by successive flows of non-indigenous elements.

The Africans, unable to limit themselves exclusively to subsistence cultivation and pasturage, thus had no other alternative but to 'integrate' themselves into the market economy. In fact, this 'forced integration' at the lowest level is a result of methods which have always been used, historically, in the relationships between colonial administrations and autochthonous populations. This is why, in the agricultural realm, (in terms of marketable goods) the co-existence of two sectors of production — one African, the other European — necessarily is advantageous to the latter, since all profitable cultivation crops are given over to it, while the African sector is forced to devote itself to *compulsory* crops on assigned plots. Such is the case with cotton in Angola whose exploitation was the subject of strict laws, which have theoretically been revoked since May 1961. The fact remains that, for over thirty years, the structure of village communities, particularly those of Catete, Muxima and Malange, was deeply upset by the enforcement of a 'cotton cultivation programme'. We know that local reactions to such measures were the source of the incidents in Baixa de Cassange. The same characteristics are also found in the case of the rice and cotton crops in Mozambique (in the Zambezi delta and the district of the Sul do Save).

A major factor in the change in the social equilibrium of the colonies — as we have already said — consists in the hiring and extensive use of contract workers (*contratados*). The long use of this system, over and above the economic ruin which it fostered, is the direct cause of the high mortality rate, genuine 'demographic anemia' which affected large areas within the borders of Angola and Mozambique.

African manpower in Mozambique is used as a 'means of earning foreign exchange', in return for commercial advantages. The local budget mentions that nearly 1/5 of recurrent income comes from 'remittances from migrant workers', that is, from a human traffic, whose annual average of 400,000 workers is largely directly towards Rhodesia and South Africa. Indeed, official sources remark on the excellence of Mozambique's geographic position as being one of the characteristics of its economy. In the development plan for 1965–67, we can read that the colony's geographic position 'creates a special vocation for an economy based on services rendered to the economies of the neighbouring hinterland'.

During a period of some 50 years (1902–58), 81,166 workers recruited in Mozambique perished in the Rand mines. According to the most recent calculations, 60% of their African miners come from territories other than those of the South African Republic. Besides the 40% coming from the Republic's own 'reserves', 36.7% come from Mozambique, 13.2% from Basutoland, 5% from Nyasaland, 3.5% from Bechuanaland, and 2.5% from Swaziland.

In Angola, out of a total population of 4,840,719, there are an estimated 2,748,000 (i.e. 57%) old enough to devote themselves to productive activity in the market economy. Of these, nearly 2,500,000 are the Africans who comprise the 'colonized society'. If 32% of this active population sector comprise the wage workers in agriculture as well as in the various transport enterprises and public works, over half are still subject to a regime of forced labour.

About 10% comprise salaried employees in commerce, the extractive and manufacturing industries, as well as the stratum of officials in the colonial administration. About 15% live in urban areas, as 'detribalized' people. 7% of the total active population comprise the members of colonial high society, the only ones to hold economic wealth and local power.

In Mozambique, out of a total of 6,543,000 inhabitants, the African active population is estimated to be 2,400,000. Over 50% of the latter is composed of contract workers, either inside the colony or elsewhere (Rhodesia and South Africa).

Almost everyone else in this colonized society are either agricultural and mine wage-workers, urban sub-proletarians, or domestic servants. Some intermediate strata exist as *assimilados*, civil servants and semi-skilled workers, of whom 1.7% are themselves employers. Let us note that 40.2% of the Indian and Chinese minorities are employers. But economic and political control is in the hands of colonial high society, of whom 51.5% are employers.

We have just analysed the nature and magnitude of the factors of change which have acted upon the structure (physiognomy) of our societies. The mechanism of economic domination peculiar to Portuguese colonialism, whose traits we have also generally outlined, causes a 'simplification' in the relationships between the conflicting societies.

The impact of European settlement not only paralyzed the normal development of the village communities, but it also burdened traditional societies with new conflicts (particularly in Guinea, Angola and Mozambique).

The integration of autochthonous masses into the market economy finally forced them into an overall state of dependency. Certainly, social differentiation grew up within the colonized society, since it is evident that the forms of economic exploitation were not felt by every stratum with the same degree of intensity. However, the privileges which the colonial administration was forced to grant to certain of them were not enough to create true 'owning classes', in overt opposition to the national liberation movement. Rather, the disintegration of the social superstructures, the progressive liquidation of the bases (both political and cultural) of our communities — sometimes at the level of the state — in short, the submission of power rooted in the people and in tradition to the new power of colonial administration completes the picture of a total situation of deep dependence.

Schematically, the rural masses facing the ultimate extremes of economic exploitation comprise the largest segment of the population, and the ones most affected by foreign exploitation. Even where industrialization is taking place, the racial hierarchy in employment blocks off the possibility of the emergence of an autochthonous and enlightened proletariat, able to play a catalytic role in the liberation struggle.

Thus the nucleus of opposition has to be formed around the strata which have had access both to privileges and the possibility of comprehending the colonial situation: civil servants, wage workers, intellectuals, and students. They will forge the ideological elements necessary in the struggle for national independence. However, the national liberation movement cannot engage in decisive action, nor find itself on an irreversible path, until it has gained strength in the countryside, and both mobilized and given an orientation to the sub-proletariat of the towns. This 'carnal relationship' between the cadres and the masses precisely illustrates the popular character of our nationalist organizations. Our programmatic orientation reflects, in fact, the deep aspirations of the working classes.

To sum up, the national liberation struggle, since it has its origin and its potential strength basis in the popular strata, is intimately linked with social liberation. In other words, the nationalist expression is oriented towards a radical change in the present system of political, social, economic and cultural domination.

6. Workers and Peasants

Editors' Introduction

In its important analysis, 'Strategy and Tactics of the ANC', the ANC analysed the role of those groups active in the South African scene which, in this view, are the 'white group', the 'African masses', and the 'Coloured and Indian people'. Within the African masses, the ANC said, there existed 'a large and well-developed working class'. It did not specify the other groups. It was concerned rather with the question of the 'special role' of this working class which it sees as a 'distinct and reinforcing layer of our liberation'. The small Unity Movement, by contrast, has long centred its political critique of the ANC precisely around this point, insisting that the peasantry, and not the working class, is the 'key to the liberatory struggle'.

This issue has been much debated among Angolan movements, too. The National Liberation Front of Angola (FNLA), the outgrowth of Holden Roberto's UPA, had long contended that it based its struggle on the role of the peasants. UNITA (National Union for the Total Independence of Angola) of Jonas Savimbi, a latter-day offshoot of the FNLA, had made a similar argument. The MPLA, by contrast, while acknowledging the centrality of the peasantry to Angolan life and politics, insisted on the importance of the role of the working class. ZAPU in Zimbabwe resolved this issue by arguing that the distinction is politically obnoxious and insisting that it is leading a 'worker-peasant revolutionary struggle'.

The role of the working class raises the question of how to classify white workers who, proletarians by European definitions, are clearly part of the privileged, wealthy upper strata of Southern Africa. The problem was, of course, particularly at issue in South Africa and Zimbabwe. Basil February, who was killed in action in an ANC-ZAPU joint operation in Zimbabwe in August 1967, reflected ANC's viewpoint in his analysis of the white worker as one of the pillars of the governing Nationalist Party 'because the government keeps him a position of privilege'. George Silundika of ZAPU similarly argued that racism 'precludes any common position between the African and European workers'.

The African Masses and the Working Class
ANC

From the statement, 'Strategy and Tactics of the ANC',
issued at its conference in Morogoro (Tanzania) in
April 1969.

The main content of the present stage of the South African revolution is
the national liberation of the largest and most oppressed group – the African
people. This strategic aim must govern every aspect of the conduct of our
struggle whether it be the formulation of policy or the creation of structures.
Amongst other things, it demands in the first place the maximum mobilisation of the African people as a dispossessed and racially oppressed nation.
This is the mainspring and it must not be weakened. It involves a stimulation
and a deepening of national confidence, national pride and national assertive-
ness. Properly channelled and properly led, these qualities do not stand in
conflict with the principles of internationalism. Indeed, they become the
basis for more lasting and more meaningful co-operation; a co-operation
which is self-imposed, equal and one which is neither based on dependence
nor gives the appearance of being so.

The national character of the struggle must therefore dominate our
approach. But it is a national struggle which is taking place in a different era
and in a different context from those which characterised the early struggles
against colonialism. It is happening in a new kind of world – a world which is
no longer monopolised by the imperialist world system; a world in which the
existence of the powerful socialist system and a significant sector of newly
liberated areas has altered the balance of forces; a world in which the hori-
zons liberated from foreign oppression extend beyond mere formal political
control and encompass the element which makes such control meaningful
– economic emancipation. It is also happening in a new kind of South Africa;
a South Africa in which there is a large and well-developed working class
whose class consciousness and in which the independent expressions of the
working people – their political organs and trade unions – are very much
part of the liberation front. Thus, our nationalism must not be confused with
chauvinism or narrow nationalism of a previous epoch. It must not be confused with the classical drive by an elitist group among the oppressed people
to gain ascendancy so that they can replace the oppressor in the exploitation
of the mass.

The African, although subjected to the most intense racial oppression and
exploitation, is not the only oppressed national group in South Africa. The
two million strong Coloured Community and three-quarter million Indians
suffer varying forms of national humiliation, discrimination and oppression.
They are part of the non-White base upon which rests White privilege. As such
they constitute an integral part of the social forces ranged against White
supremacy. Despite deceptive and, often, meaningless concessions, they share
a common fate with their African brothers and their own liberation is inex-

tricably bound up with the liberation of the African people.

Is there a special role for the working class in our national struggle? We have already referred to the special character of the South African social and economic structure. In our country — more than in any other part of the oppressed world — it is inconceivable for liberation to have meaning without a return of the wealth of the land to the people as a whole. It is therefore a fundamental feature of our strategy that victory must embrace more than formal political democracy. To allow the existing economic forces to retain their interests intact is to feed the root of racial supremacy and does not represent even the shadow of liberation.

Our drive towards national emancipation is therefore in a very real way bound up with economic emancipation. We have suffered more than just national humiliation. Our people are deprived of their due in the country's wealth; their skills have been suppressed, and poverty and starvation has been their life experience. The correction of these centuries-old economic injustices lies at the very core of our national aspirations. We do not underestimate the complexities which will face a people's government during the transformation period nor the enormity of the problems of meeting economic needs of the mass of the oppressed people. But one thing is certain — in our land this cannot be effectively tackled unless the basic wealth and the basic resources are at the disposal of the people as a whole and are not manipulated by sections or individuals be they White or Black.

This perspective of a speedy progression from formal liberation to genuine and lasting emancipation is made more real by the existence in our country of a large and growing working class whose class consciousness complements national consciousness. Its political organisations and the trade unions have played a fundamental role in shaping and advancing our revolutionary cause. It is historically understandable that the doubly-oppressed and doubly-exploited working class constitutes a distinct and reinforcing layer of our liberation and Socialism and do not stand in conflict with the national interest. Its militancy and political consciousness as a revolutionary class will play no small part in our victory and in the construction of a real people's South Africa.

Beyond our borders in Zimbabwe, Angola, Mozambique, Namibia are our brothers and sisters who similarly are engaged in a fierce struggle against colonialist and racist regimes. We fight an Unholy Alliance of Portugal, Rhodesia and South Africa with the latter as the main economic and military support. The historic ZAPU/ANC Alliance is a unique form of co-operation between two liberation movements which unites the huge potential of the oppressed people in both South Africa and Zimbabwe. The extension of co-operation and co-ordination of all the people of Southern Africa as led by FRELIMO, ZAPU, SWAPO, MPLA and the ANC is a vital part of our strategy.

What then is the broad purpose of our military struggle? Simply put, in the first phase, it is the complete political and economic emancipation of all our people and the constitution of a society which accords with the basic provisions of our programme — the Freedom Charter. This, together with our general understanding of our revolutionary theory, provides us with the strategic framework for the concrete elaboration and implementation of policy in a continuously changing situation. It must be combined with a more intensive programme of research, examination and analysis of the conditions of the different strata of our people (in particular those on the land), their local grievances, hopes and aspirations, so that the flow from theory to application — when the situation makes application possible — will be un-hampered.

Peasantry: The Key to the Liberation Struggle
Unity Movement

Excerpt from a memorandum of the All-African Convention and the Non-European Unity Movement (South Africa) to the Committee of Liberation of the Organization for African Unity (OAU) in December 1963.

In this situation the All-African Convention understood that it was of para-mount importance to begin with, to concentrate on winning the support of the peasantry. This was not only because the landless peasants comprise by far the greatest majority, but because they are the most exploited and oppressed and therefore constitute the greatest (proportion of persons) dismissed if they do not carry out government orders. The main function of the chiefs is to facilitate the recruitment of labour throughout the 'Bantustans' for the mines, the White farms and industry.

One of the most sinister features of these 'Bantustans' is the attempt to re-establish tribalism. Every African man, woman and child is to be classified under one tribe or another, whether they work in the towns or live in the Reserves. Everyone must come under tribal law, Common law has been abolished and the right of Habeas Corpus for the individual has been with-drawn. The word of the chief is law. If a man fails to obey the order of a chief, he is guilty of a criminal offence. In actual practice these laws permit of police terror throughout the Reserves and indeed they reinforce it.

This seemingly senseless and unnecessarily brutal regimentation is a logical concomitant of a forced labour system. The whole purpose is to enable the chiefs to draft labour in the required quantities. This is Verwoerd's reply to the problem of labour. At this moment populations are being reshuffled according to tribes that no longer exist. Each chief is armed not only with extraordinary powers but with weapons for his henchmen. Verwoerd sees in the chiefs his particular front-line of defence for Herrenvolkism. They are going to be used as a fifth column for the purpose of crushing the liberatory movement.

Angolan War: Peasant and Northern in Origin
GRAE

From Press Review No. 22 released on 11 December
1962 by the GRAE (Revolutionary Government of
Angola in Exile), formed by the FNLA led by Holden
Roberto. Translated from French by GRAE.

The basis of FNLA rests essentially on the black peasants sworn to forced labour, defrauded of their land and classed as 'non-civilized' by the racist government of Salazar.

93% of the total population of Angola is composed of these peasants. The working class — still quite small — stands by the peasantry in the light of the colonial economy of the country. The most active elements are organized in the Ligue Generale des Travailleurs Angolais (LGTA) which counts 3,311 members.

Likewise, the students with an FNLA leaning regrouped themselves in National Union of Angolan Students, UNEA.

The women, who have liberated themselves from colonial servitude, have entered political life with their Angolan Womens' Association.

It would be ridiculous to pretend that tribalism was the decisive factor in initiating the fighting. It is due, in reality, to geographic reasons: the only open border was that of the Congo which separated the Angolan Bakongos from the Congolese Bakongos; elsewhere the imperialists dominated the other territories which have a common border with Angola (Katanga, Northern Rhodesia, South West Africa). The impossibility, at the present, of providing military bases and safe shelters there for the non-fighting Angolan population obliges the FNLA to lengthen the lines of communication from the Congolese border and carry the war further south, little by little, in the direction of the Angolan compatriots in other tribes who, in need of sufficient arms, have not yet launched military operations on the same scale as those going on in the districts nearer the Congo.

The leftist Europeans (partisans of MPLA, because some of them come from the former Angolan Communist Party and some refer to themselves voluntarily as Marxists, welcoming the friendships of the socialist countries) must understand this situation of the war which is at the same time '*peasant and northern*' in origin. Seeing that the insignificance of the MPLA in the interior of Angola on the military plane springs from its urban and central roots in the region of Luanda, the capital, they especially recruited their members from the Angolan population classed as 'civilized' by the colonial regime; i.e., the half-castes and the '*assimilados*' (whose numbers rose to 26,000 and 30,000 respectively in 1950). From 1956 those who were very full of patriotic sentiment were able to organize, as a result of the education from which they have benefited, a framework for a minority party open to new ideas. They sometimes even had the sympathy of a part of the region around the urban centres.

But they never got very far even in this region. The principal cause of their weakness arose from the privileged position granted to the half-castes and the *'assimilados'* by the colonialists (education, exemption from forced labour, official recognition of property ownership, and of liberal professions, existing civil rights, and a standard of living far superior to that of the exploited peasant mass). This dispensation dug a social and psychological trench between them and the oppressed peasant mass.

It is understandable that many of the peasants believe that, after independence, the MPLA (from the standpoint of the lack of industrialization of the country and the weakness of national capital) will form the elements of a class of *'compradores'* if they come to monopolize the direction of the revolution in the name of their cultural superiority. (Agostinho Neto, Mario de Andrade and Viriato Cruz are to be appreciated as poets). And this in spite of their Marxist ideas. M. Houphouet-Boigny, after all, was well established as a communist in the French Parliament in 1946 . . . .

The leadership of the FNLA and its enlightened militants do not confuse the sincere patriots who fight in the MPLA with the half-castes who, remaining on Portugal's side, were given arms to use against the Africans on March 15 and the days following.

Furthermore, the FNLA assures the members of the MPLA that their integration with the FNLA would not signify the non-realization of the ideals of the 'Major Programme' of their party.

Since their Programme is not essentially different from that of the FNLA, we will present it in our next bulletin. Only the awakening of the peasantry in the course of an armed struggle resolutely turned toward the future by one ALNA can made an independent Angola, a nation capable of avoiding the traps of neo-colonialism.

Peasants — The Most Reliable Class
Jonas Savimbi

Excerpt from an interview given by Jonas Savimbi,
President of UNITA, to Yvette Jarrico in 1970.
Published in Kwacha-Angola, *(UNITA), special edition,*
1972.

In Angola 95% of the population are peasants. In our struggle, they are most reliable class. Therefore, they should join the struggle voluntarily and consciously, integrated into it by the most politically advanced elements of the party and the people. When this is achieved, we will begin to control the forest, the rural areas and surround the cities. And as the struggle develops, we will first take over the small military posts, then the military garrisons, and the cities will inevitably yield. But this depends on the course the armed struggle takes; one cannot talk about tomorrow or the next day. The armed struggle will go on and the day is not far off when the Portuguese will no longer be able to leave their cities, and be strengthened from outside. They will be obliged to give in, in one way or the other.

The Role of the Angolan Worker in the National Revolution
MPLA

Statement of MPLA in its internal organ, Boletin do Militante, *No. 4, February 1965. Translated from Portuguese.*

Trade unionism is the organization of workers for the defence of their own interests against capitalist exploitation. Our experience from the evolution of human society teaches us that the worker can only obtain his demands by uniting with other workers in the daily struggle against capitalist exploitation. This is the source of the principle of trade unionism.

But there are different types of trade unions: revolutionary trade unions of the masses, reformist trade unions, confessional trade unions, etc. Only the first one may be called a vanguard organization for the working class, since it is the only one which defends the interests of the exploited class, having a democratic structure at every level of the union movement under a form of organization based on Democratic Centralism.

Who are the Angolan workers? Workers are all those who, deprived of the means of production (land, machines, tractors, etc.) are forced to sell their labour (physical or mental) to the capitalists in exchange for a miserable wage, while the capitalists accumulate larger and larger gains, so that the workers live in impoverished conditions with an extremely low standard of living.

Angolan society is made up of the following groups: peasants, wage workers (i.e. workers in railways, ports, mines, factories, etc.), a small national bourgeoisie, and an insignificant intellectual class. The wage-earning class is one of the most developed and dynamic, due to the permanent contact which it maintains with the intellectual stratum, together with the great technical development of the urban centres in which it is located. The peasant class is also one of its natural allies since both classes share a common enemy — capitalist, colonialist and neo-colonialist exploitation — and a common objective, which is to raise their already very low standard of living. The intellectuals, together with some revolutionaries from the national bourgeoisie, struggle on the side of the working class to defeat the oppressor.

It is not by chance that the Angolan Revolution has had its beginning in the cities where there is a large concentration of workers. History tells us that on February 4, 1961, a handful of patriots set the process of armed

struggle in motion as an answer to the oppression and exploitation of the
Portuguese colonialists and their allies, the NATO imperialists.

Worker and Peasant Revolution
ZAPU

A statement of ZAPU published in Zimbabwe Review
(Lusaka), II, 5/6, May/June 1970.

It is a very common thing to hear people say workers are more useful in an
armed struggle against exploiters than peasants. Other people tend to hold
the opposite view.

In a situation like that obtaining in Zimbabwe, one would find it rather
difficult to support one stand against the other. This is because the history
of the workers is so short that the process of urbanisation is still incomplete.
It would be correct to say that workers in Zimbabwe are in fact still basically
peasants who rely to quite a large extent for their livelihood on the land to
which they go occasionally yearly.

Under such circumstances, therefore, the worker becomes the peasant,
depending on the season of the year. Having established this basic fact, we
can then try to see whether or not these people are more useful to the armed
struggle when they are in the urban areas working in the factories, hotels,
residential houses or toiling in fields out in the rural areas.

In a guerrilla struggle like the one ZAPU has embarked upon, it is vitally
important to have roots all over the country. It is necessary to operate in the
urban as well as in the rural areas.

Firstly, in the urban areas we find the majority of the enemy forces and
most of their means of livelihood and defence. In order to render the enemy
impotent, it is, therefore, important to attack his means of production and
defence. Hence the urban worker is duty bound to look into the effect of
actions like going on strike, sabotaging the enemy's means of production and
defence so as to tie him down to the urban areas where more is at stake for
him than in the rural areas.

Evidently, workers' organisations and underground machinery to sabotage
the enemy's power in the towns will thus depend upon the worker. Without
his violent actions and participation, the enemy in the urban areas would be
utterly safe. This would be bad for the struggle.

When this worker goes to the rural areas, he needs must become the armed
guerrilla fighter whose violent actions against the enemy at night must be
worse than those of a lion while his actions during the day must be as un-
suspicious as a humble dove.

The most successful worker-peasant revolutionary struggle depends solely
on how well organised the worker operates in the urban areas and how

violently the enemy is routed at night by the peasants in the rural areas.

We must be sheep to our friends but vicious tigers to our enemies wherever we are, if we really wish to win back our freedom and country. The basic aim of every worker in Zimbabwe today must be how best to destroy the enemy's means of livelihood because it is on this that he depends for power. An exploiter without means of production is as helpless as a fish out of water. The worker and peasant is the basis for success.

Social Basis of Nationalist Party Power
Paul Peterson (Basil February)

> *Part of a lecture given before 1967 by Basil February*
> *(under the pseudonym Paul Peterson) to members of his*
> *unit in Umkhonto we Sizwe (the underground organiza-*
> *tion of the ANC). Printed in* Sechaba, *VI, 7, July 1972.*

For any political party to achieve and to maintain political power, it must have the support of the majority of the electorate. In a democratic society this would mean that the party in power must have the support of the majority of the adult population.

In 1960 the census showed South Africa to have a population of 15,841,000 people. In the same year a Referendum was held to decide whether South Africa was to become a Republic. Over 90% of the electorate participated in the Referendum. The results showed that 850,458 people had voted in favour of a Republic. South Africa became a Republic because 850,458 people out of 15,841,000 had decided that it should be so! Clearly there can be no connection between democracy and South Africa.

We have introduced our discussion with a somewhat inelegant collection of figures. We want to get to grips with our problem. We want to analyse the nature and the extent of the support that the Nationalist Party enjoys in South Africa. From the figures that we have quoted it becomes clear that the right to decide who shall govern the country and how they shall govern, belongs exclusively to the 3,068,000 whites (1960 figures) in the country. But the figures also tell us that only 52.3% of the votes had gone to the Nationalists. 775,878 people had actually voted against a Republic. The task of this article is to take a closer look at that section of the white population in South Africa that keeps Vorster in power.

There are approximately 1,750,000 Afrikaners in South Africa. The Nationalist Party is the party of this section of the population. The Party was formed in 1914 under the leadership of General Hertzog as the party of those Afrikaners who refused to accept the idea of a party serving both the English and Afrikaans-speaking sections of the (white) population.

It is not difficult to understand why the Afrikaners could not accept the idea of reconciliation with the English. From the time, in 1795, when the British had first set foot in South Africa, there had been strife between Boer and Briton. The inevitable climax had come in the form of the Anglo-Boer War. For the Boers the war was the climax to 'a century of wrong'. 'There rose up before them . . . the memory of the past, . . . of the thousand and one defeats and humiliations to which they had been subjected ever since the British presence established itself in 'South Africa.' (Brian Bunting: *The Rise of the South African Reich* pp. 15–16). The war itself only served to intensify the hatred of the Boer for the British. They were chased from their homes, and their farms were burnt to the ground. Some 26,000 Boer women and children perished in British concentration camps. Ramsay MacDonald wrote prophetically that 'when every other memory of the war will have faded away, the nightmare shadows of the camps will still remain.' (Bunting p. 17).

The growth of the Nationalist Party from its birth in 1914 until the present is admirably dealt with by Brian Bunting in the book from which we have already quoted. It was inevitable that an organism born of hatred and fear should grow into a deformed and repulsive monster. We shall not try to tell that unsavoury tale once more. We need only note that, coupled with its opposition to the British, the Nationalists came to power on the basis of the most rabid and vicious racialism. This, more than anti-British sentiment, is what brought them to power. This racialism, as we shall attempt to show, is what is keeping them in power. The same racialism also contains the seeds of their inevitable defeat.

We have said that the Nationalists derive their main support from the Afrikaans-speaking section of the whites in South Africa. But even within the ranks of this small section of the population there are contradictions. The Afrikaners do not form one undifferentiated whole. Within their ranks there are classes and, consequently, class differences. At the moment these differences are hidden behind the common benefit that the white section as a whole derives from the exploitation of the non-white people of South Africa.

But society is not a dead, unmoving thing. Contradictions that may at one time be suppressed may at another time assert themselves with shattering force!

The government enjoys the support of most of the white workers in South Africa, especially that of the Afrikaner worker. In 1911, 80% of Afrikanerdom was still living on the platteland. The development of a modern economy, however, cut into the fabric of their simple way of life. Capitalism was penetrating into the innermost pore of South African society. Everything that stood in the way of the young but vigorous capitalism had to perish. The Boer with his subsistence farming was in the way. By 1925, the number of ruined and dispossessed 'poor whites' stood in the region of 300,000.

The Nationalist Party was formed in the period when the ruined Boer was starting his reluctant trek into the towns. The towns were a hostile world for the Boer. On arriving there, the Boer found that he did not have the necessary skills to compete with the immigrant white worker. He was left to find his way in the competition with the 'Black worker'.

To add to his humiliation he also found that his language was despised. It is easy to see why he saw salvation in the party of Hertzog.

The Nationalist Party and the other organisations of the *'volk'* made it their duty to rescue the helpless Afrikaner worker. Relief bodies were formed. There was a fierce struggle to have the language of the Afrikaner accepted. The Afrikaner organisations provided a cultural retreat for the homeless worker.

Over the years, therefore, the white worker has come to look to the Nationalist Party to protect him against the realities of life. This was the basis of his support for the Nationalist Party and it remains so now.

The white worker supports the government because the government keeps him in a position of privilege. Job reservation protects him from the competition of other workers. It is government policy to see to it that the white worker receives 'white man's wages'. In a word, government policy makes it very difficult for a white man to be poor!

Of course, it would be complete over-simplification to say that the white worker supports the government only because that government sees to it that he gets a good job. The white worker undoubtedly supports the ideology of the Nationalist Party. He supports the racialism of that Party.

Here someone may point out that even the outlook, the ideology of the white worker is based on his privileged position. The white worker can see that his privileged position depends on a policy of racial discrimination. As long as racialism can secure his position of privilege, he will support racialism.

From this it may be concluded that the white worker may be persuaded to discard his racialist outlook if he can be shown that racialism cannot any longer keep him in a position of privilege. In other words, if we accept that the outlook of an individual depends on his real situation in life, then we must also accept that his outlook will change when his situation changes.

This, in fact, is a profound truth. But, like any other truth, if it is carried to extremes it will merely become ridiculous. If we just accept this as a formula, then we shall conclude that we have merely to bring about a change in the position of the worker and then we shall hold our breath (or our thumb if we are so inclined) and wait for the magic change to take place. We shall be sorely disappointed. All that will happen is that we shall become uncomfortable from holding our breath.

The ideology of people is indeed based on their material conditions in life. By this we mean a certain set of ideas. For instance, a person who is oppressed by others will grow to hate those who oppress him. But the important thing is that he will not stop hating those who have wronged him the moment they stop oppressing him. That hatred will be ingrained in him. He may even pass it on to his children. In other words, even though his former oppressors have long since ceased to oppress him, even though he may not be living in the same place anymore, that person may continue to hate them.

And his children, who might never even have seen the people, will also hate them.

The example has its defects but what we wished to explain is that, although a certain outlook grows out of the situation in which the person finds himself, that outlook may remain with the person long after the original cause has disappeared. In fact, the outlook may even be adopted by others who do not even know the original cause. These persons merely accept the outlook of those around them. Very few people ever stop to think why they have a particular outlook. A common example is the attitude of many people to communism. Many people who hate communism have never bothered to find out what communism is. But they hate communism nevertheless.

The same thing applies to the white worker and his racialism. Very few white workers, we are sure, have ever stopped to consider why they are racialists. It is just ingrained in them that they should hate black people. But they hate them all the same! In other words, from having an original cause, the outlook or ideology of the person eventually becomes something that can survive even after the cause has disappeared. It leads a separate existence, independently of the original cause. But in spite of this, the material conditions under which the man lives do finally determine his outlook. Therefore, if he should retain the same outlook even after the cause has disappeared, *it now becomes possible* to change his outlook. All we must bear in mind is that his outlook will not change automatically. Nor will it change immediately.

What are the practical conclusions to be drawn from this? First, we must see to it that the material situation of the person is changed. But this will only be the beginning. Having achieved this, we must, by propaganda and otherwise, hasten and help the change in the outlook of the person.

The conditions of life of the white worker are most eloquently told by the fact that from 1935 to 1960, the wages of white miners (mine workers) rose from R1,617 per year to R2,296 per year. In the same period the cash wages of non-white mineworkers actually declined (!) from R144 to R140. Throughout the South African economy the story is the same. Always we shall find that wide gap between the income of the white worker and that of the black worker. The average income (per person) in South Africa in 1960 was R226. This figure places South Africa between the very rich and the very poor countries of the world. But this figure is very deceptive to the person who does not know South Africa. Actually, when we take a closer look, this average income is split up in the following way:

Whites: R631
Asians: R133
Coloureds: R 86
Africans: R 63

(Houghton: *The South African Economy* p. 159)

There is no need to elaborate on these figures. In any case, the immensely privileged position of the white worker in South Africa has been the subject of a considerable body of literature already. This privileged position of the white worker has a history as long as the industrialisation of South Africa itself. But in 1948, with the coming to power of the Nationalists Party, their position became firmly entrenched.

Job reservation was made law by the Industrial Conciliation Act of 1956. Under section 77 (as amended by Act 11 of 1959) the Minister of Labour may reserve certain jobs for the members of a certain race. The purpose of the Act was specifically to protect the white worker from the competition of other workers. It has resulted in a labour structure which has been called 'multi-racial teams of non-competing workers'. Furthermore, to make assurances doubly sure, the Act also provided for the racial exclusiveness of trade unions. Moreover, the Native Labour (Settlement of Disputes) Act of 1953 had already made it illegal for African workers to go on strike.

The white worker was cosily surrounded by a wall of protective legislation. But the very fact that it was found necessary to pass a law such as the 1956 Act, shows clearly how insecure and vulnerable is the position of the white worker.

South Africa is a capitalist country. For the capitalist, the main concern is to get as large a profit as possible. In other words, the capitalist is interested in exploiting the worker as much as possible. In practice this means that the capitalist pays the worker as small a wage as possible.

There are certain limits below which the capitalist cannot depress the wages of the workers. The worker must, for instance, receive sufficient to keep himself and his dependants alive. Then also, the worker must be paid enough to maintain a certain standard of living. But neither of these conditions are binding and absolute. If conditions make it at all profitable for him, the capitalist will do his utmost to depress the wages of the workers as low as possible, even below the level of bare physical survival. In the case where there is a large and constant supply of labour, for instance, the capitalist shows small concern for the health of the worker because he knows that the worker can be replaced. This is the case in a highly developed and wealthy country like America where about 4,000,000 people are unemployed. But the worker is especially vulnerable in a country like South Africa where it is illegal for him to defend himself by strike action. The worker is especially vulnerable where his trade unions are not recognised and where he has no voice in the political bodies of the country. Speaking about the conditions of the African people in South Africa. Comrade Tambo (*Oliver Tambo*, President ANC—Ed.) said that 'in the urban areas 4 out of every 5 families are starving. The rate is higher in country areas . . . The average life expectancy of an African is 37—42 years. For the whites it is 67—72 years . . .' (Address to the International Conference on Economic Sanctions against South Africa, London, 1964).

But if it is the aim of the capitalist to pay the worker such a low wage, how do we then understand the high wages that are paid to the white workers? Surely the capitalist cannot approve of this great expenditure on white wages if he could get the same job done at a lower wage. True, there are laws which prevent the capitalist from displacing white labour by black labour. But would it not be natural then to expect the capitalist to oppose these laws so as to bring about a more profitable state of affairs for himself?

In the beginning of industrialisation in South Africa, there was a real economic motive in paying white workers a very high wage. These white workers were immigrants who had to be attracted to South Africa to come to fill the need for skilled labour in the country. Neither the white nor the black workers in South Africa had these skills. But by 1922 the situation was beginning to change. By that time about four-fifths of white mineworkers were Afrikaners. The black workers had also developed considerable skill already. So much so that the Chamber of Mines decided to increase the number of black workers at the expense of the white workers. The aim of this move was to reduce costs. In the Rand Rebellion that followed, the white workers stood up in defence of their position. Smuts called out the armed might of the state. During the strike the capitalists showed that their profits were more important than the welfare of any worker, be he black or white. Many white workers were killed. Three white workers were hanged.

Today, as much as in 1922, the white worker is a luxury that the capitalist economy cannot afford indefinitely. We should point out here that we are not speaking about economies in general but of the *capitalist* economy. In other words, we are not opposed to workers, white or black, getting a high wage. Neither are we saying that it is not economical to give a worker a high wage. What we are saying is that it is against the nature of the capitalist economy to give any worker a high wage.

From the point of view of the capitalist, the white worker is a luxury which he could well do without. But for the government it is important that the white worker should continue to get a high wage so that the government can be assured of the vote of the white worker. It has been estimated that 'civil servants and employees of state capital number about one-fifth of the white population, constituting with their families a majority of the electorate'. (Bunting: *Rise of the S.A. Reich*, p. 287). As G. Fasulo commented in *Fighting Talk* in 1952: 'All the Nats have to do is to keep the dependants of the state happy and they can remain in power indefinitely . . .' And the government has made no secret of its dependence on the support of the white worker. Balthazar Vorster declared in the House of Assembly in 1956 that: 'We know one person only to whom we owe an explanation, and that is the white worker in South Africa, who has brought the Nationalist Party to the position it occupies today and who will keep it in that position in the future'. (Quoted in *The Rise of the S.A. Reich*, p. 252).

This situation represents a contradiction between the capitalists and the government, between economics and politics. But the business world cannot carry its opposition (to government policy) to the point of open defiance without undermining its own interests. On the other hand, many capitalists fear that government policy may in the long run lead to total ruin. The more this fear approaches reality, the more the capitalist may be expected to agitate for reform.

So far rumblings have been heard from the mining and from the manufacturing industry. We shall confine ourselves to the manufacturing industry. This is not so because of lack of evidence of the desire for change in mining. We are taking manufacturing industry because, as Professor Houghton says in his study of the South African economy, 'The importance of manufacturing in the future economic development of South Africa cannot be too greatly stressed because all the indications are that it must be the cornerstone of future expansion.' Manufacturing industry provided employment for 782,000 workers in 1969. 'Several government reports have stressed the importance of building up a powerful and diversified manufacturing industry.' (*The S.A. Economy*, p. 126).

The steps proposed by the Third Interim Report of the Industrial and Agricultural Requirements Commission proposes, amongst other things that: (1) Better use be made of labour, including the *increased use of Africans in industry* [my emphasis – P.P.] ; (2) There should be more equitable distribution of material income.

S. H. Frankel in 1944 and Harry Oppenheimer in 1950 both pointed out that manufacturing industry was heavily dependent on mining. Oppenheimer pointed out that manufacturing industry would have to increase its exports to become an independent and strong sector of the economy. 'This is really another way of saying,' said Oppenheimer, 'that, as a whole, industry in South Africa . . . must reduce costs.'

The Viljoen Commission of 1958 proposed amongst other things that: (1) The purchasing power of the population be increased; (2) Employment opportunities be provided for the whole population. With prophetic insistence we see the demand for the removal of Job Reservation. This, in fact, is what is meant by providing employment opportunities for all and by making more use of Africans in industry. The result will be that the white worker will be thrown into the general labour pool. The effects of competition will be felt. The capitalist will be free to employ an African at a lower wage for a job that was formerly done by a white worker. The demand that the purchasing power of the population should be increased means nothing else but that non-whites should receive higher wages. But at the same time there is a need to reduce costs, and an increase in the wages of the non-whites will have the effect of raising costs.

Therefore, at the same time as the wages of non-white workers are raised, costs of production will have to be reduced.

One way of reducing costs will be to make more intelligent use of the labour force. The worker must be allowed to develop certain skills. This means that migratory labour workers who have acquired certain skills must leave and other unskilled and untrained workers come to take their place. This is obviously a wasteful practice. The worker must be allowed to settle near his place of employment. He must have better living conditions.

Costs will also be reduced by replacing white workers by non-whites. (We must stress again that this is not the policy of the African National Congress, nor of any progressive organisation. We are here trying to see how the capitalist will reason. Our own aim is not to reduce the white worker to the starvation level at which the African worker must at present survive. Our main aim is to raise the African worker to the level that the white worker enjoys at the present moment.)

The needs of the developing economy demand the measures that we have enumerated above. And these changes threaten the privileged position of the white worker. If these changes are implemented, the white worker, in common with the other workers in South Africa, will suffer the fate of the worker in a capitalist society.

We must not conclude from this that we must merely sit back and wait for the change to take place. What we have shown here is that *tendencies toward change exist.* We have shown that these tendencies are backed by powerful industrial and financial forces in South Africa. We have shown that contradictions exist between the economic laws that operate in South Africa and the policy of the government. The government will try (is trying) to suppress these contradictions. It may even be successful for a time. But the government *cannot remove* these contradictions. The contradictions will only grow sharper.

We are not going to assume the mantle of the prophet and try to predict exactly what path the white worker will follow. At best we can indicate the possible paths and indicate how we might influence the development in the thinking of the white worker. As the attacks on his standard of living, on his social position and on his material position as a whole become more real and effective, the white worker will be forced to adopt a certain course of action to save himself from complete ruin. In our opinion there are two possible courses of action open to him. The first is a drift into a more reactionary position. The privileged position of the white worker is completely bound up with the future of the Nationalist Party. The attacks on his position will, therefore, come in the form of attacks on the Nationalist Party. The attacks on the Nationalist Party are not deliberately directed against the white worker, however, it will seem as if he is the object of the attack. The government is fully aware of this. It encourages the white worker in his fear of *'swart gevaar'* ('Black Danger'). And as the crisis becomes more intense, the propaganda of the Nationalists will correspondingly increase. The *laager* will be drawn tighter.

The success of the Nationalist Party propaganda will depend on the extent to which the white worker can be convinced that the regime is invincible. Nationalist Party propaganda will be successful if the white worker can be convinced that the government will be able to overcome the crisis. If the white worker can be convinced that the government is invincible, the white worker will be prepared to make sacrifices. In any case, the white worker will reason, the sacrifices will be only temporary.

The Nationalist Party starts off at an advantage. Their propaganda will not be falling on virgin ears. The Afrikaner is steeped in racialist ideology. He is steeped in the idea of the 'God-given' task of the Afrikaner to rule the country. The Church, the school and every other influence to which he has been subjected has convinced the Afrikaner of his Holy Mission in South Africa. The white worker, especially the Afrikaner, will therefore support the Nationalist Party. He will support it not only because the Nationalist Party promises to rescue him from the crisis but also because he is filled with hatred for the black man. He will be a good target for Nationalist propaganda. The Nationalists will try to convince him that it is the black man who has caused him to land in such a critical situation. There will be the old scare-story of the *'swart gevaar'*. If this propaganda succeeds the attention of the white worker will be turned from the real cause of his misery. His anger will be turned against the black man. This will be a masterstroke for the government. We must remember that it is the policy of the Nationalist Party that has brought about the crisis in South Africa. The Nationalist Party is, there-fore, responsible for the critical situation in which the white worker will find himself. If the white worker could understand this, he would direct his anger against the government. But the Nationalist Party, with its propaganda of the *'swart gevaar'* and the Christian mission of the Afrikaner, is turning the attention of the white worker away from the real cause of his troubles. But not only this. At the same time the Nationalists are succeeding in turning the anger of the white worker against the progressive forces.

History has many examples where the ruling classes used this trick. Hitler perfected the art when he turned the anger and frustration of the German people against the Jews. The whole of German history during the reign of the Fuhrer is very instructive from the real cause of their discontent and used for the most reactionary purposes.

We see, therefore, that although the worsening in the condition of the white worker will lay the basis for a change in his outlook, it can also be used to make him an even more fanatic supporter of the Nationalist regime. This should serve as a warning to those who see life as a simple process of cause and effect.

The revolutionary in this situation has a twofold task. He must prevent the white worker from throwing in his lot with the Vorster regime. He must also try to convince as many white workers as possible that they should side with the revolution.

These are very difficult tasks. In fact they are so difficult that most South Africans would not even bother to try. In the first place, the Afrikaner worker is going to prove a very unwilling listener to our propaganda. And even then, as we have already explained, a man's outlook does not change overnight.

The white worker is so exclusively remote that it is very difficult to reach him. Even apart from mere revolutionary propaganda, the majority of the white workers do not even read the English press. In other words, the white worker is constantly at the mercy of Nationalist propaganda that reaches him through the pages of the Afrikaans press. Trade unions are racially divided, there are Group Areas. Above all, there is the thick layer of racialism that only thickens over the years.

Furthermore, the apparent nature of the revolution antagonises the white worker. The revolution is of course, democratic and aimed at a non-racial society. But by the nature of South African society it takes the form of a struggle between black and white. The white worker cannot be expected to be bubbling over with enthusiasm to listen to people who appear to him to be intent on destroying him. Moreover, revolution does not take place in a laboratory with someone to watch over it in case something goes wrong. *Revolution is made by people, people with feelings, with hatred and bitterness and a long memory.*

There are similarities between the white workers and the workers in an imperialist country. The workers in such a country, too, get some small portion of the benefits of the exploitation of the colonial country. It is not surprising, therefore, to find that working-class leaders in such countries are notoriously reactionary as far as their attitude to the colony is concerned. But it is, nevertheless, the duty of the progressive workers in their ranks to explain to them that they should associate themselves with the struggle of the colonially exploited people. They must be shown that the colonial people and themselves have the same enemy. Working-class solidarity must be forged, across the waves as it were, between the workers of the exploiting and those of the exploited country.

But although there are similarities, we must bear in mind that there are factors which make the task of the South African revolutionary infinitely more difficult. Outstanding amongst these difficulties are racialism and the fear of the black man that has so conscientiously been instilled into the minds of the white workers.

On the whole the prospect looks grim. But we must not despair entirely. Propaganda must be consistently directed at the white workers. The nature of the revolution must be explained to them. It must be made clear that ours is not a racial struggle. It must be made clear that there is a place for all in a democratic society such as that for which we are struggling. Above all, their real situation and their real future must be explained to them. It must be made clear that the privileged and artificial position that they enjoy at the moment will not last for ever.

But our main weapon is our strength. We will not beg the white worker. We will not plead with the white worker. We will not make any concessions to the white worker. We shall be speaking from a position of strength. We must make it clear that we will win. We must make it clear that the government will crumble before our mighty onslaught. There must be no doubt in the mind of the white worker about the outcome of the revolution. *He must realise that we hold all the cards.* The future is ours. He has a place in that future.

Coldly, scientifically and confidently, we must show him that the regime will crumble. We must explain to him the trends that are at work in South Africa. He must be quite clear in his mind that the present state of affairs will not last. It cannot last. He must be made aware of the fact that Vorster and his band of lying madmen can promise him nothing but ruin and doom.

There is hope for the white worker. Much will depend on us. *But in the final analysis, the choice will be theirs.* We can do what is required of us. We can do no more. The freedom of our country is at stake.

Workers Solidarity and Racism

George Silundika

Excerpt from a speech given in 1969 at a symposium on Lenin in Alma-Ata (USSR) by George Silundika, of the Executive of ZAPU. Printed in Zimbabwe Review *(Lusaka), I, 5, December 1969.*

Comrades, a classical Marxist-Leninist is bound to pose the question: if in Zimbabwe, as in South Africa, there is so much industrialisation which survives on exploiting the African workers, why are the African workers not engaged in strikes and continual disruption of industries? Why are the white workers not combining with the African workers to march in common revolution against their employers? We also throw back the question and say, did Lenin not envisage a change of tactics by the oppressor in the face of continuous challenge?

Indeed this is the situation. The factor of racism used by the European oppressors in Africa, against the African, precludes any common position between the African and European worker. The only response that the oppressors make to the African worker for any action to assert his rights is the *gun* — hence the heavy military build-ups. It is on this basis that the revolutionary struggle in Southern Africa must not be conceived on any other basis except the armed struggle. We have taken up arms, and once again, thanks to the assistance of socialist countries. The ZAPU-ANC guerrillas are on the battlefield in Zimbabwe in anticipation of the inevitable general Southern African confrontation.

Comrades, I have used our situation to expose and demonstrate the subjective and objective conditions prevailing on the present revolutionary front against colonialism and imperialism. Meeting here as Marxist-Leninists, in honour of the tremendous contribution of Lenin, we cannot come out with praises of ourselves only. The oppressors are far from vanquished, in fact they are showing signs of resurgence. They have what is called counterinsurgency training centres, like the one in Portugal, for the training of mercenaries and all kinds of dirty work against the revolution. The imbalance in material and financial strength between armed revolutionary movements and the oppressors is too big to console ourselves; the economic and military strength of countries that serve as bases for the armed struggle is dangerously fragile. We cannot allow the revolutionary legacy of Lenin to collapse in the hands of our generation — we must fight.

7. Students

Editors' Introduction

Students always pose a problem for national liberation movements, both intellectually and practically. Practically the issue is that students are often an avant-garde group of protest and revolutionary aspirations, particularly in the early days of a movement. But in the midst of an ongoing struggle, students frequently come into conflict with leaders and cadres whose educational background may be less than theirs but who may in fact be closer in analysis and interest to the mass of the population than students.

Intellectually, the problem is one of definition. Students are a distinctive group, important politically because of their skills and organizational abilities, and highly visible. This is particularly true of any country in which higher education is a rarity. Yet, in terms of the class structure, who are they? Are they to be defined in terms of the classes from which they have sprung, or those into which their studies are clearly destining them in terms of occupation and style of life?

Furthermore, these problems are posed quite differently if, as is the case for Portuguese Africa, Zimbabwe and Namibia, the bulk of students were pursuing their studies outside (and frequently far from) their own country, than if, as is the case for South Africa, most students were to be found in universities and other institutions within the country. In the latter case, students could play a far more direct and more complex role (albeit one that must be more circumscribed in terms of language used).

For the former group, the position of ZAPU was typical. A student was revolutionary to the extent that he was linked to a revolutionary (non-student) movement. Otherwise revolutionary slogans were verbiage, and the motives of the students self-seeking. But, turning to the non-students in the movement, the PAIGC text reminded us of the firm belief that students remaining in school during the struggle, providing they are militants and studying certain things, were being useful because the party had to worry not only about the present but about the future as well.

The debate in FRELIMO illustrated well the conflicts that often arise. In 1967, Eduardo Mondlane, President of FRELIMO, issued a White Paper critical of those students who sought 'special privileges.' The student organization, UNEMO, replied to the implicitly egalitarian tone of

102

Mondlane's paper by arguing that 'Mozambique needs elites'. Soon there-after, following his assassination, there was a leadership crisis in FRELIMO which led to the ouster of Uria Simango and some others because of their elitist views of the revolution. Many of the UNEMO leaders left FRELIMO with Simango. Soon thereafter, the new president, Samora Moises Machel, sought to overcome these elitist tendencies by emphasizing the theme that students must also be producers and producers also students. And by a sort of physical alteration of these jobs, it was hoped a new spirit of fraternity would emerge.

Basically in all these countries, students were a miniscule part of the population but a large proportion of the cadres. In South Africa, students are a relatively larger percentage of the population but a smaller proportion of the cadres. Furthermore, the white student body also played an import-ant role in the country, if a sometimes ambiguous one. Hence the problem was quite different.

Historically, the National Union of South African Students (NUSAS) grouped the students in the English-language universities (as opposed to the Afrikaans-language ones) and tended to be the vanguard of left-liberal opposition to the regime. NUSAS sought to be a multi-racial organization which became increasingly difficult as government legislation removed blacks from the white universities. The statement by Duncan Innes, then president of NUSAS, in 1969 defined well the classic NUSAS position. Black students throughout the 1960s began to complain increasingly about the paternalism of the white left, including NUSAS. In 1968, this culminated in the creation of a black student organization, the South African Students' Organization (SASO) which, by the 1970s, in its policy manifesto talked of engaging in 'dialogue' with 'multi-racial organizations' like the NUSAS 'only . . . when absolutely necessary'. Faced with the emergence of SASO, the ANC gave it its blessing but sought to strengthen its own youth and student section, presumably bearing in mind the kinds of problems Mondlane had written about.

The Student and Revolution
ZAPU

Text appearing in Zimbabwe Review *(Lusaka), I, 2,*
June 1969, published by the Zimbabwe African
People's Union (ZAPU).

What role do students play in revolutions, or, more specifically, what role can Zimbabwe students play in our revolution? There is no doubt that the students themselves, with their youthful enthusiasm and eager minds, can — as they have always done — give the most articulate answers themselves.

The first question, and unfortunately, not the easiest to answer, that every student should ask himself is; 'Am I a revolutionary or not?' We will only address this to those students who have decided that they are revolutionaries.

When you decide this, you lay on yourself a burden that cannot be waived aside at will. You cannot wait for a convenient time and place to put your revolutionary ideas into effect.

Every revolutionary must always keep in mind the maxim — *The duty of every revolutionary is to make revolution* — bequeathed to us by that great revolutionary: Che Guevara. Students are well organised in student movements. Here the revolutionary must make his revolution. A student movement has to be revolutionary, if revolutionary students have to belong to it.

For a revolutionary, revolution is not only part of life, but indeed the whole of life, and, as such, the revolutionary student movement becomes the fulcrum of the student's activities.

A revolutionary student movement cannot divorce itself from the revolutionary movement in pursuit of what the students naively call 'an independent line'.

In a country in revolution like Zimbabwe, the students cannot afford the luxury of divorcing the student movement from the revolutionary movement.

Being part of the revolutionary movement you are to direct and be directed by it. The natural ups and downs of revolution no longer become 'their problem', 'ZAPU's problem'.

You can make your maximum contribution only when you can say, 'this is my problem'. Everybody has too many problems of their own to be able to put maximum effort into the problems of their friends.

The perennial problem of students from Zimbabwe of what to do after graduation is automatically vanquished by their membership of the revolutionary student movement. When you are part of a revolution, the revolution absorbs you.

If a student finds himself in a quandary as to what to do after graduation when he knows that he is part of a revolutionary movement, then he must know there is something seriously wrong with his revolutionary principles.

It is most likely that those principles, other than anything else, need a close scrutiny.

The students are the intelligentsia of the revolution and we need them. But we need them only if they become revolutionary intellectuals.

The current thinking of students tends to regard education as the all-embracing panacea of all financial and social ills. In it they see themselves being pulled out of the common fate of ordinary men and assuming the role of directing the affairs of these ordinary men from above.

True as it might be that educated people may be more capable of leadership positions, we should be aware that leadership is a position of responsibility rather than a place of privilege. The correct leadership position is from in front and not from above.

The graduating student sees himself only as a member of the bureaucratic revolutionaries — drawing up strategies for the fighting forces, and, in general, being the directing force of the revolution. This is both false and dangerous thinking.

A revolution cannot be directed from an armchair. A prerequisite for directing a revolution is to go through the crucible of revolution and thus be a revolutionary.

No amount of explications or explanations of revolution can make one really understand what it is all about. In the same manner you cannot drive a car safely, no matter how much time you spend studying, until you have had some practice — you cannot learn revolution from a book. Only out there, where you suffer all deprivations — and more — only out there, where the stakes are far too high for you to afford to lose and yet you are forever on the brink of losing: only there can you begin to know what it's all about. Only then are you seasoned enough to be called a revolutionary. Only then can we begin to understand Che: when loving life so much that you are ready to die for it; or what Frantz Fanon means by preferring victory to life.

There has been a growing tendency amongst our students to seek employment in some independent African countries or abroad on the pretext of gaining some experience for a later date when their skills will be in demand in Zimbabwe. Is it really possible that these students see no role that they can play in the struggle now? Or can there, indeed, be people who believe they stand above revolution?

We can only tell our brothers and sisters with this twisted thinking that Zimbabwe can never need them more than it needs them now.

This is Zimbabwe's hour of trial. A free Zimbabwe tomorrow will not allow today's deserters the chance to pollute and dilute her revolution. We have seen too much of that happening in independent Africa and other countries of the Third World and we are not letting the lesson go unnoticed.

To think about tomorrow's Zimbabwe and forget about today's struggle is, to say the least, acute imbecility.

Freedom is not given, it is wrested out of the powers-that-be. It is the duty of every Zimbabwean to participate fully.

The strength to endure the worst comes from the knowledge that our cause is right and noble. It is most unfortunate that there is still doubt in some people's minds as to what we are fighting for. It is true that we are fighting to kick the white foreign oppressors from our country, or, if need be, allow them to live in our country under our own conditions and bow to the complete wishes of the people of Zimbabwe. We should understand that ours is a social revolution and, in this day and age, any meaningful social revolution must be a socialist revolution. It is not sufficient for us to have an anti-imperialist front: we also have an anti-capitalist front. The ills of our society are closely connected with the unfair distribution of our country's material wealth.

When the foreigners go, we have make sure that the people shall be the masters of their own destiny and no chance should be left for the rise of another exploiting class.

105

Our Students
PAIGC

Text appearing in Libertacao, *No. 22, September 1962,*
the organ of the PAIGC. Translated from Portuguese.

Our Party, as the vanguard Party of our people's struggle, is not only concerned with the present and the near future, but also with the more distant future. Thus, it considers the situation which will obtain after independence and the difficulties which we will have to face. All African countries, due to the process of colonization, are backward countries, suffering economic and cultural underdevelopment. Our country is no exception. Our task is all the greater since we will have to overcome in very little time many difficulties which inhibit the progress of our country: illiteracy, sickness, infant mortality, a colonially structured economy, etc.

Thus, our Party, realistically, has decided to prepare those people who will in a few years contribute to the making of progress in our country. Through its external activity, it has secured a few dozen scholarships which have benefited some of the members of the Party. We have students in several European countries who have generally done very well. Many of them, the large majority of them, are among the top-ranking students in those countries. It is with great satisfaction that the Party realizes the high level of revolutionary awareness and the clear vision of perspectives and future responsibilities which are shared by our students who look at their studies as part of the struggle for liberation. The Party trusts them because they trust the Party. Our comrades study mainly medicine, nursing, economics, agronomy, and technical sciences.

They will be, in a very near future, a precious aid in the tasks required in the construction of a society free from the colonialist yoke. And in the near future, after liberation has taken place, we will create the necessary conditions which will permit education for the whole people; and we will finally end the burden of illiteracy and lack of education, and thus allow progress in our country.

But today the main task is the political struggle. This struggle, by raising our awareness and human dignity, is also an agent of education.

Each one of us must, as far as possible, aim at increasing his experience and his knowledge in the present circumstances. Those who know how to read must read a great deal and try to obtain information on the problems which interest the men of today. And as much as possible he should also help his fellows, either by sharing with them his knowledge or by teaching them how to read. The revolution which will free us is a great school, our best school!

Some of our students have come back from the countries where they are carrying out their studies in order to spend their vacation with their comrades. During this short period of time they have greatly helped those in most need. This is a correct path. Keep in mind that our students are from

the people; they are poor and simple boys from the most humble houses
of our people.

Participation of Students in the Struggle for National Liberation
Eduardo Mondlane

> *Excerpt from a White Paper issued by Eduardo*
> *Mondlane, President of FRELIMO, in 1967. Translated*
> *from Portuguese by Douglas L. Wheeler and printed in*
> African Historical Studies, *II, 2, 1969.*

As stated in the introduction, once FRELIMO was formed and structured,
it attempted to introduce students to the experience of the struggle for the
national liberation of the Mozambican People.

This attitude was as much a necessity of the situation as it was part of the
needs and aspirations of the Mozambican People. The student is part of the
People, like any other group, and the same duties fall to him [since these
duties] come from the same rights. Furthermore, *due to the situation of
illiteracy of more than 95% of the population, being a student in itself is a
privilege*, and it is normal, therefore, that this privilege postulates a major
fulfillment of duties, *especially since the benefit of a scholarship is a direct
consequence of the struggle of the masses, mainly composed of illiterates.*

But everyone realizes that *the majority of students do not aspire to have
special privileges*, since their privileged situation is somewhat *against that for
which they are struggling*, when, directly by their physical presence, or
indirectly, they contribute to the fight against Portuguese colonialism and
imperialism, responsible for the present obscurantist situation in the
Fatherland.

It is for this reason — keeping in mind as well the sum of the technical
knowledge of students and intellectuals for the sake of the development of
the struggle for national liberation, and recognizing the need for a close unity
between the student, the intellectual, and the masses, and knowing that
[students] still have a great deal to learn — that FRELIMO has established
a certain number of principles of conduct.

Quite a while ago the Central Committee of FRELIMO decided *that all
students who leave Mozambique, before pursuing their studies, must participate during a certain period in specific tasks in the struggle for national
liberation.*

Thus, from the very beginning, it was required that the student could by
this participation acquire through practice initial revolutionary training and
would fully participate in the struggle and aspirations of the masses; at the
same time, [the student would] be putting his knowledge *acquired by study
at the disposal of the national cause.*

On the other hand, it is necessary to keep in mind certain other factors and possibilities, including individual [situations] :
— Youths over 18 years of age, who have not completed primary schooling — 4th class* — are immediately integrated into the politico-military programs.
— Youths under 18 years of age, who have completed primary school, are integrated into the IM [Mozambique Institute] where they can pursue secondary studies up to the level of 2nd cycle of high school.+
— Other youths, approaching 19 years of age, who are attending advanced classes in technical and [liberal arts] high schools, be encouraged, if necessary after a period of recycling in the IM, to continue their studies in foreign Universities and Technical Schools.

The Central Committee is still attempting to place students in different countries and in this placement process, the Committee is keeping in mind the kind of training possessed by the candidates.

In this spirit, the Central Committee succeeded on the one hand to integrate students, and on the other to provide the needed training of leadership personnel so useful for the Fatherland. This [student] integration in the movement was possible, thanks to the direct effort furnished the revolution during the period preceding and following the cycle of studies in the IM, thanks again to the work done during the school holidays of the IM. Therefore, *the student went abroad precisely because FRELIMO had decided this was best*, and the student was in this way continuing as a part of the national action.

This last point deserves some attention: we should explain that, when an act is carried out due to a decision by FRELIMO, when it is carried out in a disciplined manner, it is always a revolutionary act.

In the context of the struggle for the national liberation of Mozambique, *which is our historic task in the present phase*, because FRELIMO and only FRELIMO *knows* [and] understands the real motivations of the People and clarifying their historic objectives; [only FRELIMO knows how] *to organize, to unite, to educate the people politically and to prepare them militarily, because FRELIMO and only FRELIMO was capable of defining strategy and tactics adequate in order to unleash, to develop, to consolidate, to extend and to carry to success the armed struggle of national liberation; FRELIMO* [therefore] *appears as the incarnation of the will and aspirations of the Mozambican masses, the depository of national sovereignty and leadership for the fatherland.*

---

* Fourth class, or *quarta classe* in Portuguese, represents the first major stage of primary schooling in the Portuguese system. Depending on the school and area. '4th class' certificates are attained after 3–5 years of school beyond the first year of primary school. Often such a certificate is a major prerequisite for employment in Portuguese Africa in jobs which require literacy.
+ Passing from primary to secondary school in Portuguese Africa is difficult for many students. There are three cycles in secondary school, the first two, the second three, and the last two years. Certain civil service jobs are customarily attainable after successful completion of the second cycle.

Thus, to obey FRELIMO is to obey the Fatherland, to pursue an objective which is the historic task of our People in the present phase of national liberation.

It is not necessary to be a member of FRELIMO for there to be a duty to obey the decisions of FRELIMO. In the present situation of FRELIMO, since it embodies the historic will on the People and fulfills it in the struggle it is leading, FRELIMO *appears as the will of the fatherland; its leadership cannot be questioned, because it is exercised for the sake of goals which are indisputable: independence, unity, and the liberation of the fatherland.* Therefore, *it is enough to be a Mozambican to be obliged through patriotic duty to obey FRELIMO.* It is clear that, besides being patriots, those who are also members of FRELIMO have a double duty: as a patriot and as a member of the party, subject to its internal discipline. It is clear that the first duty, the fundamental one, is that which conerns us here.

It is therefore normal that, in the phase that preceded the creation of FRELIMO, UNEMO for example, although assuming a patriotic attitude, had not desired to ally itself with or accept the political leadership of ONE party, since none of the parties then in existence was capable of assuming the leadership and responsibilities of the Fatherland; to act in any other way, UNEMO would have risked dividing students and continuing to keep a division in the patriotic ranks. But since FRELIMO was confirmed in its role as catalyst of national energy and as an expression of the hsitoric objectives of the Fatherland, UNEMO, quite rightly, has accepted *the political leadership of FRELIMO*.

When they did this, UNEMO fulfilled its patriotic duty; at the same time, there were within UNEMO students who, either because of a lack of understanding or from ignorance, were not members of FRELIMO, or they belonged to organizations which, though composed of Mozambicans, were *not* [truly] Mozambican (either because they did not embody the historic Mozambican will, leading the struggle, or because — and this is even more serious — they opposed FRELIMO, which does embody and lead the will of the Fatherland): the acceptance of the political leadership of FRELIMO on the part of UNEMO meant that all the students in that body would indirectly be integrated into the organized action of the Mozambican people against colonialism and imperialism, for the liberation of the Fatherland.

Thus it is understandable that the student, in the United States or in the Democratic German Republic, for example, attending classes, could continue to be a part of and to participate in the organized action of the People. In fact, that student sent abroad by FRELIMO (or by UNEMO which acts under the political direction of FRELIMO) *is carrying out one of the points of the FRELIMO programme:* the training of leadership groups needed for the liberation and development of the Fatherland.

It is for that reason also that FRELIMO, fully understanding its historic role as the embodiment of the will and objectives of the Fatherland, acts so that *all* Mozambicans participate in the different tasks of the national liberation, whether or not, technically, they are members of FRELIMO. And in the same way, affirming its non-partisanship, the Central Committee of FRELIMO has already had occasion to inform students orally that those students who are not members of FRELIMO and who, because of a lack of understanding or lack of information, even if they are members of pseudo-Mozambican organizations, *can, if they wish, fulfill their patriotic duty by being part of a programme in which FRELIMO will place them.*

There is one last point: the Central Committee, although it is the leadership of FRELIMO, is an organ accustomed normally to formulating the will of FRELIMO since, as already stated, it does embody the objectives of the Fatherland.

It is now necessary to discuss this because the Central Committee, responding on the one hand to the legitimate desire expressed by the majority of students to participate more directly in the struggle for national liberation (many students even wished to interrupt their studies or even to abandon their studies in order to dedicate themselves to the tasks of the struggle; the Meeting and Congresses of UNEMO always affirmed the readiness of students and their desire to play a more direct role in the struggle), *still considering the needs of our own struggle* which is encountering serious difficulties due to the deliberate obscurantist policy of the colonialists, *and also taking into account the need for revolutionary training* for leadership and future leadership groups of the Fatherland, and that this *training* can be effective only when there is close cooperation with the masses, also recognizes the financial impossibility of students returning periodically to Africa during their long holidays; *the Central Committee of FRELIMO decided and orally informed students that* students who had finished the first cycle of higher education in which they were matriculated (preparatory, preliminary instruction for arts and sciences, BA, BS, or the equivalent) *should not register for the next higher course of study without first interrupting their studies for at least a year, in order to participate directly and closely in another task of national liberation,* one different from that in which they now find themselves (that is, their own personal scientific education for advanced leadership).

Given the situation of the educational system, in the Anglo-Saxon educational system only, this interruption [of one year] is logical after the first cycle of higher education, while in other European systems, the first cycle is a preparation which requires immediate continuation on to the second cycle — diploma, licentiate.

Nevertheless, the Central Committee accepted one exception to this rule in the interruption of studies at the end of the first cycle of higher education in the Anglo-Saxon system, an exception that can be absorbed by an interruption at the end of the first cycle of the European system: in the case of youths in the Physical Sciences or related fields, or even in medical studies, they can interrupt their studies only with *serious harm which for all practical purposes would destroy previous efforts.* Since in this case the interruption has the same consequences as would those in the European system, it means a *pure loss* of time and effort put in: therefore, the Central Committee decided to allow the mentioned exception.

However, these rules, whose need is evident, carry with them in practice two major exceptions, unfortunate and unallowable.

The first is that of youths who have finished the second cycle of secondary school* — or *Form IV* — who, instead of working for a while for the Revolution before resuming their studies, leave the IM, desert the ranks of the Revolution, thus encouraged by imperialism or by its agents disguised as nationalists. In most of the cases these youths take refuge in Kenya, Sudan, and above all in the United States. In the past there were some cases in Yugoslavia, Bulgaria and Rumania, but these 3 countries, understanding the Mozambican situation and realizing that their good will in being sympathetic to the Mozambican struggle was being abused, have now ceased to be *unwilling accomplices* in these desertions.

The second exceptional case, which until now has occurred only among students in the United States is with youths who have completed the first cycle — BA — and who, instigated by imperialists and for purely egotistical reasons and their corruption, refused to interrupt their studies. It has been learned that there were cases of students who had finished their MA (licentiate, or diploma), and decided against the rules of FRELIMO and without authorization from UNEMO, to take up internships, further specialization, and to prepare for Ph. D. candidacy (DES, third cycle of higher education), doctorates, etc. . .

These students attempted to justify their undisciplined and egotistical behaviour by asserting: (1) that in the past, even before the formation of FRELIMO, there were cases of Mozambican youths who went abroad to study not returning to Mozambique; (2) that Mozambique needs leadership with superior training; (3) that future leaders, the leaders of tomorrow, the leaders of the next phase, must conveniently prepare themselves. These arguments, almost certainly infused with bad faith, cannot stand up to the reality of the facts and of the struggle.

The first argument falls on its very basis: one must reread what was written before on the history of Mozambican students abroad to see that this pretext lacks foundation. Kamba Simango returned to Mozambique and *was forced into exile*; Eduardo Mondlane was persecuted by PIDE in Mozambique and when he completed his studies, the Portuguese wanted to make him return so as to support a *colonialist propaganda manoeuvre*; and Guilherme Mabunda only now has completed his medical studies and these require a period of internship which he is now fulfilling. There are no other cases in any event during the period which precedes the formation of FRELIMO as

---

* In the Portuguese African educational system there are both technical and academic high schools. There are discernible trends in the situation of African students in the academic high schools (*liceus*) where it is difficult for Africans to get beyond the *quarta classe*, more Africans are enrolled in the technical than in the academic high schools as of the late 1960s, and a high dropout rate among Africans in higher education. See Samuels, 'Angolan Education,' 66.

well as the unleashing of the armed struggle, and for good reason.

Let us now examine the second argument. Mozambique needs trained leadership, of course! *It is for this same reason that FRELIMO has a programme.* And this programme is made possible *because there is a struggle in Mozambique.* If there are countries which offer study scholarships today, it is because the Mozambican people *are giving their blood* for the conquest of national independence, for the liberty of Mozambique, *in the cause of the freedom of humanity.* Socialist countries and various organizations show a solidarity without struggle, while the imperialist countries, the United States and various organizations which collaborate with Portugal against our People, give scholarships in an attempt to educate a leadership which will be favourable to their side. *But if this occurs, it is because there is a struggle in Mozambique.* Even those students who have deserted the ranks of the revolution and were able to get scholarships *are benefiting directly from our struggle on the international plane.*

Mozambique needs a revolutionary and trained leadership, leaders whose technical training is supported by a revolutionary will and idea, leaders who possess a true dedication to the people and to the revolution, who can be remembered only in the heat of the people and the struggle, in fidelity to the needs of the Fatherland, formulated by FRELIMO which embodies its will and objectives in the present historical phase. This is one of the reasons why FRELIMO obliges the IM students to work during their holidays, to participate directly in the tasks of the Revolution before going abroad, and [it encourages them to] interrupt their studies after the first higher cycle, etc . . . This serves to 'immerse' the student, the intellectual, and the future trained leadership in the bosom of the Revolution.

Everyone must understand this: although the Fatherland needs trained leaders, today as well as tomorrow, it *only needs leaders who are revolutionary,* otherwise even the colonialist [or 'colonialist-trained'] leaders would be excellent for us, since they have academic titles and technical qualifications. But we do not need them because *their knowledge is used to oppress the people,* since their wills, ideas and interests oppose the very revolution that serves the people.

It is fundamental to realize that *the struggle is the most important and best training school there is in the world.* We have comrades who yesterday did not know how to read and who today defeat the colonial army led by officers graduated from Military Academies, who are doing their apprenticeship, and who have torrents of counter-revolutionary knowledge. We have increased production in the zones under our control with our 'ignorant' peasants under the direction of our Central Committee where the only numerous diplomas perhaps are from primary schooling. Nevertheless, we have gotten results superior to those of the companies and the colonial state with all their engineers, agronomists, laboratory experts, technicians, etc . . . We teach more children and adults to read and write than the colonialists and, in the meantime, unlike them [the colonialists] we have no primary school graduates, privately schooled teachers, etc. . . This then is the great lesson of the popular war, the revolution which is now occurring in our Fatherland, in so-called Portuguese Guinea, in Vietnam, or in any part of the world. *The revolution also needs and cherishes its students, leaders and revolutionary intellectuals, but they can get more of an education in the revolution than in the university.*

The standard of living of the students, even though limited, is far and away better than that of most of the inhabitants of our land, and, besides, the material opportunities open to students after graduation are enormous; it is evident, too, that the revolution cannot compete in salaries with imperialism or with the international companies, especially since presently there are neither salaries nor minimum comforts which are the norm in any University. On the other hand, the education provided by Portuguese high schools, seminaries and technical schools, by imperialist teaching establishments, by the cooperation of information media and at the disposal of imperialism is used to inculcate in students, in the leadership and intellectuals, the dangerous idea that they are superior to the masses and that they are entitled to a privileged social and material situation. These are the germs planted in the mind which open the door to many desertions and treacheries, not only in our country but also in all the countries dominated by imperialism. Only our national faith, our revolutionary convinctions, practice in the struggle, and communion with the masses permit us to meet the challenge of this situation.

The imperialist propaganda of corruption stresses, above all, that the students are the leaders of tomorrow, the future leaders. We must firmly denounce this imperialist poisoning which is indecent, criminal, and which tries to make our students into accomplices of imperialism through the exploitation of the blood and sweat of the People.

Leaders are forced, whether or not they are intellectuals, to participate in the different tasks of the revolution, in the sacrifices and daily dedication to the People, in revolutionary study and practice. And there is no other kind of leader, nor can there be. It is the revolution that trains the leaders, and our young students should be *vigilant* faced [as they are] with imperialist intoxication, with imperialist corruption: only with vigilance and a reinforcement of revolutionary convictions and love of the people can we avoid corruption and treason: being a part of the struggle gives us the needed defences.

Furthermore, we should say, in the spirit of self-criticism that should always condition us, that the Central Committee due to inadequacies, albeit not serious, must also share the blame in this problem.

The demands of the struggle often cause us to neglect the political education of students abroad, and this neglect is excessive due to ephemeral contacts and texts. On the other hand, the decisions and writings of the Central Committee are not often given proper written publicity, thus facilitating the spread of false information and a lack of understanding of the real situation. Finally, the Central Committee has been hesitant in its decisions when faced with abuses and the flagrant lack of discipline of certain people, and although the Committee never has, at least morally, sanctioned this behaviour, there are those who could interpret tacit approval — albeit in bad faith — from this silence.

Mozambique Needs Elites
UNEMO

Excerpt from the UNEMO (Mozambique) National Union of Students White Paper of 1968, replying to Mondlane's paper. Translated from Portuguese by Douglas L. Wheeler and printed in African Historical Studies, *III, 1, 1970.*

No one can question the fact that Mozambique needs an educated elite* with higher training. According to a common expression, we shall say that we should not be concerned with quantity so much as with quality: 'Ponderantur et non numerantur' — weigh them and do not count them. The same idea was expressed by a French General at the Treaty of Versailles: a flock of sheep commanded by a lion is worth more than a pride of lions led by an ass. Mr. Mondlane cries that we need an outstanding elite and that he encourages students to pursue their studies after a stay in Dar es Salaam. Until now how many had that good fortune after returning to Dar? Moreover, promises of scholarships are so strong that he creates the impression that FRELIMO is the one who takes money from its own coffers to pay for higher education. Mr. Mondlane should keep in mind the following: that no student will now believe his promises of study after a period in training, for three reasons:

(a) FRELIMO did not make good its promises;

(b) FRELIMO has difficulty, like any other organization, in obtaining scholarships immediately for so many students who want to continue the promised higher education;

(c) It has been proved that Mondlane wants no intellectual rival. There is no other reason because he persecutes and continues to persecute so many Mozambicans whose names could well be cited here.

Dr. Mondlane asserts that: 'It is necessary for these future leaders to be well prepared, the leaders of tomorrow, the leaders of the next phase.' Why is this false? Is all this not necessary? The argument betrays itself. Why does he say on page twelve (12) that '. . . this serves constantly to involve the student, the intellectual, the future technical elite'? Why did Mondlane come to know that students necessarily must take part in the government of Mozambique later? This does not mean that it is the intention of the students to dethrone Dr. Mondlane, or to exploit the people or to prepare [themselves]

---

* 'Elite' translates the Portuguese word '*quadros*', which may also be translated 'cadres'.

with ambitions of being 'great people' in Mozambique. But it is a fact that Mr. President Mondlane should admit (very unfortunately, nevertheless, for his presidential aspirations) that if Mozambique wishes to progress, it must be in the hands of competent people — which is not to say that the people must be excluded or that all students want to be or must be leaders. Far from it! We have no base of power, but in sane logic, those who should direct the destinies of a country in this twentieth century are those who are well prepared. Still, whether or not Mister Mondlane wants to admit it, all students are going to bring progress in Mozambique by means of serving, helping and cooperating with the people.

Producers and Students
Samora Machel

> *From the directives issued by Samora Machel, President of FRELIMO, at the beginning of the production cycle for 1971—72 and widely circulated. Reproduced under the title 'Sowing the Seeds of Liberation' in* Mozambique Revolution *(Dar es Salaam) No. 49, Oct.—Dec. 1971.*

We shall soon be starting to prepare the land for new crops.

To many people production may seem a rite, a necessity, just something we are obliged to do in order to eat and clothe ourselves. It is true that production is aimed at satisfying our basic biological needs, but we also need it to free ourselves from poverty, to better know, control and use nature, and to educate ourselves politically. We are revolutionaries, our activities always have political meaning and content. Therefore our production, besides having an economic meaning and content, must have also political content.

In the enemy zone, under capitalism, under colonialism, there is also production. There, too, man wields the hoe to break the soil. There too, on the factory machine which we do not as yet have in our zone, — man makes things. Yet we say that production in the enemy zone is exploitation, whereas in our zone production liberates man. But it is the same hoe, the same man, the same act of breaking the soil. Why then is there this dividing line? Almost everyone knows the G3 gun. In the hands of the enemy the G3 is used to oppress and slaughter the people, but when we capture a G3, it becomes an instrument for liberating the people, for punishing those who slaughter the people. It is the same gun, but its content has changed because those who use it have different aims, different interests . . .

In FRELIMO we always emphasise the importance of production. To our army we give the tasks of fighting, producing and mobilising the masses. To our youth we give the tasks of studying, producing and fighting. In our discussions, in our documents, we constantly stress the importance of production, pointing out that this is an important front in our fight and a school for us. We can see that production is satisfying our everyday needs at the same time as liberating and uniting us. But we do not as yet see that production is a school, that we learn through production. Some people might be surprised that in our schools there are those who devote long hours to production, and that our army also has this task. These people might feel that this is absurd, that it would be more worthwhile for the pupils to spend this time reading books, attending classes, that the army's job is to fight and not to produce. But we also learn through production. Our ideas do not fall from the skies like rain. Our knowledge and experience do not come from dreaming in our sleep. Without ever having been to school, our illiterate peasants know more about cassava, cotton, groundnuts and many other things than the honourable capitalist gentleman who has never touched a hoe. Without knowing how to read, it is clear that our mechanics know more about car engines, how to assemble and repair them and how to mend broken parts, than the honourable capitalist gentleman who has never wished to soil his hands with motor oil. We see our 'ignorant' masons, our 'stupid' carpenters and labourers, so despised by the capitalist gentlemen, making beautiful houses, beautiful furniture which the honourable capitalist gentleman appreciates immensely and which he has no idea how to make. This clearly shows that we learn through production.

What we learn we do, and when we do, we see what is wrong. So we learn also from our mistakes and achievements. The mistakes show where there are shortcomings in our knowledge, weak points which have to be eliminated. This means that it is in the process of producing that we correct our mistakes. Production shows us that, if good tomatoes are going to grow in it, this soil needs more manure and this kind of manure, that there more water is needed. It was by making experiments which failed that our pupils learned how to make soap. It was by making soap that they improved the quality of the soap.

Production is a school because it is one of the sources of our knowledge, and it is through production that we correct our mistakes. It is by going to the people, that we both learn and teach the people. If our army did not produce, how would we have grown cassava in Tete when the people had no knowledge of cassava? If we had contented ourselves with making speeches about cassava, would the cassava have grown? What better way of defending our production in Tete against bombing raids, chemical weapons and enemy incursions than diversification of production, introduction of new crops and crops which are resistant to enemy action?

How can the people improve their production methods, how can they know what is wrong and what is right, unless they produce? We are in the habit of saying that it is in the war that we learn war, which means in fact, that it is by carrying out a revolution that one learns how to carry out a revolution better, that it is by fighting that we learn to fight better and that it is by producing that we learn to produce better. We can study a lot, but what use is tons of knowledge if not taken to the masses, if we do not produce? If someone keeps maize seeds in a drawer, will he harvest ears of maize?

If someone learns a lot and never goes to the masses, is never involved in practice, he will remain a dead compendium, a mere recorder who is able to quote by heart many passages from scientific works, from revolutionary works, but who will live his whole life without writing a single new page, a single new line. His intelligence will remain sterile, like those seeds locked in the drawer. We need constant practice, we need to be immersed in the revolution and in production, to increase our knowledge and, in this way, to advance our revolutionary work, our productive work.

The seed of knowledge only grows when it is buried in the soil of production of struggle. If we have already so greatly transformed our country, if we have won so many successes in production, education, health and combat, it is because we are always with the masses. We learn from them and pass on what we learn to them. We consistently apply what we know to production, correct our mistakes and enrich our knowledge. But we should not be satisfied.

Practice is not enough. One must also know, study. Without practice, without being combined with force, intelligence remains sterile. Without intelligence, without knowledge, force remains blind, a brute force.

There are comrades who look down on study because they do not know its value. Study is like a lamp in the night which shows us the way. To work without studying is to advance in the dark. One can go forward, of course, but at great risk of stumbling or taking the wrong path. At some bases, among some comrades, the regular habit has been established of devoting some time to study. This is good, but it is not enough. All leaders and cadres, together with the units must organise consistent and regular study programmes. Depending on the situation at least one hour a day should be devoted to study activities. Study should be organised in the spirit of collective work, collective consciousness, with small groups in which some teach others and everyone fights ignorance together. Because our starting point is a fairly weak one, we advise that in this first phase every effort should be made to raise the level of basic knowledge, especially by wiping out illiteracy in the units and among the cadres.

The Political Commissar, in co-operation with the Department of Education and Culture and working closely with the Provincial organisations, must organise the programme of fighting illiteracy and ignorance in such a way that each FRELIMO base becomes a base for fighting against obscurantism. Closely related to this programme should be a programme of seminars for comrades with higher scientific knowledge — agronomists, engineers, mechanics, sociologists, nurses, etc. — to help raise the general level of knowledge of leaders and cadres in the districts and provinces. These should be specialised seminars on precise subjects such as irrigation, hygiene, mill construction, the introduction of new crops and the introduction of new production methods.

In this way our comrades will be able to relate their scientific studies to practice, and raise the level both of their own work and of the work of the masses. Soil without manure produces weak plants, but manure without soil burns the seeds and also produces nothing. Our intelligence, our knowledge, are like that manure. Manure must be mixed with soil, intelligence with practice. Because their very existence depends on exploiting us, capitalism and colonialism keep knowledge away from the masses, creating an educated elite which does not work and is used only to better exploit the masses.

We say that it is the workers who must have knowledge, who must rule and who must benefit from labour. This is what we say and practice. And this is why our Armed Struggle has been transformed into a Revolution, why everything is in constant transformation and we are liberating the creative energy of the masses. This, finally, is why the enemy hate us. Nothing exists without production, and nothing exists without workers. The planes and bombing raids, the colonialist crimes, are aimed at keeping the workers producing for the capitalists, at keeping them exploited. The target of our bullets, the purpose of our struggle is, definitively, to end the exploitation of man by man, colonialism being its principal form in our country today. Our objective is to hand production over to the creative ability of the masses.

We are going to enter our eighth year of war. Next year we will celebrate the 10th anniversary of the founding of our Front. We are growing a great deal, but to grow more, to meet the growing needs of the war and the people, it is essential that our production increase in both quantity and quality, that more things be produced in our country.

Revolution liberates man. It liberates his intelligence and his work. This liberation manifests itself in the development of our production, which serves the people, which serves the struggle. Therefore, at this time when preparations are being made in agriculture for sowing the crops of the new season, we say to all the comrades:

To produce is to learn. Learn in order to produce and struggle better.

The Role of Students
Duncan Innes

> *Excerpt from a 1969 speech, 'Our Country, Our Responsibility', by Duncan Innes, then president of the National Union of South African Students (NUSAS).*

South Africa is our country and our responsibility. If we are concerned for the future of our country, as I am because I do not believe she has a secure future, then we must ask ourselves what we can do for our country and for our future. We must ask ourselves what we, as students, as tomorrow's leaders, can do. We must ask ourselves what NUSAS can do . . .

Our role then, as I see it, the role of NUSAS, the role of South African students, is to hold our basic policy before us as an ideal and to work with all our strength for the implementation of that ideal. Our role must be to point out the injustice of our society. This is to our duty, to do both as citizens of South Africa and as members of the community of mankind. Let the South African people never be able to say, as the German people said after they had seen the mangled horrors of Auschwitz and Buchenwald, 'We did not know this was happening.' In 10 years' time, let this not be the pathetic cry of White South Africa. We know! We are aware of what is happening! It is our duty to make South Africa aware of what we know.

There are those who would say that all is peaceful in South Africa. Let them remember the thousands of banned men and women, who lead twilight existences in our land.

There are those who would say that the African is happy in South Africa. Let them remember Sharpeville.

There are those who would say that the African is well-treated in South Africa. Let them look to the filth of the African locations.

There are those who would say that South Africa is a sunny, healthy land. Let them look to the dead in Limehill.

And when they say to us, as they will: Why do you point out these things? Are you a Communist? Are you a Leftist? Are you an enemy of South Africa? Then reply to them that you are none of these things. Tell them that you are someone who believes that every man who is born has a right to life, that every man who is born has a right to develop himself to his full potential. Tell them that, when you point out injustices in your country, you do so not because you wish to harm your country, but because you wish to remove the injustices and thus improve the image of your country.

There is much in this country that needs to be improved, for in a land such as this, where the majority have no freedom, none of us can be free. If a Government can condemn one section of the population, there is no reason why it cannot condemn another. The African who struggles for equal rights and equal opportunities is condemned; the White man who defends the African's right is also condemned. The 180-day law, bannings, passport removals, and deportations are the order of the day. And we must remember that, because one person has lost a passport, all of our passports are in jeopardy. We must remember that, because one man has been banned, all of us can suffer the same fate.

There is no criterion by which we may judge whether we are safe or not. The law can be no criterion because the courts are discarded by our rulers. You do not have to commit a crime to be condemned by our Government. You simply have to do something that these enlightened dictators do not like at one particular time. With that criterion no-one is safe. Not even the verkramptes, or ultra-conservatives, who are harassed as much by the Special Branch as we are . . .

And what freedom do we, in South Africa, have today anyway?

Do we have the freedom to love whom we choose? It is against the law to love someone whose skin is of a different pigment of ours. We can only love those whom our rulers have by law approved. Do we have the freedom to go wherever we choose in our country or can we go only to those places which are marked by our Government for Whites only? If we are in a hurry, do we have the freedom to catch the first taxi or bus that arrives, or must we wait for one that is marked for Whites only?

Do we have the freedom to invite the MCC cricket team to visit our country, or must we first dictate who their team is to be? Do our athletes have the freedom to compete internationally, and I mean all our athletes? Do we have the freedom to read great books and see great films, or are we only allowed access to those our rulers deem fit for us?

These are but a few of our unfreedoms. They are only the beginning. There will be more unfreedoms for us to chalk up on our 'Book of Rules'.

We can, of course, sit back and accept all of this. We can argue that there is nothing we can do now, and that in time all these problems will sort themselves out. This is a fallacy. Time alone can change nothing. It is through our efforts now that time will eventually reflect change. But we must make the effort now!

Let us stand up for our ideals. Let us dare to struggle and let us dare to win. Let us dare to dream of a future in which all the people of South Africa will be able to join hands together and to cry out in the words of the old Negro spiritual:

'Free at last, free at last; thank God Almighty, we're free at last.'

Black Student Policy Manifesto
SASO

An official statement of the South African Students Organization (SASO), adopted in 1972.

(1) SASO is a Black Student Organisation working for the liberation of the Black man first from psychological oppression by themselves through inferiority complex, and secondly from the physical one accruing out of living in a White racist society.

(2) We define Black people as those who are by law or tradition, politically, economically and socially discriminated against as a group in the South African society and identifying themselves as a unit in the struggle towards the realisation of their aspirations.

(3) SASO believes that:

(a) South Africa is a country in which both Black and White live and shall continue to live together;

(b) that the White man must be made aware that one is either part of the solution or part of the problem;

(c) that, in this context, because of the privileges accorded to them by legislation and because of their continual maintenance of an oppressive regime, Whites have defined themselves as part of the problem;

(d) that, therefore, we believe that, in all matters relating to the struggle towards realising our aspirations, Whites must be excluded;

(e) that this attitude must not be interpreted by Blacks to imply 'anti-Whitism' but merely a more positive way of attaining a normal situation in South Africa;

(f) that in pursuit of this direction, therefore, personal contact with Whites, though it should not be legislated against, must be discouraged, especially where it tends to militate against the beliefs we hold dear.

(4) (a) SASO upholds the concept of Black Consciousness and the drive towards black awareness as the most logical and significant means of ridding ourselves of the shackles that bind us to perpetual servitude.

(b) SASO defines Black Consciousness as follows:

(i) Black Consciousness is an attitude of mind, a way of life.

(ii) The basic tenet of Black Consciousness is that the Black man must reject all value systems that seek to make him a foreigner in the country of his birth and reduce his basic human dignity.

(iii) The Black man must build up his own value systems, see himself as self-defined and not defined by others.

(iv) The concept of Black Consciousness implies the awareness by the Black people of power they wield as a group, both economically and politically and hence group cohesion and solidarity are important facets of Black Consciousness.

(v) Black Consciousness will always be enhanced by the totality of involvement of the oppressed people, hence the message of Black Consciousness has to be spread to reach all sections of the Black community.

(c) SASO accepts the premise that, before the Black people join the open society, they should first close their ranks, to form themselves into a solid group to oppose the definite racism that is meted out by the White society, to work out their direction clearly and bargain from a position of strength. *SASO believes that a truly open society can only be achieved by blacks.*

(5) SASO believes that the concept of integration cannot be realised in an atmosphere of suspicion and mistrust. Integration does not mean an assimilation of Blacks into an already established set of norms drawn up and motivated by white society. Integration implies free participation by individuals in a given society and proportionate contribution to the joint culture of the society by all constituent groups. Following this definition therefore, SASO believes that integration does not need to be enforced or worked for. Integration follows automatically when the doors to prejudice are closed through the attainment of a just and free society.

(6) SASO believes that all groups allegedly working for 'integration' in South Africa — and here we note in particular the Progressive Party and other Liberal institutions — are not working for the kind of integration that would be acceptable to the Black man. Their attempts are directed merely at relaxing certain oppressive legislations and to allow Blacks into a white-type

society.

(7) SASO, while upholding these beliefs, nevertheless wishes to state that Black Consciousness should not be associated with any particular political party or slogan.

Dialogue with multiracial organisations:

(1) SASO believes that dialogue with student organisations such as NUSAS and UCM should only be engaged in when absolutely necessary. i.e. in matters affecting either one or all as student organisations or where so doing is in the interests of black students.

(2) SASO believes that there can never be cause for joint consultation with any of these organisations on anything relating to the SASO political stance.

Black Theology

SASO is committed to the promotion of Black Theology which is essentially a re-examination of the black man's religious make-up and an attempt to unite the Black man to God. SASO sees Black Theology as an existential theology that grapples with the Black man's day-to-day life experience.

Foreign Investments:

(1) SASO sees foreign investments as giving stability to South Africa's exploitative regime and committing South Africa's trading partners to supporting this regime. For this reason, SASO rejects foreign investments.

(2) Further, SASO sees the ameliorative experiments like those of Polaroid as, at worst, conscience-salving and at best, resulting in the creation of a change-resistant middle class amongst the few Blacks employed by foreign firms.

On Namibia:

SASO recognises the indisputable right of the people of Namibia to conduct their own affairs without any interference from South Africa and expresses solidarity with the students and the people of Namibia to rid themselves of this unwarranted occupation.

On Dialogue between African States and South Africa:

(1) SASO rejects all attempts at dialogue between African States and South Africa.

(2) SASO believes that South Africa is intent on stretching her tentacles through trade links throughout Africa so as to hold Africa in her grip.

(3) SASO further believes that no amount of preaching will alter South Africa from her course towards total and lasting subjugation of the Black peoples of South Africa.

Black Students and the South African Revolution
ANC

Excerpt from a statement by the National Executive of
the ANC, 'The Time for Action Has Come', adopted at
their meeting in Zambia, 27–31 August, 1971.

(1) This meeting notes with pleasure that the African students in particular, and other Black students generally, have emerged as a powerful potential revolutionary force capable of playing a vital role in the South African revolution.

(2) The establishment of the South African Students Organisation, whose main aims are to unite all Black students, to project the true image and dignity of the Black man, and to assert the right and ability of the Black man to lead where in the past he followed white leadership, is a welcome and necessary trend in the situation prevailing in our country.

(3) This meeting therefore recommends:
(a) That the NEC takes steps to keep all South African students outside South Africa fully informed on the trends and political developments in our country.
(b) That a regular News Bulletin addressed to the Youth in South Africa be issued by the Youth section inside South Africa.

(4) This meeting instructs the NEC to strengthen the ANC Youth and Students Section so that it can effectively perform the following tasks, inter alia –
(a) To play a more active role in organising and keeping in more dynamic contact with our Students and Youth all over the world;
(b) To organise political lectures and seminars in all areas where we have a number of Students and Youth concentrated and thereby orientate them towards more active participation in the South African revolution;
(c) To plan educational programmes for selected ANC Students, with the object of meeting the short- and long-term needs of our struggle and our people;
(d) To initiate preparations for the convening of a general conference of all our students and Youth abroad.

8. Women

Editors' Introduction

Women's liberation posed a problem for the national liberation movements in two ways. On the one hand, the movements felt that they needed to define the relationship of the problem of women's oppression with that of their national oppression. It was a question of priorities and they felt that the problem in their countries was different from that to be found in Western industrialized countries. The statement of the ANC addressed itself to this distinction.

The other problem was the opposite one. While some white women in the West might define women's liberation in such a way as to ignore the problem of national liberation, conversely some members of national liberation movements might brush aside the existence of any problem at all. It was the fact that 'women's liberation was a fundamental necessity of the revolution, a guarantee of its continuity, a condition of its triumph' that Samora Machel, president of FRELIMO, emphasized in his speech of 1973.

Women's Liberation
Zanele Dhlamini

> *An article prepared by Zanele Dhlamini on the*
> *occasion of South African Women's Day (August 9) for*
> Sechaba, *VI, 9, September 1972.*

To understand what the Women's liberation movement today represents, we must understand the general situation which is developing in the Western world.

Western democracy is faced with a general crisis in that there have come to the surface many problems which it has failed to remedy. Even in its most idealistic form it pretends to be a government for all the people. It seeks to convince the ordinary people that it is the best and only government they could have. However, every day we realise that, in fact, this democracy does not, and cannot, resolve their problems. Both England and the U.S.A. are still facing the problems of institutional poverty, rising unemployment and discrimination against large sections of the people. Hence the beginnings of a general awareness which in the United States is best expressed by the Black Panther Party's slogan of 'All Power to the People'. A slogan which says no more no less than is claimed by Western democracy's 'government of the people, by the people, for the people'. Yet the fact that such a slogan can be so threatening to the powers that be is a very strong indictment against the way this democracy is actually practised. What the Black Panther Party's slogan represents is the consolidation of a general anti-imperialist struggle. A struggle against a democracy which is on behalf of a minority group.

Many people realise more and more that, instead of being themselves subjects and creators of history as they have been led to believe, they have in reality, to a great extent, been objects of history. By and large, women in the Western world have been objects of history. Various sections have, of course not to the same extent, been passive recipients of policy. Suffragettes protested; workers have formed trade unions which have consistently tried to protect the interests of workers. Latterly, we have seen students in Europe, America and Japan demanding to be full and active participants in formulating policies governing their universities. Some have gone further to identify with the demands of workers and the struggles for national liberation overseas.

Women in the Western world, en masse, are now experiencing this general awakening. Women, like all other dominated sections of society, are fighting against an oppressive system which excludes them from participating in the formulation of policies even within the very boundaries of a bourgeois democracy. The movement is about the awakening of the masses of women to take up their legitimate role in society.

The forms of struggle differ from country to country. The priorities and focus of attack are dictated by the prevalent conditions and the levels of consciousness of the women themselves. It also reflects the political climate and the influence of the various groups and classes. In the U.S.A., organisations range from the moderately liberal NOW which makes limited legalistic and social reformist demands, to the socialist oriented CELL 16, a Boston feminist organisation, which makes more fundamental anti-imperialist demands.

Against this background, I wish to examine the condition of the Black women of South Africa who live under the policies of Apartheid, and also to look at the very important role, I think, they have to play in the liberation of all South Africans.

South Africa is a racist country. Administrative policies are made to affect various racial groups differently. The White women, although accorded normal voting rights, do suffer the limitations faced by women under all Western bourgeois democracies. One or two serve in the White racist parliament and probably in other fields too. By and large they are grossly underrepresented in the corridors of power. Whenever they have been recruited and trained for active (*Laager*) or reserve military service and for police duties, it has only been as tools of the oppressive White government machinery, controlled and led by men. They have been recruited in order to strengthen the government forces against the militant efforts of the oppressed Black majority. They have been called upon when Black protest has been threatening and when there has been numerical necessity to crush them.

'By the Women's Enfranchisement Act of 1930, which gave the vote to white women only (despite the previous pledges of Hertzog and Malan that Coloured women would be included), the European electorate increased from half a million to one million, and the effect of the African vote was more than halved.'[1] (It was finally destroyed in 1936.) Ordinarily, the number of White women in government service, the military, industry and management is negligible compared to their numbers in society and the opportunities supposedly available to them as members of a supreme White race. Divorce laws, laws governing succession, illegitimacy and administrative promotions are biased in favour of their men.

Their experience, however, can never be comparable to that of Black women. With all their limitations, South African White women have still been put on a pedestal. A pedestal based on false and mythical bourgeois standards: that they are fragile, decorative, weak (feminine) and incapable of the simplest work that Black women perform daily for both their masters and for themselves. The White men feed the illusion with minor 'gentlemanly' tasks of door opening and cigarette lighting. With Black domestic service cheaply available for their household and various family responsibilities, White women have theoretically all the leisure in the world. They go out to work to earn pin-money and to avoid boredom at home.[2]

These women will not have real liberty without a change in the situation of Blacks because theirs and the Blacks' situation are manifestations of the same exclusive bourgeois democracy. I have said 'real liberty' because in the experience of South Africa we have seen that Whites can enjoy many unreal liberties, liberties which are guarded by machine guns, Saracens and submarines directed against 'fellow-citizens'.

A system which discriminates against its own kith and kin is not about to act 'lady bountiful' towards those it regards as less than human.

Working on the premise that 50% of the population of any society is female, we can assume conservatively that in South Africa (population 21 million) there are 7½ million Black women, 2 million White women, 1 million Coloured and 300,000 Indian women. (Indian and Coloured women suffer the same conditions as African women. The differences are only of theoretical interest to social anthropologists.) Any position, therefore, adopted by Black women, who constitute more than a third of the total population and half of all oppressed peoples, has to be very important in terms of liberation.

Black women in South Africa are at the bottom rung of all oppressed groups as workers. When employed they earn the least and do the most menial jobs.

Of the 800,000 Black women classified in 1960 as economically active

active, more than 50% were in domestic service; 25% were farm labourers or employed inside and outside the farmer's house; 25,000 were professionals, , mainly nurses and teachers. The remainder were factory hands or clericals in the private sector. The average cash wage paid to black domestic servants in Johannesburg per month is $21.98.

Professionals like nurses earn thus:

Black nurses	$ 924 – $1,260
Black 'nursing sisters'	$1,176 – $1,680
White 'nursing sisters'	$2,856 – $4,200

Those employed in the food and canning industry often earn less than $8.40 per week.

The potential Black female work force (i.e. 15–60 years) is recorded as 38%. The figure is obviously much higher because Black children do not have compulsory education nor are there enough schools to admit them all. They become available for economic exploitation at a much earlier age as cheap child labour. Often they stay at home to release their parents for employment. Otherwise, they hussle in the streets picking pockets or otherwise fending for themselves in rather unconventional ways. Only a minority of Black children go to school.

Most of the unaccounted for women live in villages and African reserves as peasants where they work harder than anybody else for even less. They try to keep families alive and together where the country's migratory labour policy is to contract men away from their homes for extended periods of time while only women, children and old men remain behind. the former to till the soil, build houses, tend the cattle and generally take charge of the problems of daily living.

In describing the peasant conditions, Govan Mbeki cites instances where unpaid compulsory labour adds insult to injury to the peasants in the reserves. Men are drafted into work teams to dig holes for the creosote poles or erect barbed wire fences. Women must provide and cook food for these teams. 'If a women has to leave her children without a meal, it is an eventuality that the government officially happily overlooks. What matters is that she should provide the food to the teams when her turn comes. A complaint against the harshness of the law is punished as incitement to disobedience . . . Every widowed women, for though a women is in every other law a 'child', dependent on the male heir, in matters of taxation she assumes the position of the absent male taxpayer.'[3] (All Black men over 18 years of age must pay a poll-tax whatever their economic or physical condition.)

Apartheid hits Black women far beyond wage discrimination. Women are ill-educated and under-trained. Job reservation, determinants and regulations plus influx control regulations affect them as brutally as their men. Like them, they can neither be members of legally recognized trade unions nor can they withdraw their labour for collective bargaining. (Under the Terrorist Act, such action would be regarded as subversive because it aims at changing the existing social, political or economic conditions.)

While men are absent at the mines, in prisons or farm labour camps, women both in cities and villages are left to suffer the harassment of the police and other effects of various government anti-Black schemes. Under the Bantu Resettlement Scheme, 'a phenomenal number of women and children are being moved around, thus suffering poverty, malnutrition, broken families and privations of land and cattle.'[4] *The Rand Daily Mail* (July 23rd, 1970) published a story of four Zulu women and their 41 children who lived in tents for 2½ years, 'a brave, but futile resistance against constant urging by government officials to move into a concentration-camp type of township,' i.e. after they had been evicted from a farm where their husbands formerly worked. Mrs. Lena Mnisi and her 4 children were sent off to Paarl in 1966 away from her husband because he was a 'disqualified person' — he had not worked continuously for one employer for 10 years. In July 1970, when her husband qualified, she only received a temporary permit and was fined $42 in November 1970 (or six weeks imprisonment) for being illegally in the area. Replying to protests, Koornhof, Deputy Minister of Bantu Administration, said: 'If African men were allowed to contract marriages freely with women not qualified to be in the area, the number of Africans would increase.'

In the small town of Excelsoir, 14 Black women were recently arrested and imprisoned because, as the Minister of Justice, Mr. Pelser, put it: 'There has been a whispering campaign' — rumours had been rife in the White community about the number of African women with 'bastard' children. The 14 women and five white farmers were arrested. The farmers were immediately released on bail of $250 each. Nobody came forward to help the women. Now they are out of prison. They have the difficult problem of finding employment, and, worse still, they may be hounded out of the location.[5]

Barry Higgs writes that in 1969 'there were 5,000 trials under the Immorality Act in South Africa.' He estimates that one in every 200 White males came up in court for sexual 'offences'. The great majority involved White men and African or Coloured girls generally much younger than the men. 'Rape of non-White women by White men is statistically far more frequent than rape of White women by non-White men. Blacks convicted of rape of White women are generally sentenced to death. No White man has ever been executed for raping a Black women.'[6]

These facts clearly indicate that Black women in South Africa have a triple yoke of oppression. They suffer all the degradations of White racism. They are exploited as workers and peasants. And they are females in a clearly patriarchal family structure, where traditionally precedence is given to males in both public and private life. H.J. Simons has written extensively on the subject of African women and their legal status in South Africa.[7]

Black women live under three legal systems (customary law, Native law and European law), none of which accord her a position equal to that which she in fact holds by virtue of her influence, her economic independence and her social and political dynamism. Clearly, she has no legal rights. Black women are treated as minors under perpetual guardianship of their fathers, brothers or husbands who intercede for them in legal matters and enter into all sorts of contracts on their behalf. At the risk of being counter-revolutionary in terms of present-day women's liberation analysis, (viz. the core of the contradictions in society is sex exploitation of females by males rather than the Marxian class contradictions);[8] I would argue that female oppression via Black males is the least of the Black women's burdens. The sexism Black women suffer most is from the White establishment. Black male prejudices have not dehumanized, degraded and brutalized Black women to remotely the same extent their white racism and capitalist exploitation are doing. Black men are no index of equity for Black women. They do equally dreary jobs for a pittance. In fact, their lives and conditions are often worse off under apartheid. They live in constant fear of arrest under the Pass Laws and suffer incredible humiliations in the prisons and what is called 'mine compounds' away from their families. Educated women of the Western industrialized countries are livid because they do not have the same work opportunities as their men: they want communal day care for their children, unrestricted abortion and birth control plus equal sharing of home duties, like raising babies, with their menfolk, among other reasons because technology and bottle-feeding make this possible. These are legitimate demands reflecting their experience within their society today.

South African Black women would not better their condition much by acquiring the status of Black men. Besides, the women have been doing what is considered men's work for a very long time. Communal care of children and other dependants is probably what has helped them survive the inroads of apartheid which disrupt and threaten to destroy Black family life. Unrestricted birth control and abortion assume a political dimension, where government policy is to reward the birth of extra White children and encourage White immigration into South Africa, while it campaigns for family reduction among Blacks.

This looks particularly sinister when the Black numbers are already reduced by the acknowledged high incidence of still-births, high infantile mortality rates, malnutrition, adult starvation, death sentences and socio-political murders. 'From international figures it appeared that South Africa accounted for nearly 50% of all legal executions in the world.'[9]

Numbers are the only strength South African Blacks have in the face of a hostile government. Black women are, therefore, not about to campaign for their own annihilation. Division of nursery duties will be problematic where modern technology has not yet reached Black kitchens and nurseries. The mother seems to be still indispensable for the children's survival.

It is no exaggeration to say that through the common experience of racist and capitalist exploitation over the years Black women and Black men in South Africa have achieved what Angela Davis calls a deformed kind of equality.[10]

To some extent they have had to deal with each other, as people, in much more real terms rather than play the games of Ladies and Gentlemen. Problems of survival have taught the Black man that the Black woman, who traditionally took the back seat, is no frivolous nit-wit incapable of caring for herself and family in his absence, i.e. when he is unemployed, in prison, detained or has fled the country for political reasons.[11] She has had to work for wages, feed and clothe the family and educate the children to the limits that the South Africa situation will permit. She does this without being spared any of the harsh laws of apartheid policies. In fact, sexist as the oppressor is, he tends to project his own sexual prejudices into the laws he imposes onto the Blacks — some of which never were under customary law, e.g. depriving women of property rights and installing younger males as guardians of their older widowed or single female relatives.

It is obvious that feminist issues exist in South Africa, but the Black women will have to work out their own priorities according to their experience and the future society they wish to see.

Some Black South African women have made their views known. Florence Mphosho, a dedicated member of the African National Congress and a previous staff member of the WIDF (Women's International Democratic Federation) says that 'the revolution will help to liberate women . . . Politics is the best school for the development of true comradeship and equality between men and women.'[12] Kate Molale, of the Federation of South African Women, in a message to all women, told an ADN reporter that 'the women of the world can help the women of South Africa by launching a campaign against the sale of arms to the racist regime of South Africa by Western Powers, for the release of all political prisoners and to end all apartheid and racial laws.'

Black women have participated in the fight for their land and their rights throughout the bloody history of colonialism and internal oppression and there is documentary evidence of this. In recent times Charlotte Maxeka was one of the founders of the African National Congress in 1912.

Women have formed religious, political, social, educational and economic (stock-fares) organizations to combat problems created by the policies of apartheid. En masse (22,000 in Pretoria in 1957) they have demonstrated against the extension of Pass Laws to women. They also campaigned against Bantu Authorities in Pondoland in 1960. Others have since then persisted to publicly challenge apartheid against all odds when recent legislation was made even harsher. Winnie Mandela, Thokozile Mngoma and Martha Dlamini, among others, were held in jail for more than a year in 1970 under the Terrorism Act. Dorothy Nyembe is serving a prison sentence of 15 years for her political beliefs.

Clearly, the sexism of the oppressor should not divert us from attacking racism and capitalism in a very direct way. Sexist concessions to Black women will not change the South African situation. Besides, no real liberation will be achieved by women — Black or White — while the racist, capitalist attitudes prevail. All that can be achieved is very limited reforms and concessions. A more constructive way to deal with the feminist problems amongst the oppressed is to launch a revolution within the revolution so that women in the South African struggle can participate as a massive, conscious

and equal partner in solving *all* the problems that affect the re-education and
'consciousness raising' of both men and women towards a transformation of
social roles affecting both public and private lives. It will be the women's
responsibility to make sure that the successes achieved carry on to the resulting government and are not reversed by the new masters as has been
experienced elsewhere.

In conclusion, I would like to refer to an article on women's liberation
appearing in the *Sechaba* of July 1970, sub-titled: 'A discussion of the
issues with reference to the African revolution'; that is, at the risk of being
pedantic. Some of the issues referred to were: (1) Alternatives to the nuclear
family; (2) demands for free contraception and advice; (3) abortion on
demand.

The first one is clearly not a Black South African issue. The following
excerpt from a letter written by a poor mother in the U.S.A. arises from
issues similar to the latter two. 'You murder me, women's liberationist, every
bullshit demand you make; not because what you ask is wrong, but because
of what you leave out. Where is free childbirth in your platform, where is
decent pre-natal care? Where is nourishing food for me, so my child isn't
born premature and retarded? So he doesn't die in infancy? Where is a decent
place to live, enough clothes, freedom from disease and filth . . .?'[14] There is
everything to be gained by all individual women in making those three
demands, even though they reflect the needs of only a particular class and
condition of women. In South Africa it is mainly the needs of the non-poor
White woman. There is no need for Black women to echo them. *'For what is
done or learned by one class of women becomes by virtue of their common
womanhood the property of all women . . . eventually.'* (Elizabeth and Emily
Blackwell, 1859).

Notes
1. Mbeki, Govan, *South Africa: The Peasants' Revolt*, Britain, Penguin Books, 1964, p. 27.
2. It is claimed that the problem of poverty amongst Whites has been eliminated. Watts, H. I. *Poverty: Some Implications of Inequality*, Johannesburg, Spro-Cas No. 4, 1971, pp. 51, 53.
3. Mbeki, Govan, *op. cit.*, pp. 99 and 108.
4. Desmond, Cosmas, *The Discarded People*, England Penguin Books, 1971.
5. *Sechaba* (April 1971) Vol. 5, No. 4, p. 11.
6. Higgs, Barry, *Sex and Race, Sechaba*, Vol. 4, No. 6, June 1970, pp. 3 and 8.
7. Simons, H. J., *African Women — Their Legal Status in South Africa*, London, C. Hurst and Co., 1968.
8. Firestone, Shulamith, *The Dialectic of Sex — The Case for Feminist Revolution*, New York, W. Morrow and Co., Inc., 1970, p. 6. 'We can attempt to develop a materialist view of history based on sex itself.'
9. Horrell, Muriel, *A Survey of Race Relations in South Africa*. S.A. Institute of Race Relations, Jan. 1971, p. 44.
10. Davis, Angela, *Reflections on the Black Women's Role in the Community of Slaves,' Black Scholar — Journal of Black Studies and Research*, Vol. 3, No. 4, Dec. 1971.

11. Horrell, Muriel, *op. cit.*, pp. 42, 43. In 1967, '496,071 sentenced and 257,651 unsentenced prisoners had been admitted to gaol.' 'In the same year, 222,600 Africans were in prison for up to one month.' For the same period (1968–1969) breast-fed infants admitted to gaol with their mothers, or born during the mother's detention, were:—

	White	Black	Total
With Mother	3	4,697	4,700
Born in Detention	1	186	187

12. *Sechaba*, Aug. 1970, Vol. 4, No. 8.
13. *Sechaba*, Vol. 4, Nos. 11/12, Nov/Dec. 1970, pp. 19.
14. Anonymous, *Women – A Journal of Liberation*, Vol. 2, No. 3, p. 51.

A Fundamental Necessity of the Revolution

Samora Machel

Excerpts from the Opening Speech of the First Conference of Mozambican Women by Samora Moises Machel, president of FRELIMO, on Mar. 4, 1973. Translated from Portuguese.

The main objective of the Conference lies in the study of questions dealing with women's emancipation, and in the search for the types of action which will bring about her liberation. But a question arises: Why the concern for woman's liberation? And still another question arises: What is the reason for the holding of this Conference?

There are among us – the organization is well aware of this fact – people who believe that we must consecrate all our efforts to the struggle against colonialism, and that the task of women's liberation, in this case, is purely secondary since it is a useless and strength-consuming task. And further, they add that the present situation in which we live, with its lack of schools, few educated women, tradition-bound women, does not provide us with the basis for any significant action; for this reason, we must await independence, the construction of an economic, social and educational base before undertaking the battle.

Some others, interpreting the Statutes tendentiously, state that it is necessary to respect certain traditional local particularisms, since attacking them at this stage makes us risk loss of support by the masses. These people ask: What is the relevance of a women's liberation movement when the majority of the women are totally indifferent to the question? Their conclusion is that it is an artificial liberation, imposed on the women by FRELIMO. This is a very serious question. It requires study and clear ideas.

The liberation of women is not an act of charity. It is not the result of a humanitarian or compassionate position. It is a fundamental necessity for the Revolution, a guarantee of its continuity, and a condition for its success.

132

The Revolution's main objective is to destroy the system of the exploitation of man by man, the construction of a new society which will free human potentialities and reconcile work and nature. It is within this context that the question of women's liberation arises.

In general, the women are the most oppressed, the most exploited beings in our society. She is exploited even by him who is exploited himself, beaten by him who is tortured by the *palmatorio*, humiliated by him who is trod underfoot by the boss or the settler. How may our Revolution succeed without liberating women? Is it possible to liquidate a system of exploitation and still leave a part of society exploited? Can we get rid of only one part of exploitation and oppression? Can we clear away half the weeds without the risk that the surviving half will grow even stronger? Can we then make the Revolution without the mobilization of women? If women compose over half of the exploited and oppressed population, can we leave them on the fringes of the struggle?

In order for the Revolution to succeed, we must mobilize all of the exploited and oppressed, and consequently the women also. In order for the Revolution to triumph, it must liquidate the totality of the exploitative and oppressive system, it must liberate all the exploited and oppressed people, and thus it must liquidate women's exploitation and oppression. It is obliged to liberate women.

Considering that the fundamental necessity of Revolution is its continu-- ance by future generations, how may we assure their revolutionary training if the mother, as the first educator, is marginal in the revolutionary process? How can we make of the home of the exploited and oppressed a centre of revolution and militancy, a transmitter of our views, a stimulus of commit- ment for the family, if the woman is apathetic to this process, indifferent to the society which is being created, and deaf to the people's appeal?

To say that women do not feel the necessity to defend their liberation is an argument that holds no water when looked at carefully.

Women do feel the impact of domination and the necessity of changing their situation. What happens is that the domination of society upon them, by choking their initiative, frequently prevents them from expressing their aspirations, and from conceiving of the appropriate methods for their struggle.

It is at this stage that FRELIMO intervenes, as a vanguard aware of the men and women of Mozambique, of the oppressed people. FRELIMO formu- lates the line to be followed and indicates the methods of struggle. We must understand this phenomenon in order to avoid useless and dishonest discussions.

The question, therefore, is which is the most suitable moment to launch the struggle for women's liberation. We cannot limit the revolutionary process to certain aspects only and neglect others, because the Revolution is a global process. Otherwise, the Revolution will be blocked and destroyed. The evil roots which we neglect to remove or whose removal is postponed until later will become cancerous roots before that 'later' ever arrives.

Under present conditions FRELIMO can no longer undertake an armed struggle without the making of the Revolution itself. The condition for the development of the armed struggle is striking at the roots of exploitation. It is erroneous to believe that we must postpone the liberation of women until later, for that would mean that we allow reactionary ideas to gain ground and to combat us when they are strong. It is not sensible not to fight the crocodile when it is still on the banks of the river, but to wait and fight it when it is in the middle of the river.

Our armed struggle, acting as an incubator, creates the necessary conditions for receptivity by the masses to ideas of progress and revolution. Not to undertake a battle when conditions are ripe shows a lack of political vision, i.e. a strategic error . . .

It is obvious that if we speak of the liberation of women we must mean that we consider her oppressed and exploited. One must understand the bases of such oppression and exploitation.

Let us begin by saying that women's oppression is a consequence of her exploitation, since oppression in a society is always the result of an imposed exploitation. Colonialism did not come to occupy our lands in order to arrest us, to whip us or beat us on the palms. It invaded us in order to exploit our riches and our labour. It has introduced the system of oppression in order the better to exploit us, to overcome our resistance and to prevent a rebellion against exploitation. Physical oppression with courts, police, armed forces, prisons, torture, and massacres. Moral oppression with its obscurantism, superstition, and ignorance, whose purpose is to destroy the spirit of creative initiative, to eliminate the sense of justice and criticism, to reduce a person to passivity, and to the acceptance of the normality of a condition of exploitation and oppression. Humiliation and contempt become part of this process since the person who exploits and oppresses has a tendency to humiliate and to scorn his victim, and to consider him an inferior being. Racism thus appears as the ultimate form of humiliation and contempt.

The mechanism of the alienation of women is identical to the mechanism of alienation of the colonized man in a colonial society, or to that of the worker in capitalist society.

From the moment that primitive humanity began to produce more than it was able to consume, the material bases were created for the creation of a social stratum which would from then on appropriate the results of the work of the majority.

It is this appropriation of the work of the masses by a handful of elements of a society which is at the basis of the system of man's exploitation of man and at the heart of the antagonistic contradiction which has been dividing society for centuries.

Ever since the appearance of this process of exploitation, women as a group, like men, have been submitted to the domination of the privileged classes.

The woman is also a producer and a worker, but with certain special qualities. To possess women is to possess workers, unpaid workers, workers the totality of whose labour power may be appropriated without resistance by her husband, i.e. her boss and sovereign.

To marry women in an agrarian society is a sure means of accumulating much wealth. The husband has at his disposal unpaid manpower, which makes no claims, which does not rebel against exploitation. We can see the importance of polygamy in the rural areas of an agrarian economy. And since society understands that the woman is a source of wealth, it demands that a price be paid. The parents thus require from the future son-in-law a price — *lobolo* — in exchange for their daughter. The woman is bought, inherited, as if she were a material good, a source of wealth.

But still more important, and quite different from the slave, for example, who is also a source of wealth and an unpaid worker, the women offers two other advantages to her owner; she is a source of pleasure; and above all she is a producer of other workers, a producer of new sources of wealth.

This last aspect is particularly significant. Thus the husband has the right, in such a society, to repudiate the woman or to demand the return of his *lobolo* if she is sterile or if he thinks she is. We thus observe that, in many societies where there is a consciousness of the value of the labour of the children borne by the women, the principle is established that the children belong to the mother's family, or clan. In our society, this is also the practice until the husband pays the totality of the *lobolo*, i.e. the price for the purchase of his wealth. It is in this context that we find the over-emphasis on the fertility of women, the transformation of the man-woman relationship into a mere act of procreation.

There is a further problem. The exploiter, due to his control of the masses, acquired great wealth, large fields, cattle, gold, jewellery, etc. In spite of these riches, as any man, he was still mortal. The problem thus arose as to the future of that wealth; in other words, the question of inheritance came to the fore. The woman is the producer of heirs. We can thus understand how the point of departure for the exploitation of women and her consequent oppression is to be located in the system of private property, in the system of man's exploitation of men.

It is important to understand correctly the nature of the contradiction, or contradictions, which are at play, since it is only in the light of such understanding that we shall be in a condition to define the objects of our attack, and to conceive of an adequate strategy and tactics.

We have seen that the basis of the domination of women was to be found in the system of organization of the economic life in society: in private property of the means of production, which necessarily leads to the exploitation of man by man.

This means that the essential contradiction between women and the social order, over and above the specific conditions of her situation, is the contradiction between herself and the exploitation of man by man, between woman and private property over the means of production. In other words, the contradiction is the same as that which exists between the popular working masses and the exploitative social order.

Let us be clear on this point: the antagonistic contradiction is not found between man and woman, but rather between woman and the social order, between all exploited women and men, and the social order. It is her condition of exploitation which explains her absence from all tasks of thought and decision in society, which causes her to be excluded from the elaboration of the thought and decisions which organize economic, social, cultural and political life, even when her interests are directly at stake. This is the main aspect of the contradiction: her exclusion from the decision-making sphere of society.

This contradiction may only be resolved by means of the Revolution, since it is only the Revolution which can destroy the pillars of an exploitative society, and reconstruct society on a new basis which may liberate woman's initiative, integrate her as a responsible agent in society, include her in the taking of decisions. Consequently, in the same way as there cannot be a Revolution without the liberation of women, the struggle for the liberation of women cannot succeed without the victory of the Revolution itself.

We must add that the ideological and cultural bases of the exploitative society which keep women under control are destroyed by the ideological and cultural processes of Revolution which impose new values, methods, new content in education and culture onto society.

Besides this antagonistic contradiction between the woman and social order, there arise also other contradictions which, even if secondary, oppose women to men. The marriage system, the marital authority based exclusively on sex, the frequent brutality of the husband, his systematic refusal to consider women his equal, are all sources of friction and contradiction.

There are even times, in certain extreme cases, when secondary contradictions, because they are not correctly solved, become severe enough to result in serious consequences, such as divorce. But it is not such happenings, serious as they may be, that will alter the nature of contradiction.

We must emphasize this aspect, since we witness at present, mainly in the capitalist world, an ideological offensive which, under the aegis of women's liberation, pretends to transform into an antagonistic relationship the contradiction with man, thus dividing men and women — exploited beings who ought to combat together the exploitative society. In reality, beyond the demagogy which masks the real nature of this ideological offensive, it is an offensive by capitalist society in order to confuse women and to divert their attention from the real aim.

In our ranks there occur small manifestations of this ideological offensive. We hear, here and there, women murmuring against men as if it were the sex difference that was the cause of their exploitation, as if men were sadistic monsters who take pleasure in women's oppression.

Both men and women are the products and victims of the exploitative society which has given birth to them and educated them. It is essentially against this society that both women and men must together struggle. Our practical experience has proved that the progress that has been obtained in the liberation of women is the result of the successes achieved in the common struggle against colonialism and imperialism, against the exploitation of man by man, and for the building of the new society.

9. The Modes of Cultural Oppression

Editors' Introduction

The most insidious of the ways in which colonial powers maintained their authority was by cultural oppression. Few people accepted for its own sake the legitimacy of political domination. And most people were sceptical of the economic arguments advanced to justify colonial rule, suspecting them of being self-seeking. The argument that was always most effective was the cultural one — the conqueror as the bearer of civilization. This argument was more effective not because it was true but because conquest led to self-doubt, and in a state of self-doubt, some of the conquered began to believe the ideology of the new masters.

Consequently, a central task for the movements was the task of demystification. To the argument that the conquered had no culture worth preserving, the articles of the MPLA and the ANC answered quite simply, it is not so. What was true was that the seeming absence of 'culture' was the result of the destruction or weakening of indigenous cultural institutions by the colonial power.

At this point, the conqueror retorted with a more subtle argument. Perhaps you *had* a culture, but we brought you a new and better one. For the Portuguese, this argument was presented in the form of a beautiful web of theory, called *Lusotropicalism*, which argued that the Portuguese civilization was specially and magically non-racial. This theory was put forward not by a Portuguese, in fact, but by a Brazilian named Gilberto Freyre. The movements in Portuguese Africa found this myth one of the very first obstacles they had to overcome. In 1955, Mario de Andrade wrote an article under a pseudonym (Buanga Fele) exposing this myth. It was published in the prestigious organ of African cultural reassertion, *Presence Africaine* (Paris).

The article by ZAPU attacking birth control may seem very far removed from Andrade's discussion of Lusotropicalism. But in fact it was the same issue. In Zimbabwe, the conquerors asserted their cultural wisdom (in this case, the wisdom of birth control). What ZAPU said was that the cultural clothing hid a policy of political and economic significance, and one not in the interests of the oppressed African majority.

But, said Cabral, it is not enough to proclaim a 'return to the source'.

In whose interest do we proclaim it, and for whose benefit? In delineating a distinction between the cultural perspective of the petty bourgeoisie and that of the masses, Cabral warned against the pitfalls of a narrow 'cultural nationalism'.

Cultural Racism
MPLA

This statement, entitled 'The Effects of Colonialism on the Colonized African Peoples', is found in the MPLA publication, Angola in Arms, *V, 2, August 1971.*

One of the most serious aspects of colonialism has been its effect on the culture of the African peoples.

A social system based on the exploitation of man by man in its most extreme form, seen as a whole, colonialism means the economic plunder of the land of the politico-social servitude of man. But it is not only this. Based on the enslavement of man, as in every situation of privilege in history, colonialism seeks to perpetuate this enslavement. Firearms and the whip not being sufficient, colonialism resorts to the destruction of the African, in this identifying him with any other colonial and making him lose his identity with himself through the destruction of his culture. Therefore, colonialism is also cultural genocide. It has plundered the land and debilitated men. It tried to wipe out their past in order to depersonalise them in the present and obstruct their future. Depersonalised meant 'tamed', which ensured the perpetuation of the colonial relationship.

This is how colonialism understood it and how it acted.

To avoid uprisings, the ideal conditions for enslavement had to be created, imbuing the slave with acceptance of his situation, that is making the slave accept being a slave.

How? Firearms and the whip could not serve this purpose. There was only one way to proceed: to destroy the colonial's culture and make him either submit or be alienated by the 'superior culture' of his oppressor.

Attacking culture has been the most tragic of colonialism's manoeuvres to enslave peoples, since it afflicts men, their institutions, their mode of behaviour and their way of thinking. And its consequences are even more serious in that while it is 'profitable' to the oppressor in the long run, it is also only in the long run that its effects can be rooted out.

A subtle and imperceptible weapon, it is nevertheless the most effective one for the colonialists' desired perpetuation of their privileges. 'The better to dominate and exploit him (the colonial), colonialism places him outside the historical and social, the cultural and technical circuit,' writes Albert Memmi in his 'Portrait of the Colonial'. But what is meant by culture?

Avoiding all over-simplified definitions of 'the sum of knowledge', whether it be at the individual level or that of the people, we find that their culture is the body of ideas and patterns of behaviour which come from them, all of which is related to a body of social structures which supports them. To this must be added also technology, which is essential to the survival of any community, as well as a measure of feeling, which gives culture certain nuances from one people to another.

From this we will agree that there is not only one culture. Given the different material conditions under which it exists and upon which it develops, and the variations in the realm of feeling, one is forced to admit that there are different cultures.

Culture is a repository with which each individual identifies himself as belonging to a people. That is, it is an acting and thinking entity to which he wants and feels himself to belong.

In the colonialist attempt to destroy the colonial, the intention is precisely to break this link of the individual's identification with the entity to which he belongs. In the initial phase, they start by denigrating the values of the colonised — cultural racism is the beginning of cultural assassination and its manifestation. Similarly, they deny that the colonial has a past — deliberately drawing a curtain of oblivion over the past. Then they loudly proclaim that the values of the black man (or of any other colonial) are immoral and un-aesthetic, or insignificant, that his is an 'inferior culture'. 'The black man has no history,' is said with the utmost insolence and emphasis, so as to lead to the logical conclusion that the history of the black man started with colonialism

There follows a whole process of manipulation to create in the black man an inferiority complex towards that which is his by inculcating in him the idea 'everything African is vile.' The colonial stops using that which belongs to him as his cultural heritage. An inferiority complex about African culture having been created in him, he tends to deify European culture. The deification of the allegedly superior European culture is the most characteristic feature of the alienated colonial.

Colonialism kills the colonial spiritually and creates barriers which prevent the black African from situating himself in time and finding himself, making of him an empty receptacle to be filled with manipulated education. If the colonial should want to put an end to the sub-human condition, he has to forget what he is and 'rehabilitate' himself through the mode of reasoning of the oppressors, adopting their values and language. All that is African has to be left behind and only in the family circle can he perhaps retain his links with that which is his. The nature of his country is unknown to him, his people's history forbidden him, and the heroes of his people are classed as murderers and shameful opponents of 'progress', brought by the European, of course. The colonised man knows nothing about his country or its people.

Hence the disuse, if we may use the term, of African culture which leads to its being forgotten. This is the amnesia colonialism wants. Amnesia and an inability to understand both past and present historical events. In addition to not having a memory, the black man (the colonial) must not be able to see ahead.

Then comes the next phase of the process, that of getting the 'superior culture' of the master accepted in the present.

It is here that the problem of the effects of colonialism on culture becomes most critical. In fact this is the culminating moment when the colonial moves away from himself, i.e. from his people, to adopt the culture which is alien to him.

Portuguese colonialism calls this 'assimilation'. It makes a great deal of noise about it and presents it as the alleged cornerstone of its method of colonising or, as they say, of 'civilising'.

The ideologies of Portuguese colonialism claim that Lusitanian colonisation is 'different'; that Portugal, which alone has divine attributes, can adapt to any ecological and cultural environment, having an enviable ability to get close to the people there. Everything was done without friction and what happened was a result of osmosis between the Portuguese and the people there, through natural interpenetration. Hence the 'different' way of colonising – sorry! – of 'civilising'! But history shows that this tendency towards assimilation has happened only in one direction: it is the black man (the colonial) who, if he wants to affirm himself, has to adopt the patterns of the oppressor.

This cultural racism was even institutionalised in the 1933 Salazarist constitution, which is still in force and which says that the 'native', to be considered 'assimilated', must, among other things, adopt European ways of life and renounce African customs and traditions, i.e. African patterns of thought and behaviour. This means that the African has to renounce African culture if he wishes to lose his slave status in the eyes of the coloniser.

Nothing could show more clearly that cultural destruction forms a part of the essence of Portuguese, just like any other, colonialism. In the process of 'assimilation', the African has almost always to adapt to an education unconnected with his own world, and follow patterns of learning which are at odds with the ecological reality of the environment of his future activities.

Training and education, those essential aspects of culture, often take place in different fields and also different places. Therefore, if, despite everything, early training still manages to uphold traditional values, i.e. African culture, it is not completed and backed up by appropriate formal education, since the formal education given to the budding *'assimilado'* is intended precisely to destroy all African values in him.

It is easy to see what distortions and traumas are caused by this situation.

The so highly lauded interpenetration finally results in a hierarchy of values. Elements of African culture rarely appear in the 'superior culture' of the European. They are wholly rejected or, at most, tolerated either because they do not offend European canons or because of the touch of exoticism they provide, all of which merely goes to show how 'magnanimous' the masters are. 'Now you can see that we have nothing against African culture, that we do not want to destroy it. Indeed, we even use and accept some aspects of your culture.' Thank you very much! The truth of the matter is that such aspects that are adopted are few and it can virtually be said that in the formal education handed out by colonialism African culture is rejected as a whole, especially since the rare aspects 'used' are watered down through adjustment to European models.

(Then they say that 'this is proof of the inferiority of African culture'! You see, if it had more 'good' features for adoption, our culture would certainly have adopted them, as it has the few features 'made use of'.) 'Assimilation and colonisation are contradictory, since they tend to smash the colonial relationship, to suppress privileges, to remove the difference between colonisers and colonised,' A. Memmi states in his 'Portrait of the Colonial'. This means, therefore, that 'assimilation' cannot go beyond a certain point if it is not to become a negation of that which it serves — colonialism.

In substance a farce, 'assimilation' does however have an important part to play in the act of colonisation, that of benumbing and destroying black African culture (or any other colonised culture).

For the newly independent African states, the most serious heritage is that which results from this facet of colonialism. The problem of culture is of particular importance and requires urgent solution, especially since the attacks on African culture continue even after independence.

One of the major weapons of neocolonialism and imperialism is still the conquest of the mind, of the 'soul' of the colonised man. It is not surprising that we should see a proliferation of 'cultural centres', libraries, 'friendship circles' etc. in the newly independent African countries. Colonialism and neo-colonialism are identical in their essence, the one using some of the methods of oppression of the other.

Neocolonailism is also a powerful gag to stifle peoples culturally so as to continue colonial relations indefinitely. The independent African countries need to display a will of iron in reviving African culture. This task of restoring the African to himself is now one of the most crucial problems in the construction of the new independent African states.

But construction implies renovation, so that in African re-personalisation it is necessary to react against the patterns of education imposed by the coloniser — often mechanically transferred from his country to the colonised country — and make every effort to define African culture, or to redefine it for the requirements of progress.

Both things must be done courageously, with all the political and economic responsibilities and consequences implied. The definition of a cultural policy is an urgent need in the independent African countries if they wish to free Africa more rapidly from the effects of colonialism and to struggle more effectively against the economic and political dependence to which many African countries are still subjected.

Culture in Chains
ANC

A statement found in the ANC's Sechaba, *VII, 2,
February 1973.*

No man is an island, and no man has yet been found who is content to create
in an ivory tower without thought of his creation ever being brought to the
notice of another human being. Even the casual diarist, who hides his inmost
thoughts from those closest and dearest to him, thinks of posterity. The lover
must have a mistress or the image of a mistress before he can dash off a
sonnet. The prisoner in solitary confinement or in the death cell will scribble
something on the wall in the hope that someone else will read and learn of
his condition. The suicide leaves a note because he cannot bear to be misunderstood. The man who sings in his bath hopes that someone will overhear
and know that he is happy.

The apartheid laws deliberately place barriers in the way of communication, and these barriers are so obstructive that it is a tribute to the human
spirit that anything gets through at all. The very word 'apartheid' means the
condition of separateness, and in terms of the apartheid laws there is no
South African people but only a number of separate racial groups whose
contact with one another must be reduced to the minimum.

Under the Population Registration Act of 1950, the population is divided
into three main categories — Whites, Africans and Coloureds, and the Government is given the power to proclaim sub-categories within the African and
Coloured categories. The following categories have been proclaimed for
Coloured persons — Cape Coloured, Malay, Griqua, Chinese, Indian, other
Asian and other Coloured. (For trade purposes Japanese have been classified
as honorary Whites). The Africans, again, are classified into ten ethnic sub-
groups — Xhosa, Zulu, Northern Sotho, Southern Sotho, Tswana, Tsonga,
Swazi, Venda, Southern Ndebele and Northern Ndebele. By law the racial
identity of every person is entered in a population register, and every South
African citizen must carry an identity card stating his racial classification.

The purpose of these racial classifications is to make communications
between the various groups more difficult, so that the White racists may
continue in power on the well-worn basis of 'divide and rule'. Politically this
separation is today enforced by the Prohibition of Political Interference Act
of 1968 which prohibits any person belonging to one population group from
(a) becoming a member of any political party of which any person who
belongs to another population group is a member, and (b) addressing any
meeting of which all or the majority belong to another population group or
to other population groups. Thus multi-racial parties are illegal. So are multi-
racial trade unions.

Outside the political sphere separation is also enforced. Under the Group
Areas Act separate areas are set aside for residential occupation by the
various groups, and it is illegal for a White to enter an African area without

a special permit from a Government official. White and Black cannot sit down together in a restaurant to have a meal. Cohabitation between Black and White is a criminal offence punishable by up to seven years imprisonment. Marriage between Black and White is legally impossible. Black and White actors cannot appear together on the stage. Black and White cannot be members of the same audience at a play or concert. Black and White sportsmen cannot belong to the same team, or even compete against one another in separate racial teams. Qualified Black nurses cannot attend White hospital patients.

These are the general rules which govern social contact between the races in South Africa. There are exceptions here and there. Permission is occasionally given for a Black VIP to be allowed a meal in a White restaurant or accommodation in a White hotel. Black sportsmen are occasionally allowed to compete in White sporting fixtures so that South African official representatives can adduce arguments to facilitate the return of South Africa to the international sporting fields from which she has been barred because of her apartheid policies.

There are also illegal breaches of the rules. Some lightskinned Blacks cross the colour line whenever they can escape detection. There have been occasions when Whites have blackened their faces and worn Black attire (such as Indian saris) in order to gain admission to segregated Black shows from which they would otherwise have been barred.

But the exceptions merely prove the rule. Nor does the separation stop at the Black-White barrier. Even the Whites are separated, (although not by law) with Afrikaans and English-speaking Whites belonging to separate institutions from one end of their lives to the other. At school Afrikaans-English separation is enforced by law, which lays down that children must be educated in their mother tongue. Outside of school, separation is enforced by social and politically encouraged custom whereby there are parallel institutions for the two groups in every sphere of life – separate chambers of commerce, teachers' and students' organisations, youth organisations, and the like. The purpose of this separation between the two White groups is to establish the hegemony of the Afrikaners in every sphere of life, and to ensure that Afrikaans culture is not submerged by the stronger world-wide English culture.

Describing South Africa as a collective White dictatorship, a Cape Town university professor, Jan Loubser, in a speech on October 9, 1972 said that within the White group there was a dictatorship of the Afrikaner over the English-speaking South African, 'Over the past 24 years (since the first Nationalist Party Government came to power in 1948) an Afrikaans imperialism has developed over the English speakers,' he said. 'This imperialism is evident in the police, the armed forces, in the radio service and in many other institutions,' all of which are dominated by Afrikaners. Were it not for the economic power the English-speaking section wielded, said Professor Loubser, their position today would have been very much the same as that of the Africans.

What does all this mean for the creative artist in South Africa? In the most obvious sense, the cultural facilities available to the Black majority are far inferior to those of the Whites — and in some cases simply non-existent. In the giant African township of Soweto, from which Johannesburg draws most of its labour force, there is only one cinema for a population of nearly one million, and the number of films which may be seen by audiences at that cinema is grossly restricted by a censorship which places all Africans on the same level as White children under the age of 16. The best libraries in the country are barred to Blacks. Very few Blacks have ever seen the inside of a theatre or a concert hall.

But there is an even deeper sense in which cultural deprivation cripples the artistic spirit. Nobody — literally nobody — knows life in South Africa well enough to describe it adequately, let alone tell the truth about it, the whole truth and nothing but the truth, as is expected from the artistic as well as the legal witness. The artistic vision is restricted by the apartheid barriers, and even the most vivid imagination is no substitute for experience.

In the Western capitalist countries there are, true, class barriers which divide the nation. But a writer or a painter can cross these barriers. He can merge himself with any section of the community, and live their day to day life just as they do. The educated middle class writer can go 'slumming' for his raw material, as Gissing, Kingsley, Mrs. Gaskell and others did in Victorian times when they became aware of the way in which the industrial revolution had divided the people of England into two nations. Or the poor boy can rise to the top, as Dickens did, observing and noting the habit and condition of the various strata as he passes through.

But in South Africa the wall is impenetrable. No White man can live in a Black township, eat, drink and sleep there, make love and marry there, bring up a family there, starve and die there. He may observe a little from outside the fence, but he can never get inside a Black skin and feel in his bones what it is like to be Black. He may imagine hunger, but it takes one who has known hunger in a certain milieu to describe the way in which hungry children, having eaten their portions but remained unsatisfied, continue to scrape their spoons round the bottom of their porridge bowls in the hope that somehow the metal may be transformed into a further quantity of food . . . an image captured in all its pathos and simplicity in one of the early short stories of the African writer Alfred Hutchinson, who died recently, in Nigeria at the tragically early age of 48.

No writer in South Africa can see life steady and see it whole. Out of his own experience he can only tell what he has seen and known, and this is inevitably only part of the total picture. No White writer has yet managed to create a real and convincing Black character, and vice versa. Nor has any writer, White or Black been able to describe the relations between White and Black which are accurate and valid for both parties. A Nadine Gordimer can tell the reader in delicate and precise prose how a White liberal looks at the Black world, she can even portray accurately how a Black appears in the eyes of a White observer, but she cannot get inside the Black body and look out-

145

wards.

Similarly, the White characters in the novels of Peter Abrahams are carica-tures, stiff and unreal. They speak and act abruptly, crudely, like puppets lacking flesh and blood. Alan Paton's Black priest in *Cry the Beloved Country* is a sentimentalised White do-gooder with a Black habit, a sort of religious Black-and-White minstrel. Such creative failures are inevitable in a divided society.

A subsidiary problem for the South African writer is — for whom does he write? What is the market for his work? To whom does he address himself? This is partly a question of language. The African who writes in his mother tongue, even the Afrikaner, starts with a tremendous handicap by comparison with the English-speaking South African who has a world language at his disposal. It is partly a question of economics. Book production for a tiny market is unprofitable.

But above all it is a question of attitudes. The political and literary lin-guafranca of Black South Africa is English, which enables all Africans to communicate with one another across the ethnic border, and also to address Whites in their own country and abroad. Paradoxically, the group which suffers most from apartheid in culture is the Afrikaner tribe, who are the most isolated in their own homeland in which they enjoy political hegemony. Afrikaans — as the language of the conqueror, the administrator, the police-man, soldier, location superintendent, and pass officer — is detested by the non-Afrikaans majority in South Africa.

The newspapers which are directed towards the African market — even those owned by supporters of the Nationalist Government — are written in English. So are most of the books produced by non-Afrikaans writers.

Today, we notice a new phenomenon. A section of the Afrikaans intelli-gentsia are finding it more and more difficult to speak to their own people because they find themselves out of sympathy with its objectives. Moral conflict has almost destroyed a writer like Uys Krige, who loves his lan-guage and its heritage, but finds himself not only unable but possibly also unwilling any longer to communicate with his fellow Afrikaners who are moving in a direction where he cannot follow. The poet, Breyten Breyten-bach, because he married a Vietnamese women, is unable to live in South Africa where his marriage would not be recognised, and so is today an exile in Paris, though acknowledged as the greatest Afrikaans poet of his generation. Many Afrikaans novelists have achieved publication with parables and fantasies because to handle the truth is too difficult or too dangerous. And many are reduced to silence.

The Johannesburg *Sunday Times* wrote on October 22 1972: 'The completed manuscripts of several prominent Afrikaans authors are being preserved until South Africa's censorship laws are abolished or sufficiently relaxed to permit their publication. In this way a treasure house of Afrikaans literature is being built up for the enjoyment of future generations.'

The paper quoted one of the leading Afrikaans authors. Andre Brink, as saying: 'The Publications Control Board and the Government, which condones its operations, are strangling Afrikaans literature. They are creating a desert in the development of our culture.'

Brink had had his latest novel, *Die Saboteurs*, accepted by a British publisher for translation and publication in English, but said: 'I have withdrawn it from publication abroad because I want it first to be published in Afrikaans here, in my own country. The book has a special meaning and a message for Afrikaners who, I feel, should read it first.'

There were other Afrikaans writers, said Brink, who were grappling with the same problem. 'They are prepared to preserve the manuscripts intact for publication 100 years hence if need be, rather than agree to deletions or censorship in any other way. In this way, contemporary literature will not be lost.'

The South African Government is spending hundreds of millions of rand every year in its bid to keep the South African peoples apart from one another, but stronger forces, both political and economic, are forcing them together in a common mould. In the ranks of the South African liberation movement, it has been demonstrated that South Africans of all races, creeds and colours can work together as equals to achieve their common objective — freedom. When the apartheid walls have finally been broken down, the tremendous creative forces of the peoples of South Africa will be unleashed, not only to create a better material world, but also a richer and more profound culture than was ever dreamed of in the past.

What is Lusotropicalism?
Buanga Fele (Mario de Andrade)

Excerpt from an article by Mario de Andrade under the pseudonym, Buanga Fele, in Presence Africaine, *n.s., IV, Oct.–Nov. 1955.*

Segregation and assimilation are the political formulae by which colonization ensured its privileges against the legitimate vitality of colonized peoples.

It was a question of keeping a barrier between the standards of living of the two groups and of avoiding the questioning of the rights of Europeans to rule in the political and economic spheres.

But assimilation and segregation take on various forms according to the historical, demographic, and economic givens of the particular colonial complex. The Union of South Africa, with a large self-governing population of Europeans amongst Black people four times their number, does not react in the same way as does Great Britain in Nigeria where the people are better organized to fight colonialism. In the Belgian Congo both assimilation and segregation go efficiently hand in hand in a rich country, and accomplish for the time being the colonizer's dream of order. Portugal is too poor in its demography and metropolitan resources to expect that segregation can accomplish results in Africa in any way other than by systematic limitation of the social mobility of the indigenous population and by sacrificing a part of the white man's prestige. Compromises are hard to avoid when one is poor.

In Brazil and in the African colonies, we sometimes see the Portuguese agreeing to do certain tasks which would be deemed *'unworthy of whites'* by other Europeans.

This is the basis used to justify the argument that Portuguese whites take spontaneously to life in the tropics and engage in widespread intermarriage. The history of colonization shows us, in fact, that the Portuguese in the beginning of their tropical colonization were without the social or ideological framework, or the economic stability, required to establish racial prejudices. A large number of sociologists and historians (including certain professors at the Sorbonne) thus believe in a generosity peculiar to the 'race' and character of the Portuguese.

Let us rather consider how the Portuguese express their colonialist ideology. It is Mr. Marcello Caetano (in *Tradicoes, principios e metodos da colonisacao Portuguesa*, Agencia Geral do Ultramar, Lisbon, 1951) who enlightens us in this matter: 'The colonial administration of modern Portugal is based on four fundamental principles: political unity, spiritual assimilation, administrative separation, economic solidarity.'

Spiritual assimilation (to restrict our discussion to this one principle) means 'a certain concession of respect for the *nature* of the autochthonous peoples, while nonetheless attempting to teach them the faith, culture, and Portuguese civilization with a view to their eventual integration in the Lusitanian community.' In other words, Mr. Marcello Caetano, theoretician of Portuguese colonization, means by spiritual assimilation what Malan meant by *apartheid*: the segregation of Black people from modern life. The natives being the material basis of the accumulation of colonial capital, the administration has every reason to respect, even to favour their existence.

Let us look at an African colony such as Mozambique and examine its demographic reality closely: the total population is 5,732,317; the Europeans number 48,213 (including 45,599 Portuguese); the 'Yellows' 1,613; the Indians 12,630 and the *Metis* (the statistics do not make clear their origin) 25,149; thus a total of 5,640,363 Blacks, supposedly *'non-civilized'* or *natives*, and 4,349 so-called *'civilized'* or *'assimilated'*. Now it is clear that economic exploitation is based in this colony essentially on the 5,640,363 Blacks who are paralysed by a special status. Thus assimilation is a practice restricted to a few in the colonial cities. The ludicrous number of Blacks *'civilized'* or *'assimilated'* by the Portuguese is a good proof of it.*

As for considering intermarriage to be a policy actually desired and established by the colonial power, the demographic evolution of certain colonies demonstrates its falsity: since 1940—50 the white population has increased by 79% in Angola, whereas the native population has increased merely by 10%.

It therefore became necessary to define characteristics of Portuguese colonization. Salazar's government was once again able to find the right 'man' able to elaborate a sociological theory appropriate for the circum-stances. It found him in Brazil, 'a brother country'.

Since Gilberto Freyre — this right man — had already in some way created a precedent in his analyses of Portuguese colonization in Brazil, he had but to enlarge his field of observation, i.e. to go from one continent to another.

The official trip which Gilberto Freyre, the Brazilian sociologist, took round the Asian and African countries under Portuguese domination must be seen as a modern colonial mystification. Freyre did nevertheless claim he reserved total freedom of action when he accepted the Portuguese Government's invitation to study on the spot the colonial societies of Portuguese background. But it was a useless precaution! Far be it from us to accuse G. Freyre of 'selling himself to the Fascist Salazar', as so many others have hastened to suggest. We simply believe it would be useful to examine what he calls a cultural complex and a civilization — Lusotropicalism — and its implications in Africa.

For clarity of presentation, we should start with the evolution of thought of G. Freyre. Actually, his basic sociological theories can be found in *The Masters and the Slaves*. In the words of the author himself (preface to the 1st Portuguese edition, 1931), the book is 'an essay on genetic sociology and social history whose objectives are to determine and sometimes to interpret some of the most significant aspects of the formation of the Brazilian family'. This family, as we know, was based on an agrarian slave economy.

The relationships between the master who was a settler, and the slave who served him, and which were maintained for two centuries, result in what is termed by Freyre the 'colonial success' of the Portuguese. The Lusitanian settler belonger to a people which had, at the time of the 'discovery' of Brazil, already demonstrated its ability to live in the Tropics — such is the starting-point of the Portuguese 'skill in colonization'. What are the secrets of the victory of the Portuguese? They are his mobility, his ability to mix, and the facility with which he becomes acclimatized. Freyre thus concludes:

> Considered as a whole, Brazilian history was, as has been already shown in the first pages of this essay, a process of equilibrating antagonistic forces. Antagonisms of civilization and in the economy. The European and the native civilization. The European and the African. The African and the native. Agrarian economy and pastoral. The Catholic and the heretic. The Jesuit

* Population Table
(Statistical data obtained from the Census of 1950)

	Guinea	Angola	Mozambique
Total population	510,777	4,145,266	5,732,317
Blacks	503,935	4,036,687	5,640,363
'Civilized' Blacks	1,478	30,089	4,349

and the large property owner. The *bandeirante* and the mill
owner. The Paulist and the immigrant. The Pernambucan and the
peddler. The rich landowner and the pariah. The university
graduate and the illiterate. But most important of all, more widespread and more profound! the antagonism of the master and the
slave.

It is a fact that in all these clashing antagonistic forces there
have always been *forces of fraternization and of vertical mobility*
that could minimize their shock or harmonize them, and which
are peculiar to Brazil: miscegenation; dispersion of inheritance;
the easy and frequent interchange in the occupation of high
political and social positions by half-breeds and natural sons; the
lyric Christianity 'a la portugaise'; moral tolerance; hospitality
towards strangers; inter-communication among the different areas
of the country.

It is not our purpose here to judge G. Freyre's historical method, his
genetic formulation of the origin of the Brazilian family. In all this we pick
out some hasty generalizations on the peculiarity of the Portuguese colonist.
He wants, on the one hand, to argue the existence of humanitarian attitudes
on the part of the Portuguese colonist towards every ethnic group with which
he comes into contact. On the other hand, he claims categorically that all
Portuguese colonial societies are cross-bred. Not concerning himself with the
economic and political aspects of the colonial problem – wrongly, we believe
– Freyre prefers to dwell on the Negro influence upon Brazilian sexual and
family life. It is precisely the refusal to consider the colonial mechanism as
being an enterprise of economic exploitation directed by a political power
structure which accounts for the weakness of his sociology.

After all, cross-breeding was largely practised in Brazil not out of moral
considerations, or because of political vision, but as a result of a simple
circumstance – the scarcity of white women.

However, the fully developed concept of 'Lusotropicalism' appears clearly
only in 1940 in a book which Freyre entitled *O Mundo que o Portugues criou*
('The World that the Portuguese Created'). There we find the claim that
'Portugal, Brazil, Africa, Portuguese India, Madeira, the Azores, and the Cape
Verde Islands constitute today a community of sentiment and culture.' We
can already see the leitmotif of Lusotropicalism – the existence of a
community of sentiment and culture of all tropical countries placed under
the political control of Portugal and the direction of Christianity. And how
did this community come into being? The author answers that this:

> community of intimate sentiments and common external culture
> in the most obvious and concrete forms is the consequence of the
> process and conditions particular to Portuguese colonization. In
> Asia, as well as in Brazil, in the Atlantic islands and to a certain
> extent in Africa, there have been developed in men, due to the

Portuguese method of colonization, the same essential qualities
of cordiality and sympathy characteristic of the Portuguese
people. This people is the most Christian of modern colonizers
in its relationships with so-called inferior people, the most over-
flowing with sympathy.

What is the role of Christianity in all this? Since it seems that 'the most
Christian of modern colonizers' has not felt any remorse for its practice of
slave-trading over four centuries, a practice which continues today in the
form of forced labour in Guinea, Sao Tome, Angola, and Mozambique.
Freyre believes *religiously*, one might say, in the peculiar hereditary capacity
of the Portuguese to live under the tropical sun, taking unto himself a wife of
colour. Informed by this prejudice, it is understandable that the heart of the
colonial question escapes him. His conception of Lusitanian culture is quite
simple — it is that complex of typically European values which the colonizer
has transmitted and established: mores and customs, beliefs, as well as
technology — in short, a way of life.
We should dispel all ambiguity. There could not come into being a new
form of culture (the Lusitanian culture in the tropics) in the colonial conditions of productive relations. What kind of harmonious or warm participation
in this cultural idealism, in this mystification, could there be in Africa under
Portuguese domination, where the native cultures are systematically
destroyed by a ferocious assimilation policy, where men are detribalized,
where whole populations are reduced or forced to labour? . . .
Lusotropicalism, an invalid explanation of Brazilian history, is entirely
false under the colonial circumstances of Africa. This 'sociological theory'
supposed the acceptance of a coming together of the various elements of the
colonial population in the social, economic, cultural and political arenas. But
the assimilation policy, as it is understood and practised by the Portuguese
colonial administration, paralyzes the natives and assimilated Blacks and to a
certain extent the mulattoes by eliminating them from this coming together.
What is the basis then of a 'Lusotropical' civilization?
The essay which G. Freyre has included in his book, *Um brasileiro em
terras Portuguesas* ('A Brazilian in Portuguese Lands,' Lisbon, 1952) allows
us to see more clearly the essential theses of Lusotropicalism. According to
him:

> The Portuguese added from the beginning to his quality of
> European, an Arab influence with a predisposition to amorous
> adventures under the sign of Dark Venus . . . The Portuguese is
> a people less imperially European, but rather bound by blood,
> culture, and life tries to cross-breed peoples . . . We may assert
> that the Portuguese easily becomes, because of his culture,
> the 'Lusotropical' who finds in the Tropics the natural and
> congenital surroundings for his development. He has added to the
> economic, religious and political incentives for expansion this
> taste (which is absent in other Europeans) for living, loving and

procreating in the tropics; by fraternizing with the women, the men, and the values of the tropics, rather than by solely exploiting men, destroying their values and raping the women of the conquered lands.

According to the brilliantly superficial pen of G. Freyre, we can thus read that Lusotrpicalism is simultaneously a concept, a theory, a system, and a method of colonization.

We may thus define it as being: (1) a congenital attraction of the Portuguese towards coloured women in his sexual relationships; (2) the unselfishness of the Portuguese in their economic exploitation of the tropics; (3) the maintenance of social relations with the inhabitants of tropical countries such that there is created 'vertical mobility' in social and political life.

And hence the corollary: a part of Africa, Asia, Oceania and America, dominated by a small number of brave Portuguese who brought in their blood the tropical heritage acquired in their cross-breeding with the Moors, bears the stamp of a community of sentiment and culture — the 'Lusotropical' civilization.

Portuguese colonization could not find a better justification! . . .

We conclude that this 'cultural complex' invented by Freyre is without foundation in reality. There has never been in the tropical countries under Portuguese domination, certainly not in Africa, an act of marriage between two cultures, a form of contact which might have been desirable, but rather the relation of a dominating culture to dominated ones. Freyre has not said a word about *natural children of Lusotropicalism*. During his trip he did not see new men of a 'Lusotropicalism' character.

We have limited ourselves to giving a few concrete examples of this mystification, all taken from Freyre's work. But we were forced to start this way, since 'Lusotropicalism' arose out of a false interpretation of the genesis of Portuguese maritime expansion. Actually, we plan eventually to study the chronicles of the 14th and 15th Centuries — a sort of secret history of Portuguese colonization — to draw the picture of a particular type of colonizing mentality. The following quotations are drawn at random from the documents of the time which guided the men of Portuguese colonization (Cf. A *espansao quantrocentista Portuguesa,* by Magalhaes-Godinho, Lisbon):

'The honour and status of the knight grows great by the exercise of arms.'

'Theft and piracy are more worthy of the knight than commerce.'

'Commerce with the infidels is just, as long as it contributes to the prosperity of Christian nations.'

'The exhaltation of the faith demands war on the infidels as well as the conversion of souls.'

'It is just to enslave the infidels since lost souls are not true lords of their bodies; so will the souls be saved and the bodies will end their bestial life.'

'It is just to appropriate the lands of the infidels, since the latter have taken them from their real owner, God, by usurpation.'

'It is just to search for profit, as long as it does not interfere with the service of God.'

The most savoury aphorism is perhaps this definition given by the
Portuguese historian, Magalhaes-Godinho: 'The Portuguese built in the 16th
Century a commercial Empire whose soul was spices, whose foundation
piracy and pillage, whose nerves cannons.'

The equilibrium of these forces is obvious: the foundation and the nerves
are assuredly a constant in a system whose variable is the soul. There is the
evidence which draws aside the veil from the fraud of 'Lusotropicalism'.

African Population – Growth Strangulation
ZAPU

An article in ZAPU's Zimbabwe Review *(Lusaka), II,
1/2, Jan./Feb. 1970.*

A Family Planning Clinic has been constructed and completed in the grounds
of the Harare Hospital, Salisbury. It is directed towards African family
planning. The director of this project is a Mrs Spilhaus of the Family
Planning Association of Rhodesia. This project has been made possible by
contributions from some international 'welfare organisations', presumably at
the request of the Family Planning Association of Rhodesia. It is reported
that International Planned Parenthood and Oxfam plus proceeds from the
Rhodesian State Lottery combined to enable the project.

This development is a culmination of years of penetration by European
social workers into African family life. It started off by formation of African
women's clubs to undertake home occupational activities such as sewing,
knitting, cooking and hygiene in mothercraft. Clubs such as Radio Home
Club, Ruwadzano (not the Church one), Women's Council, and many others,
were formed in different areas of the country. In every one of them the representative of either the British Governor, the District Commissioner or
some other official of the police or civil administration was the patron.
These have usually been the wives of these officers. Competitions are held
within and between a number of these clubs. On occasions of prize-giving
the District Commissioner of the area is usually the honoured guest including
some 'Madame' so-and-so from the state or bourgeois society.

Of late, since last year in fact, a training centre has been established at
Domboshawa. Domboshawa is an old establishment school. It used to be the
training centre for Africans in joinery and agricultural demonstration. It is
most famous for producing agricultural demonstrators who move around
African peasant areas (now only nominally) to teach the best methods of
crop production. The regime has now and again used Domboshawa for what
is called 'training' of Chiefs. The most recent highlighted activity in Dom--
boshawa was the convening by the Rhodesian regime of a gathering of chiefs
– a gathering called the Indaba – at which the chiefs were drilled in support-

ing the regime. Methods of brinkmanship were used, blackmailing the chiefs over their positions if they did not show support. It is here also where the British Minister, Bottomley, was taken to meet the chiefs and listen to their chorus in support of Smith.

All this goes to define what Domboshawa is used for by the regime. The institution is some twenty miles out of Salisbury. The next interesting use of Domboshawa by the regime was around 1966 when it came to light that women, particularly young ones, were being enticed there to ungergo training in intelligence and spying for the regime. This was directed specifically against the guerrilla movement as well as expanding the internal informer system. The scheme is continuing with obvious difficulties of recruitment because, apart from chronic sell-outs, the African population in general resents and resists being exploited for the benefit of the regime.

Now women, so-called 'community development' workers, are being trained in Domboshawa. The first output of these women was fielded in January this year. There are twenty-seven of them. The basis of their selection is that they must be married and should have been members of one or more of the clubs referred to above. They are taught by a Miss Winfred Wilson. The institution of their training is government and they are outright government employees. What are they supposed to do? They are supposed to cycle around every kraal in the countryside and put themselves at the disposal of the women in the villages on family problems, particularly as regards birth.

On the surface all this exercise is so much of a welfare that it would look immoral to work against it. The fact of the matter is that the women being trained in Domboshawa are birth control agents. In another sense they are used as spies and informers to the regime of what they see in African villages, particularly on such activities as are against the regime. It is not by sheer coincidence that the opening of the Family Planning Clinic has been taking place at the same time as the fledging of the twenty-seven women for carrying out the birth control campaign. It is one co-ordinated exercise.

Why is there so much concern about introducing birth control among Africans and making it appear a grave issue of the moment? The Africans themselves have never shown any bother over the number of children they are having. On the contrary, the greatest concern in African families today is that disorganisation of African life due to enforced migration of Africans for work

and settlements is depriving the African family of expansion and stability. The whole campaign suggests that a big family is an offence against life and progress and is ill motivated. The women who cycle around African homesteads are briefed to argue that to have an improved economic life and enjoy it it is necessary to exercise birth control.

The birth control campaign in Zimbabwe is objectionable, to say the least. The whole population in Rhodesia today is five million, on one hundred and fifty thousand square miles. England, which is almost half the size of Zimbabwe (Rhodesia), carries a population ten times that of Rhodesia, that is, fifty million people. The United Kingdom can easily afford to carry another twenty million people. In these terms Zimbabwe needs a much higher birth rate to make use of all the space of the God-given land. These settler family planners and their agents are cheating African mothers into believing that, by applying birth control, there will be a greater likelihood of saving more money thus increasing the possibilities of buying better furniture, a motor car and sending the only child or two, to expensive and, of course, bourgeois types of school. This is a simple trick of making sure that any money earned by the African must be quickly and substantially returned to the British controlled banks. It is like the argument of a man who steals nine of your ten cows and then puts forward a theory of how to save milk, from one cow and how good it is to possess one cow.

It is not difficult for the Africans of Zimbabwe to understand the systematic curtailment of their economic, population and intellectual potential. Only a few years ago the regime, emphasising the pastoral life of the Africans as an excuse, shifted whole communities to arid areas. When these communities started converting these areas into vast arable land, the regime, using an economic argument of better crop production, enforced reduction of each field to about six acres, average. This was claimed to be intensive crop production. There was complete disregard of the size of the families to be maintained. African stock was also reduced to very small numbers per person. Some families were deprived of all their cattle. This was direct undermining and strangulation of the African means of subsistence. The calculated effect of this imposed poverty was to compel African males to industrial areas where they could be exploited as 'cheap labour'.

Religious missionaries initiated African education and still carry ninety per cent of African education, particularly primary education in the rural areas and also the country's secondary and teacher training institutions. The regime was, belatedly, involved in these schools through a percentage of grants and payment of teachers' salaries. Now the regime has sacked all African teachers who had not as yet taken their training course but had recognised performances all the years. This January the regime has decided to take off five per cent from the salary of African teachers teaching in missionary schools. Eight years of primary school education has been reduced to seven years, sadly enough, with a poorly constructed syllabus. Children passing to secondary schools were double the available number of places in the whole country. These children are now frustrated. Their intellectual potential is withered and their labour is at the mercy of settler employers for exploitation.

The above illustrations serve to put the birth control exercise as schemed by the Rhodesian regime in the correct context and proper perspective. After depriving the African people of their land and cattle, thus putting an economic squeeze on the Africans, the settlers are now seeking to trim and tie down the size of African families to that squeeze. There is no point in producing learned figures as to how planned African family life as part of a planned countrywide economy could increase the fortunes of Rhodesia. The economy is solely and wholly controlled by the Western capitalists and their settler agents on the spot. An African family which surrenders itself to be trimmed to the economy of the settlers is not helping itself at all but is contributing to the fortunes of the settlers and their mother companies in Europe and the United States.

The economy of Rhodesia, like the economy of all capitalist states, rests on exploited masses. The exploiting class maintains its position through vigilance on three fronts:
(a) the exploited masses, figure-wise, must not expand to such strength as cannot be estimated vis-a-vis the force used to suppress them;
(b) the exploited masses must not be allowed to arm themselves at all, even with knives, stones or sticks, since their automatic retaliation is a certainty;
(c) the exploited masses must not be paid such money or given such technical training as could enable them to develop their own capital; in short, they should always be kept at a begging level of impoverishment.

Clearly, therefore, it is for the precise purpose of maintaining the political and economic privileges of the settlers that birth control is being campaigned for among the Africans in Zimbabwe. The regime has openly expressed its worry over African population growth. On statistics available to it, African population grows at the rate of 3½ per cent. An economic expert from Pretoria, Professor Sadie, some two years ago was engaged by the regime to make an economic survey of Rhodesia and advise on its relationship to population growth. His major conclusion was that the African population was growing at a rate dangerous to the stability of the country. He advocated for swift policies on birth control among Africans. This is what we are seeing today this Domboshawa scheme of community development workers and the Family Planning Clinic built at Harare.

As pointed out earlier, the issue here is not that of understanding or otherwise the concept of a planned economy, it is the basic philosophies and principles of life involved. Why all the missionary zeal to save the Africans from the 'dangers' of big families as though it is something bordering on a sin or a disease? Africans regard humans and their association as their priority value; therefore the greater the number of humans with a closer association, the greater is the life contentment derived. The concept being fostered behind the Rhodesian birth control campaign (or so-called 'community development' under a disguise) is said to be 'improvement' of African economic welfare. It is an attempt to treat Africans to an accumulation or capitalistic concept. 'Prefer more money and more wealth than more children', is the idea. 'Find pleasure in material care and accumulation than in human care and association' is another way of putting the ideas being fostered.

The argument here is not that there is no relationship between the number of children and one's means to feed them, it is that they are not exclusive of each other. They can be mutually regenerative in the direction of increase all through.

Three technical points rule out the birth control campaign in Rhodesia:
(a) the privileged economy of the settlers in Rhodesia cannot constitute a standard to draw conclusions on what population it can carry; it is an ideologically ill-constructed economy;

(b) the vast unoccupied space of the one hundred and fifty thousand square miles of land in Rhodesia, including the farms being currently used by settlers and absentee investors and the unexploited resources of the country, impose an obligation on the Zimbabwe population to fill these spaces and enjoy these resources through an accelerated and increased birth rate;
(c) it is foreign to the African family concept and was certainly not intro-- duced on African initiative.

Whilst the settlers are, on the one hand, fielding this birth control campaign among Africans on the excuse of a population strained economy, they are, on the other, advertising for increased immigration from Europe which crosses, along the high seas, with tons and tons of Zimbabwe minerals being exported to feed companies in Europe, America and Japan. Who can fail to realise the whole trick in the circumstances?

International organisations like Oxfam and International Planned Parenthood are running a serious risk of antagonising themselves against the African population of Zimbabwe by contributing to causes which are neither approved nor initiated by the Africans. The birth control campaign in Rhodesia, as argued above, is against African valued traditions and is politically ill-motivated to the benefit of the British settler oppressors. There is no doubt that in Zimbabwe the African population will find its obligation to resist the campaign. If the African women agents who are being trained in Domboshawa for such suicidal campaigns do not take advice and stop being used against their people, they will have to face the consequences.

Culture, Colonization, and National Liberation
Amilcar Cabral

A speech given by Amilcar Cabral, Secretary-General
of the PAIGC, upon the award of an honorary doctorate
by Lincoln University (USA) in 1972.

The people's struggle for national liberation and independence from imperialist rule has become a driving force of progress for humanity and undoubtedly constitutes one of the essential characteristics of contemporary history.

An objective analysis of imperialism in so far as it is a fact or a 'natural' historical phenomenon, indeed 'necessary' in the context of the type of economic-political evolution of an important part of humanity, reveals that imperialist rule with all its train of wretchedness, of pillage, of crime and of destruction of human and cultural values, was not just a negative reality. The vast accumulation of capital in half a dozen countries of the northern hemisphere, which was the result of piracy, of the confiscation of the property of other races, and of the ruthless exploitation of the work of these peoples, will not only lead to the monopolization of colonies, the division of the world, and imperialist rule.

In the rich countries, imperialist capital, constantly seeking to enlarge itself, increased the creative capacity of man and brought about a total transformation of the means of production thanks to the rapid progress of science, of techniques and of technology. This accentuated the pooling of labour and brought about the ascension of huge areas of population. In the colonial countries where colonization on the whole blocked the historical process of the development of the subjected peoples, or else changed them radically in the name of progress, imperialist capital imposed new types of relationships on indigenous society, the structure of which became more complex, and it stirred up, fomented, poisoned or resolved contradictions and social conflicts; it introduced, together with money and the development of internal and external markets, new elements in the economy; it brought about the birth of new nations from human groups or from peoples who were at different stages of historical development.

It is not to defend imperialist domination to recognize that it gave new nations to the world, the dimensions of which it reduced and that it revealed new stages of development of human societies and in spite of or because of the prejudices, the discrimination and the crimes which it occasioned, it contributed to a deeper knowledge of humanity as a whole, as a unity in the complex diversity of the characteristics of its development.

Imperialist rule on many continents favoured a multilateral and progressive (sometimes abrupt) confrontation not only between different men but also between different societies. The practice of imperialist rule — its affirmation or its negation — demanded (and still demands) a more or less accurate knowledge of the society it rules and of the historical reality (both economic, social, and cultural) in the middle of which it exists.

This knowledge is necessarily expressed in terms of comparison with the dominating subject and with its own historical reality. Such a knowledge is a vital necessity in the practice of imperialist rule which results in the confrontation, mostly violent, between two identities which are totally dissimilar in their historical past and antagonistic in their different functions. The search for such a knowledge contributed to a general enrichment of human and social knowledge in spite of the fact that it was one-sided, subjective, and very often unjust.

In fact man has never shown as much interest in knowing other men and other societies as during this century of imperialist domination. An unprecedented mass of information, of hypotheses and theories has been built up, notably in the fields of history, ethnology, ethnography, sociology, and culture concerning people or groups brought under imperialist domination. The concepts of race, caste, ethnicity, tribe, nation, culture, identity, dignity, and many other factors have become the object of increasing attention from those who study men and the societies described as 'primitive' or 'evolving'.

More recently, with the rise of liberation movements, the need has arisen to analyse the character of these societies in the light of the struggle they are waging, and to decide the factors which launch or hold back this struggle. The researchers are generally agreed that in this context culture shows special significance. So one can argue that any attempt to clarify the true role of culture in the development of the (pre-independence) liberation movement can make a useful contribution to the broad struggle of the people against imperialist domination.

In this short lecture, we consider particularly the problems of the 'return to the source,' and of identity and dignity in the context of the national liberation movement.

The fact that independence movements are generally marked, even in their early stages, by an upsurge of cultural activity has led to the view that such movements are preceded by a 'cultural renaissance' of the subject people. Some might go as far as to suggest that culture is one means of collecting together a group, indeed one *weapon* in the struggle for independence.

From the experience of our own struggle and one might say that of the whole of Africa, we consider that there is too limited, even a mistaken idea of the vital role of culture in the development of the liberation movement. In our view this arises from a fake generalization of a phenomenon which is real but limited, which is at a particular level in the vertical structure of colonized societies — at the level of the *elite* or the colonial *diasporas*. This generalization is unaware of or ignores the vital element of the problem; the indestructible character of the cultural resistance of the masses of the people when confronted with foreign domination.

Certainly, imperialist domination calls for cultural oppression and attempts either directly or indirectly to do away with the most important elements of the culture of the subject people. But the people are only able to create and develop the liberation movement because they keep their culture alive despite continual and organized repression of their cultural life and because they continue to resist culturally even when their politico-military resistance is destroyed. And it is cultural resistance which, at a given moment, can take on new forms (political, economic, military) to fight foreign domination.

With certain exceptions, *the period of colonization* was not long enough, at least in Africa, for there to be a significant degree of destruction or damage of the most important facets of the culture and traditions of the subject people. Colonial experience of imperialist domination in Africa (genocide, racial segregation and apartheid excepted) shows that the only so-called positive solution which the colonial power put forward to repudiate the subject people's cultural resistance was *'assimilation'*. But the complete failure of the policy of 'progressive assimilation' of native population is the livng proof of the falsehood of this theory and of the capacity of subject people to resist. As far as the Portuguese colonies are concerned, the maximum number of people assimilated was 0.03% of the total population (in Guinea) and this was after 500 years of 'civilizing mission' and half a century of 'colonial peace'.

On the other hand, even in the settlements where the overwhelming majority of the population are indigenous peoples, the area occupied by the colonial power and especially the area of *cultural influence* is usually restricted to coastal strips and to a few limited parts in the interior. Outside the boundaries of the capital and other urban centres, the influence is almost out. It only leaves its mark at the very top of the colonizers' social pyramid — which created colonialism itself — and particularly it influences what one might call the 'indigenous petit bourgeoisie' and a very small number of workers in urban areas. The influence of the colonial power's culture is almost nil.

It can thus be seen that the masses in the rural areas, like a large section of the urban population, say, in all, over 99% of the indigenous population are untouched or almost untouched by the culture of the colonial power. This situation is partly the result of the necessarily obscurantist character of the imperialist domination, which, while it despises and suppresses indigenous culture, takes no interest in promoting culture for the masses who are their pool of manpower for forced labour and the main object of exploitation. It is also the result of the effectiveness of cultural resistance of the people who, when they are subjected to political domination and economic exploitation, find that their own culture acts as a bulwark in preserving their *identity* where the indigenous society has a vertical structure; this defence of their cultural heritage is further strengthened by the colonial power's interest, in protecting and backing the cultural influence of the ruling classes, their allies.

The above argument implies that, generally speaking, there is not any marked destruction or damage to culture or tradition either for the masses in the subject country or for the indigenous ruling classes (traditional chiefs, noble families, religious authorities). Repression, persecution, humiliation, betrayal by certain social groups who have compromised with the foreign power, have forced culture to take refuge in the villages, in the forests, and in the spirit of the victims of domination. Culture survives all these challenges and, through the struggle for liberation, blossoms forth again. Thus the question of a 'return to the source' or of a 'cultural renaissance' does not arise and could not arise for the mass of these people, for it is they who are the repository of the culture and at the same time the only socio-structure who can preserve and build it up and *make history*.

Thus, in Africa at least, for a true idea of the real role which culture plays in the development of the liberation movement a distinction must be made between the situation of the masses, who preserve their culture, and that of the social groups who are assimilated or partially so, who are cut off and culturally alienated. Even though the indigenous colonial elite who emerged during the process of colonization still continue to pass on some element of indigenous culture, yet they live both materially and spiritually according to the foreign colonial culture. They seek to identify themselves increasingly with this culture both in their social behaviour and even in their appreciation of its values.

In the course of two or three generations of colonization, a social class arises made up of civil servants, people who are employed in various branches of the economy, especially commerce, professional people, and a few urban and agricultural landowners. This indigenous petit bourgeoisie, which emerged out of foreign domination and is indispensable to the system of colonial exploitation, stands midway between the masses of the working class in town and country and the small number of local representatives of the foreign ruling class. Although they may have quite strong links with the masses and with the traditional chiefs, generally speaking they aspire to a way of life which is similar if not identical with that of the foreign minority. At the same time, while they restrict their dealings with the masses they try to become integrated into this minority, often at the cost of family or ethnic ties and always at great personal cost. Yet, despite the apparent exceptions, they do not succeed in getting past the barriers thrown up by the system. They are prisoners of the cultural and social contradictions of their lives. They cannot escape from their role as a marginal class, a 'marginalised' class.

The marginal character of their role both in their own country and in that of the colonial power is responsible for the socio-cultural conflicts of the colonial elite or the indigenous petit bourgeoisie, played out very much according to their material circumstances and level of culture but always resolved on the individual level, never collectively.

It is within the framework of this daily drama, against the backcloth of the usually violent confrontation between the mass of the people and the ruling colonial class that a feeling of bitterness or a *frustration complex* is bred and develops among the indigenous lower middle class. At the same time they are becoming more and more conscious of a compelling need to question their marginal status, and to rediscover an identity.

Thus they turn to the people around them, the people at the other extreme of the socio-cultural conflict — the masses.

For this reason arises the problem of the 'return to the source' which seems to be even more urgent than the serious isolation of the petit bourgeoisie (or native elites) and their acute feelings of frustration, as is the case when African diasporas are sent to countries with colonial or racist traditions. It comes as no surprise that the theories or 'movements' such as *Pan Africanism* or Negritude (two pertinent expressions arising mainly from the assumption that all black Africans have a cultural identity) were propounded outside Black Africa. More recently, the Black Americans' claim to an African identity is another proof, possibly rather a desperate one, of the need for a 'return to the source' although clearly it is influenced by a new situation: the fact that the great majority of African people are now independent.

But the 'return to the source' is not and cannot in itself be an *act of struggle* against foreign domination (colonialist and racist) and it no longer necessarily means a return to traditions. It is the denial, by the petit bourgeoisie of the country, of the usurped supremacy of the culture of the dominant power over that of the dominated people with which it must identify itself. The 'return to the source' is therefore not a voluntary step, but the only possible reply to the demand of concrete need, historically denied, and enforced by the inescapable contradiction between the colonized society and the colonial power, between the mass of the people exploited and the foreign exploitive class, a contradiction in the light of which each level of social stratum or indigenous class must define its role.

When the 'return to the source' goes beyond the individual and is expressed through 'groups' or 'movements', the contradiction is transformed into struggle (secret or overt), and is a prelude to the pre-independence movement or of the struggle for liberation from the foreign yoke. So, the 'return to the source' is of no historical importance unless it brings not only real involvement in the struggle for independence, but also complete and absolute identification with the hopes of the mass of the people, who are struggling not only against the foreign culture but also on the foreign domination. Otherwise, the 'return to the source' is nothing more than an attempt to find short-term benefits, knowingly or unknowingly a kind of political opportunism.

One must point out that the 'return to the source', apparent or real, does not develop at one time and in the same way in the heart of the indigenous petit bourgeoisie. It is a slow process, broken up and uneven, whose development depends on the degree of acculturation of each individual, of the material circumstances of his life, on the forming of his ideas and on his experience as a social being. This unevenness is the basis of the split of the indigenous petit bourgeoisie into three groups when confronted with the liberation movement: (a) a minority, which, even if it wants to see an end to foreign domination clings to the dominant colonialist class and openly oppose the movement to protect its social position; (b) a majority of people who are hesitant and indecisive; (c) another minority of people who share in the building and leadership of the liberation movement.

But the latter group, which plays a decisive role in the development of the pre-independent movement, does not truly identify with the mass of the people (with their culture and hopes) except through struggle, the scale of this identification depending on the kind or methods of struggle, on the ideological basis of the movement and on the level of moral and political awareness of each individual.

Identification of a section of the indigenous petit bourgeoisie with the mass of the people has an essential prerequisite: *that, in the face of destructive action by imperialist domination, the masses retain their identity*, separate and distinct from that of the colonial power. It is worthwhile therefore to decide in what circumstances this retention is possible; why, when and at what levels of the dominated society is raised the problem of the loss or absence of identity, and in consequence it becomes necessary to assert or to re-assert in the framework of the pre-independence movement a separate and distinct identity from that of the colonial power.

The identity of an individual or of a particular group of people is a bio-sociological factor outside the will of that individual or group, but which is meaningful only when it is expressed in relation with other individuals or other groups. The dialectical character of identity lies in the fact that it identifies and *distinguishes* that an individual (or a group) is only similar to certain individuals (or groups) if it is also different to other individuals (or groups). The definition of an identity, individual or collective, is at the same time the affirmation and denial of a certain number of characteristics which define the individuals or groups, through *historical* (biological and sociological) factors at a moment of their development. In fact, identity is not a constant, precisely because the biological and sociological factors which define it are in constant change. Biologically and sociologically, there are no two beings (individual or collective) completely the same or completely different, for it is always possible to find in them common or distinguishing characteristics. Again the identity of a being is always relative, even circumstantial, because defining it means picking out more or less strictly and cautiously the biological and sociological characteristics of the being in question.

One must point out that in the fundamental duality given in the definition of identity, sociology is a more determining factor than biology. In fact, if it is correct that the biological element (inherited genetic structure) is the inescapable physical basis of the existence and continuing growth of identity, it is no less correct the case that the sociological element is the factor which gives it objective substance, by giving content and form, and allowing confrontation and comparison between individuals or between groups. To make a total definition of identity the inclusion of the biological element is indispensable, but does not imply a sociological similarity, whereas two beings who are sociologically exactly the same must necessarily have similar biological identities.

This shows on the one hand the supremacy of the social over the individual condition, for society (human for example) is a higher form of life; it shows on the other hand the need not to confuse, in arriving at identity, the *original identity*, of which the biological element is the main determinant, and the *actual identity*, of which the main determinant is the sociological element. Clearly the identity of which one must take account at a given moment of the growth of a being (individual or collective) is the actual identity, and awareness of that being reached only on the basis that his original identity is incomplete, partial and fake, for it leaves out or does not comprehend the decisive influence of social conditions on the content and form of identity.

In the formation and development of individual or collective identity, the social condition is an objective agent arising from economic, political, social and cultural aspects which are characteristic of the growth and history of the society in question. If one argues that the economic aspect is fundamental, one can assert that identity is in a certain sense an expression of the economic reality. This reality, whatever the geographical context and the path of development of the society is defined by the level of productive forces (the relationship between man and nature) and by the means of production (the relationship between men and classes within a single society). But if one accepts that culture is a dynamic synthesis of the material and spiritual condition of the society and expresses the close relationship both between

man and nature and between the different classes within a single society
we can assert that identity is at the individual and collective level and
beyond the economic condition, the expression of a culture. This is why to
attribute, recognize or declare the identity of an individual or group is above
all to place that individual or group in the framework of a culture. Now as
we all know, the main prop of culture in any society is the social structure.
One can therefore draw conclusion that the possibility of a given group keeping (or losing) its identity in the face of foreign domination depends on the
extent of the destruction of its social structure under the stresses of that
domination.

As for the effects of imperialist domination on the social structure of the
dominated people, one must look here at the case of classic colonialism
against which the pre-independence movement is contending. In that case,
whatever the stage of historical development of the dominated society, the
social structure can be subjected to the following experiences: (a) *total
destruction*, mixed with immediate or gradual liquidation of the indigenous
people and replacement by a foreign people; (b) *partial destruction*, with the
additional settling of a more or less numerous foreign population; (c) *supposed
preservation*, brought about by the restriction of the indigenous people in
geographical areas of special reserves usually without means of living, and the
massive influx of a foreign population.

The fundamentally horizontal character of the social structure of African
people, due to the profusion of ethnic groups, means that the cultural resistance and degree of retention of identity are not uniform. So, even where
ethnic groups have broadly succeeded in keeping their identity, we observe
that the most *resistant* groups are those which have had the most violent
battles with the colonial power during the period of effective occupation,*
or those who because of their geographical location have had least contact
with the foreign presence.**

One must point out that the attitude of the colonial power towards the
ethnic groups creates an insoluble contradiction: on the one hand it must
divide or keep divisions in order to rule and for that reason favours separation if not conflict between ethnic groups: on the other hand to try and keep
the permanency of its domination it needs to destroy the social structure,
culture, and by implication identity, of these groups. Moreover it must
protect the ruling class of those groups which (like, for example, the Peul
tribe or nation in our country) have given decisive support during the colonial
conquest a policy which favours the preservation of the identity of these
groups.

As has already been said, there are not usually important changes in
respect of culture in the upright shape of the indigenous pyramid or of the
indigenous social pyramids (groups or societies with a State). Each level or

---

* In our country: mandjaques, pepels, oincas, balantes, beafadas.
** Pajadincas and other minorities in the interior.

class keeps its identity, linked with that of the group but separate from that of other social classes. Conversely, in the urban centres, as in some of the interior regions of the country where the cultural influence of the colonial power is felt, the problem of identity is more complicated. While the bottom and the top of the social pyramid (that is the mass of the working class drawn from different ethnic groups and the foreign dominant class) keep their identities, the middle level of this pyramid (the indigenous petit bourgeoisie), culturally uprooted, alienated or more or less assimilated, engages in a sociological battle in search of its identity. One must also point out that though united by a new identity — granted by the colonial power — the foreign dominant class cannot free itself from the contradictions of its own society, which it brings to the colonized country.

When, at the initiative of a minority of the indigenous petit bourgeoisie, allied with the indigenous masses, the pre-independence movement is launched, the masses have no need to assert or reassert their identity, which they have never confused nor would have known how to confuse with that of the colonial power. This need is felt only by the indigenous petit bourgeoisie which finds itself obliged to take up a position in the struggle which opposes the masses to the colonial power. However, the reassertion of identity distinct from that of the colonial power is not always achieved by the lower middle class. It is only a minority who do this, while another minority asserts, often in a noisy manner, the identity of the foreign dominant class, while the silent majority is trapped in indecision.

Moreover, even when there is a reassertion of an identity distinct from that of the colonial power, and the same as that of the masses, it does not show itself in the same way everywhere. One part of the middle class minority, engaged in the pre-independence movement, uses the foreign cultural norms, calling on literature and art, to express rather the discovery of its identity than to draw on the theme of the hopes and sufferings of the masses. And precisely because it uses the language and speech of the colonial power, the minority only occasionally manages to influence the masses, generally illiterate, and familiar with other forms of artistic expression. This does not however remove the value of the contribution to the development of the struggle made by this petit bourgeoisie minority, for it can at the same time influence a sector of the uprooted or those who are latecomers to its own class and an important sector of public opinion in the colonial metropolis, notably the class of intellectuals.

The other part of the lower middle class which from the start joins in the pre-independence movement finds in its prompt share in the liberation struggle and in integration with the masses the best means of expression of identity distinct from that of the colonial power.

That is why identification with the masses and reassertion of identity can be temporary or definitive, apparent or real, in the light of the daily efforts and sacrifices demanded by the struggle itself — a struggle, which while being the organized political expression of a *culture* is also and necessarily a proof not only of *identity* but also of *dignity*.

In the course of the process of colonialist domination, the masses, whatever the characteristic of the social structure of the group to which they belong, do not stop resisting the colonial power. In a first phase — that of conquest, cynically called 'pacification' — they resist gun in hand foreign occupation. In a second phase — that of the golden age of triumphant colonialism — they offer the foreign domination passive resistance, almost silent, but blazoned with many revolts, usually individual and once in a while collective. The revolt is particularly in the field of work and taxes, even in social contacts with the representatives, foreign or indigenous, of the colonial power. In a third phase — that of the liberation struggle — it is the masses who provide the main strength which employs political or armed resistance, to challenge and to destroy foreign domination. Such a prolonged and varied resistance is possible only because while keeping their culture and identity, the masses keep intact the sense of their individual and collective dignity, despite the worries, humiliations and brutalities to which they are often subjected.

The assertion or reassertion by the indigenous petit bourgeoisie of identity distinct from that of the colonial power does not and could not bring about restoration of a sense of dignity to that class alone. In this context we see that the sense of dignity of the petit bourgeoisie depends on the objective moral and social feeling of each individual, on his subjective attitude towards the two poles of the colonial conflict, between which he is forced to live out the daily drama of colonization. This drama is the more shattering to the extent to which the petit bourgeoisie in fulfilling its role is made to live alongside both the foreign dominating class and the masses. On one side the lower middle class is the victim of frequent if not daily humiliation by the foreigner, and on the other side it is aware of the injustice to which the masses are subjected and of their resistance and spirit of rebellion. Hence arises the apparent paradox of continuing colonial domination; it is from within the indigenous lower middle class, a social class which grows from colonialism itself, that arise the first important steps towards mobilizing and organizing the masses for the struggle against the colonial power.

The struggle, in the face of all kinds of obstacles and in a variety of forms, reflects the awareness or grasp of a complete identity, generalizes and consolidates the sense of dignity, strengthened by the development of political consciousness, and derives from the culture or cultures of the masses in revolt one of its principal strengths.

10. The Christian Churches

Editors' Introduction

For most of Africa, the arrival of Christianity was part and parcel of the expansion of the European world economy which began in the 16th Century and which led to the colonization of Africa, largely in the latter part of the 19th Century. The European colonial powers were Christians, the white settlers were Christians, and the missionaries were Europeans. Furthermore, when Europeans spoke of bringing 'civilization' to Africa, one central feature of the definition of civilization was Christianity.

In Southern Africa, there were no African Moslems (though this is not true of Portuguese Guinea, located in West Africa). This is one explanation of the particularly high rate of conversion of the indigenous population of Southern Africa to Christianity. Of course, the particular form of Christianity that had the most adherents varied according to the colonial power's preferences: primarily Catholicism in the Portuguese territories; Lutheranism in Namibia (because of the German influence); Protestantism (in one form or another) in South Africa; a balance of Anglicans, Methodists, and Presbyterians in Zimbabwe.

The leadership of the national liberation movements usually were products of mission schools. Some owed their educational career to missionary institutions. These man were at one and the same time appreciative of the advantages they had obtained from the Christian churches and fundamentally critical of the overall position of these churches. One such man was Eduardo Mondlane, the founding president of FRELIMO. We include two statements by him. The first was written when he was a student in the United States in 1952, before the rise of the national liberation movement, in which he raises rather gently some questions about the historic role of Christian missions in Southern Africa. The second was a speech made in 1964 and, when already president of FRELIMO, Mondlane was asked to speak at a meeting of the Mediterranean Congress for Culture. By now his cricitism of the Church was far sharper.

We include as well two pieces on the relationship of Christian doctrine and colonial practice. Joshua Nkomo, president of ZAPU reminded the Church of its duty to defend 'Christian principles'. The ANC pointed out the ironic contrast between the South African Government's pose as the bastion of Christian civilization and the slowly emerging critiques of government policies by leading churchmen.

In Portuguese Africa where the Catholic Church loomed large, there was concern naturally with the religio-political role of the Vatican. We include three items: a criticism by the MPLA of the Pope's visit to Portugal in 1967, an open letter from the three CONCP movements to the African Episcopal Conference (of the Catholic Church), held in Kampala in 1969, and a statement by FRELIMO after the Pope in 1970 had received the leaders of the CONCP movements in audience in Rome. We attach ZAPU's analysis of this audience too, wherein it drew the lesson for Zimbabwe.

Christian Missions Under Test
Eduardo Mondlane

> *An article by Eduardo Mondlane, later to be president*
> *of FRELIMO, in* Archways, *a YM-YWCA publication,*
> *Winter 1952.*

When the first Christian missionaries sailed from Europe or America for Africa, Asia, and the Pacific Islands, they were mainly motivated by the words of Jesus when he said, 'Go ye, therefore . . . baptizing them in the name of the Father, Son, and the Holy Ghost.' This was strictly interpreted to mean saving their souls from everlasting damnation. They were activated by a spiritual command for strictly spiritual purposes. Whenever they were forced to minister to the material needs of the new converts and the pagans, it was made strictly clear that it was a means of reaching the spiritual needs.

This approach implied that it is possible to separate spiritual needs from material needs.

It was mainly due to this tendency of the early missionaries to dichotomize all life that the humanists and those who follow a materialistic view of life objected to the missionary enterprise. Also, the fact that the missionaries were driven by the avowed purpose of spreading the gospel aroused antagonism from the students of cultures, technically known as anthropologists, although today many of them would approve.

I will not attempt to analyse the theological and philosophical implications of that early approach of the Christian Missions, for I am not qualified to do so. But I am interested in noting the changes that took place, especially in the majority of the missions that are working in the more industrialized areas of Southern Africa.

Anyone who visits Southern Africa today will notice that most mission stations are located in what are called 'Native Reserves', far from the cities and industrial centres, where most Europeans live. Although it is not easy to generalize on that which deals with human behaviour, I'd venture this explanation: the early missionary, being interested in the spiritual more than the material needs of the people, concentrated his energies on teaching the Natives the Bible and things connected with theology, and the practical methods of preaching, in order to get as many converts as possible. Many of the very early schools in Southern Africa were really Bible Schools. Whatever science and technology was taught was only a means of preventing the converts from corrupting themselves through over-indulgence in leisure. In many cases practical lessons in masonry and general agriculture were given to enable the Natives to produce food for immediate consumption.

In so far as politics is concerned, unless the convert was either a chief of the tribe or an important member of the tribal council, he was discouraged from participating in it. The missionaries seem to have based their faith on what Jesus said to Pilate, namely that 'My kingdom is not of this world . . . .' They were supposed to belong to a 'new world' that would come soon, either with the physical death of each individual or with the second coming of Christ. I have heard thousands of sermons preached by Africans as well as Europeans and Americans on this subject. To a great extent this is still the basis of the faith of many African Christians today.

Meanwhile, European nations were busy occupying most of Africa and dishing it out to different nations as colonies. In the wars that took place as a result of the European occupation, most missionaries kept their hands off, and in those few cases where they participated they favoured their national governments with the hope that they would have better chances of winning souls for Christ.

Military occupation was accompanied by economic exploitation. The grabbing of traditional African land by Europeans and the subsequent displacement of thousands of African families followed. The discovery of gold, coal, copper and diamonds made things worse. The able-bodied men were either forced to go to work in the new mines or lured in one way or another to move to the new industrial areas. Those families that remained in white man's land were placed in the position of semi-slavery by their white lords.

The development of slums in the new cities, such as Johannesburg, Pretoria, Durban, and Elizabethville is another problem that destroyed the hopes of those who thought that, if the Natives who were dispossessed of their land, and went to live in European towns, they would be better off. The development of crime of all sorts, venereal diseases, tuberculosis, and other new and more dangerous diseases made its impact felt in the lives of the people.

In the face of these and other negative social effects, the missionary was forced to sit down and rethink many of his earlier assumptions. Without changing, too much his basic faith in God, his love for all men, and the desire to save them from perpetual damnation, the missionary set out trying to meet the demands of the new situation.

There are as many approaches to the new problems as there are missionaries in the field, but I would not be too wrong if I said that the majority of the missionaries are not only aware of the social, economic, and political questions, but also are worried about how to deal with them. This is something to be thankful about. A number of American missionary societies are hoping to meet the new problems by recruiting their candidates from all fields of life. A year or so ago, the Methodist Church sent about fifty young missionaries to Africa on a programme of three years. These young missionaries are trained in engineering, agriculture, building, social work, nursing, medicine, preaching, etc.

By this new emphasis, the cleavage between the material and the spiritual is being narrowed down.

As Dr. Emory Ross says, the cultural life of the African has always been 'one whole'. If the Christian faith wants to survive as a way of life for the Africans, yes, even for all the peoples of the world, it must satisfy the needs of the people as a whole. The time of the 'pie in the sky' religion is gone. The Christian Church must try to answer the intellectual, material, and spiritual questions of the people.

The Role of the Church in Mozambique
Eduardo Mondlane

Section of an address by Eduardo Mondlane, president of Frelimo, to the Mediterranean Congress of Culture, 20—24 June 1964.

Earlier in this paper, we hinted at the rationalizations given by the Portuguese Government as to why it insists on pushing the Catholic Church into the forefront in the education of the African people. The Portuguese Government claims that it has two purposes in Africa: one is to improve the material life of the African, while the other is to encourage the Portuguese Catholic missionary to improve the Africans' spiritual and intellectual life. Whatever there is in the form of concrete programmes for putting into effect the first part of the Portuguese colonial policy was discussed, at least in part, in the outline above. The second part of the policy is being realized through the use of the Roman Catholic missions. While the Colonial Act provides for freedom of conscience and the freedom of the various religions, at the same time and in a contradictory manner it provides for a special protection and assistance to the Roman Catholic mission programme. Departing from an earlier attitude held during the first two decades immediately following the establishment of the Republic, the Portuguese Government recognized the rights and special functions of the Church, which are 'to Christianize and educate, to nationalize and civilize the native populations'.

In Mozambique this policy is governed by appropriate constitutional provisions, beginning with the Missionary Accord of 1940, which spelled out in some detail the principles contained in the Concordat of 7 May 1940 between the Vatican and Portugal, and the Missionary Statute of 1941. In these agreements, the Portuguese Government was committed to subsidizing the Church's missionary programme, and limiting the activities of non-Catholic foreign missionaries. In the estimated population of Mozambique of 7 million, the number of people who subscribe to the Roman Catholic faith is estimated at 500,000. These are served by about 100 mission and parish churches, led by secular priests and fathers of various orders, including Franciscans, Dominicans, Benedictines, Lazarists and those of the Holy Ghost Congregation. In 1959 there were in Mozambique 240 priests and fathers. Of these, only three priests were Africans. Some of the most important activities of the Catholic Church are 'the founding and directing of schools for European and African students, elementary, secondary and professional schools and seminaries . . . as well as infirmaries and hospitals.' The whole responsibility for educating the African people has been entrusted to the Roman Catholic Church, exclusive of the government; this in spite of the fact that the overwhelming majority of the Africans are not Christians, let alone Roman Catholic. To this programme was also attached the responsibility of preparing those individuals who were to become assimilated to the Portuguese culture. The Portuguese believe that there is a better chance for an African to become a Portuguese in spirit if he is a Roman Catholic. This belief was often expressed by officials of the government, as illustrated by a statement in 1960 by Dr. Adriano Moreira, then Under-Secretary of State for Overseas Administration.

While emphasizing that political loyalty did not depend upon Christian qualification, Dr. Moreira declared that Catholic missionary activity was inseparably linked to patriotism and that the formation of Christian qualities led to the formation of Portuguese qualities. It is this attitude which led to the separation of education of the African children from that of the Europeans. This separation of the educational system of the two racial groups is all the more peculiar when one takes into consideration the fact that, elsewhere in the world, the Catholic Church insists on educating the children of its members. Yet in Mozambique, the children of the Europeans, who are more than 95% Roman Catholic, are left in the hands of the secular schools of the State. The intention of this policy is to indoctrinate the children of the majority of the native, black Mozambicans with Christianity, thereby assuring the government of a population which is loyal to Portugal.

How the Portuguese could believe this fantasy is very difficult to understand, in view of the example shown by other African states where the proportion of Christians, especially Roman Catholics, is much higher than in Mozambique. Our own neighbour, Tanganyika, has not only a higher Roman Catholic population, but it also has the first and only black African Cardinal the Catholic Church has ever had, and its first prime minister, who later became its first president, is a devout Roman Catholic. There is no evidence anywhere in Africa to support the idea, cherished by Portuguese officials, that the more Catholics they will be able to create in Mozambique, the more

Portuguese Mozambique will be.

This attitude of the Portuguese Government is so entrenched that it constantly influences policy, even where decisions involving the admission of foreign Christian missionaries, Catholic or Protestant, into the country are concerned. Since the 17th Century, foreign missionaries have been suspected of 'denationalizing the natives', and of acting as advance agents for foreign governments. When these missionaries are Protestant, the situation becomes worse; fears and resentments are multiplied. Consequently, for many years the Protestant missions in Mozambique have been hampered and quite often thwarted by a powerful combination of Catholic clergy and officials of the colonial government. From time to time public statements are made by high officials of the colonial government attacking Protestant missions, accusing them of fomenting anti-Portuguese sentiments amongst the African population. Lately accusations have been levelled against Protestant missionaries, alleging that they were responsible for the rise of nationalism in both Angola and Mozambique. This in spite of the fact that the leadership of the nationalist movements of the two countries is mixed, religiously speaking. In our own Mozambique Liberation Front, the majority of the members of the Central Committee, which directs the whole programme of the struggle, are either Roman Catholics or come from Catholic families. The man in charge of our military action programme is a practising Roman Catholic. The largest number of our students abroad, who have run away from Portuguese schools either in Mozambique of Portugal, are Roman Catholic. In the summer of 1961, when more than 100 university students from Portuguese colonies in Africa ran away from Portuguese universities to France, Switzerland and West Germany, over 80 of them declared themselves to be either Roman Catholic or to come from Catholic families . . .

In general, the Portuguese Catholic hierarchy supports the programme of the Salazar regime both at home and overseas. Most Portuguese Catholics are Portuguese first and Catholics second. To many of them, being Portuguese and being Catholic are one and the same thing. Consequently, we know of no instance during the last 40 years when the Roman Catholic Church of Portugal felt compelled to protest officially against the many excesses of the Portuguese Government's colonialist actions against the African people. On the contrary, the highest officials of the Church have tended to come out in support of the status quo.

The only exception to this rule has been the position of one leader of the Catholic Church in Mozambique, the Bishop of Beira, Monseigneur Sebastiao Soares de Resende. For a number of years, this churchman dared to question the Government for its treatment especially of African cotton growers. He wrote in his monthly pastoral letters, published in a Church publication, criticising the manner in which the Government was carrying out some of its African policies, but with little or no success. His intention, however, was to liberalize the policy rather than change it radically. When, finally, some of his criticisms began to annoy the Salazar regime, he was ordered by the Vatican to stop publishing them. Subsequently, the Government curtailed some of the privileges which he had previously enjoyed, including taking away his responsibilities as the Director of the only secondary school in Beira. Bishop Resende is one of those Portuguese liberals who believe in the possibility of the creation of a new Brazil in Africa, where Portuguese culture would flourish even after independence. The impression one gets of his position, as gleaned from some of his pastorals and a daily newspaper which he is supposed to control, is that Bishop Resende can conceive of an independent Mozambique only within a community of Portuguese interests, cultural, religious and economic. However, since he has never felt compelled to formally state his position, we will refrain from speculating further.

The clearest statement ever made by a Portuguese Catholic leader of any standing concerning the question of self-determination and independence was by Monseigneur Custodio Alvim Fereira, Auxiliary Bishop of Lourenco Marques. If his position is to be taken as representative of the Roman Catholic Church, then the Church is unequivocally against independence. In a recent circular which was read in all Cath olic Churches and Seminaries in Mozambique, Bishop Pereira outlined ten points intended to convince the clergy that independence for the African people is not only wrong, but against the will of God. The Statement ran as follows:

I. Independence is irrelevant to the welfare of man. It can be good if the conditions are present — the cultural conditions do not yet exist in Mozambique (*sic*).

II. While these conditions are not being produced, to take part in movements for independence is acting against nature.

III. Even if these conditions existed, the Metropole has the right to oppose independence if the freedoms and rights of man are respected and if it (the Metropole) already provides for the well-being, and civil and religious progress of all.

IV. All movements which use force (terrorists) are against the Natural Law, because independence, if it is to be assumed that it is good, must be obtained by peaceful means.

V. When the movement is a terrorist one, the clergy have the obligation, in good conscience, not only to refrain from taking part, but also to oppose it. This (obligation) derives from the nature of his mission (as a religious leader).

VI. Even when the movement is peaceful, the clergy must abstain from it in order to have spiritual influence upon all people. The Superior of the Church may impose that abstention; he imposes it now from Lourenco Marques.

VII. The native peoples of Africa have the obligation to thank the colonialists for all the benefits which they receive from them.

VIII. The educated people have the duty of debunking those with less education of all the illusions of independence.

IX. The present independence movements have, almost all of them, the sign of revolt and communism; they have no reason;

we must not, therefore, support these movements. The doctrine
of the Holy See is quite clear concerning atheistic and revolutionary communism. The great revolution is that of the Gospel.

X. The slogan 'Africa for the Africans' is a philosophical
monstrosity and a challenge to the Christian civilization, because
today's events tell us that it is Communism and Islam which wish
to impose their civilization upon the Africans.

The reaction of our people to the above situation was, as can be expected,
a demand for our freedom now.

Christian Principles and Expediency

Joshua Nkomo

*From the pamphlet by Joshua Nkomo, president of
ZAPU, entitled* The Case for Majority Rule, *published
in New Delhi, ca. 1964.*

It must be remembered that the official religion of this country is
Christianity. It is therefore essential that the standards of the affairs of the
State must be measured up to Christian ethics and values.

Britain also has Christianity as her official religion. But this is what Mr.
Smith said at his Sinola meeting: 'There was a time when the British and
Rhodesian moral codes were the same. It is obvious today that our moral
codes are different.' The pertinent question is: Who has gone off the rail
— Sir Alec Douglas-Home or Mr. Smith?

This article would be incomplete if I did not comment on the part played
by the Church in the affairs of this country. When I say the Church, I mean
the missionaries of all denominations that assisted in the development of
the country. No one can deny the fact that there was a time when the entire
education of the African people was provided by the Church with very little
or no assistance from the Government. Up to this day the Church still
shoulders more than 90% of African education. The churches have played no
small part in the provision of medical services, particularly in the outlying
districts. Of course, the African people themselves played an important
part in providing these services.

Lest I be misunderstood, let me hasten to add that the Church has not
been spotless regarding the wrong things that have been perpetuated in this
country. As a matter of fact, I am at variance with the Church on a number
of issues. However, these do not call for comment here.

I point out these things because it seems that many people do not understand the position of the Church in our society. I am not at all suggesting
that the Church should take part in party politics. But I do say that the

Church, as the conscience of the people, has the right and duty to make its voice heard on such a definite question of right and wrong as the one that confronts us in this country.

The Church will destroy itself if it sacrifices Christian principles and ethics on the altar of expediency.

Vorster and the Christians

ANC

An article in Sechaba *(ANC), III, 2, February 1969.*

John Vorster, we are told, is Prime Minister of Western Christian civilisation's bastion state in Africa. His Republic is the bulwark of Christianity's survival, against the hordes of heathens and communists that 'infect' the continent. His apartheid represents a shining light of Christian values in a world made 'decadent' by liberalism and democracy. So we are told. But Mr. Vorster, it seems, can't get along with the Christians. He has been accusing some of them of blasphemy, liberalism and leftism. And he has threatened that, if they persist in their present attitudes, the cloth will not protect them from his wrath.

What are these attitudes that set the Christian Prime Minister to abuse Christian priests as though they were dangerous revolutionaries?

They have condemned the vicious, anti-human philosophy of apartheid — the very least, one would have thought, that a Christian who claims to believe that all men are the children of God should do. One clergyman, the Rev. Wimmer, was quoted in the *Rand Daily Mail* in September as saying that: 'The Government, like us, cannot serve two masters, and in serving apartheid, it has rejected God and . . . cannot claim to be Christian.'

And 12 leading Churchmen, from the Dutch Reformed Church, Anglican, Methodist, Presbyterian, Congregational and Lutheran Churches, have written to the Prime Minister condeming apartheid as 'obviously not in accordance with the intention of God as revealed to man in His word.'

And a long time they took, coming to that conclusion . . . But in South Africa, even if you are a Church Minister, you are taking your courage in both hands when you criticise apartheid. Mr. Vorster rants, and Mr. Vorster threatens — you cannot do a Martin Luther King in South Africa, he tells them. Don't try to play the martyr. Cut it out! he yells hysterically. Cut it out! Martyr? Martin Luther King? Did he choose that example by accident? Is it fanciful to see that as an incitement to some lunatic assassin to rid the Prime Minister of these turbulent priests?

Racialist South Africa has a long history of hating those Christians who were not prepared to limit their Christianity to a decent weekly attendance at Church, while the servants prepared the Sunday dinner. Vorster himself refers to the troubles of the voortrekkers with missionaries — their crime was to have fought to end the evil practise of slavery at the Cape. And the voortrekkers never forgave them for it. In recent years, we remember how Father Trevor Huddleston and Bishop Reeves were hounded out of South Africa. Their crime was to have identified themselves with the struggles of the oppressed, and to have had the courage to speak out against apartheid.

Funny, isn't it, that the crusaders of Western Christian civilisation just can't get on with the Christians.

Pope — Ally of Salazar
MPLA

Editorial in Angola in Arms *(MPLA), IV, 1, May—June 1967.*

On the 13th of May 1967, Pope Paul VI visited Portugal. Thus, with this visit, the Pope manifested openly his support to the fascist regime of Salazar. On the 13th of May, 1967, Pope Paul VI visited the shrine of Fatima in Portugal. At the airport when the Holy Father's plane landed, he was received by the President of the Portuguese Republic, Americo Tomas and by the dictator himself, besides many other prominent personalities of the colonial-fascist regime and of the Church.

At Fatima, there is celebrated every year the appearance of the Virgin Mary. It was 50 years ago that three little Portuguese pastors declared that they had seen and heard the voice of the Virgin. It was therefore the 50th anniversary that was being celebrated at Fatima.

It was this fact which Paul VI used as a pretext to go from the Vatican to Portugal. Although he had stated before leaving his headquarters that the visit had no political attributes, and beside the fact that he remained only a few hours in Salazar's territory, the positive political effect which the fascists got cannot be ruled out or denied by the Pope. This trip was a guarantee of the support given to the repressive regime by the Vatican.

Not so many people would have voiced their condemnation of the Pope's trip, as was the case, if Portugal had a just and democratic regime; if the right to independence of the peoples under its colonial rule was being respected by the Portuguese regime; if Portugal were not waging a criminal war against the people of the three African territories she is subjugating; if the Portuguese regime respected the right to freedom of the Portuguese people itself.

But Portugal has one of the most anti-democratic regimes in the world today. Portugal is also the only country which stubbornly insists in maintaining, by force, her African colonies.

In Portugal, the Salazar regime suppresses all the essential liberties of its own people by taking away the right of Portuguese citizens to choose their own system of government, in free elections. To impose upon its people his iron rule, Salazar has created one of the most severe police, PIDE, among other instruments of repression no longer used in any part of the world today. The Portuguese economy is in the hands of a very restricted number of bourgeois who export most of the benefits acquired through the system of exploitation in the colonies, to the advantage of the foreign monopolists with whom they are associated.

In the colonies Salazar continues to negate the right to independence and sovereignty of the peoples. By adopting the most retrograde attitude of trying to go against the laws of history, the fascist regime of Salazar has installed in the colonies a police apparatus of a tremendous capacity; Salazar has sent to these African territories more than 100,000 troops, mobilised the settlers to combat on the side of the colonial army and is seeking to corrupt the Africans to oppose themselves to the freedom war of our people. However, all this is in vain. In Angola, the people under the leadership of the MPLA is today, more than ever before, determined and mobilised for the war for Independence. Our people is today, more than even before, fully sure that our war can only end with victory for Angola.

Behaving hopelessly, the barbarian Portuguese colonialists are murdering defenceless men, women and children; burning, bombing and destroying whole villages; they are exterminating the people's cultivated lands, and are killing the cattle to destroy the material subsistence base of the people.

It was this policy of cruelty and violence that the Pope, in the interest of the Church of which he is the supreme representative, came to ratify during his visit to Fatima.

But this attitude of the Pope should not astonish anybody. Nothing new was revealed to us, for we always knew the Pope as a consistent ally of Salazar, as a staunch protector of the fascists and colonialists. Throughout its history the Catholic Church has given its support to the colonialist policy of the oppressive classes in Portugal and elsewhere.

Although the Christian religion has inherent in itself a humanitarian and sound character, this quality has been used by the Church itself as an instrument for the domination of some peoples by others, of some classes by others. Thus, in the past, the Catholic Church sided with the bourgeoisie and it was used as an instrument of this class; it sided with and protected the colonialists; and with the wealthy against the poor.

In Angola at the beginning of the period of 'maritime discoveries', the first contacts of the Portuguese colonialists with our people were made by the Catholic missionaries. They were the agents of the colonialists who penetrated the interior of our country 'preaching the faith', to convert our people to submission and humiliation, and to forsake the attitude of resistance to the colonialist invader. They were also the ones who paved the way for the soldiers who consolidated the conquests by violence, who sacked, who robbed, and murdered with the blessing of the Church.

At the beginning of the armed revolt in our country and with the advancement of our struggle for liberation, the Catholic Church didn't take a position in favour of the nationalists. To the contrary, the Church always sided and collaborated with the colonialist Church repressive apparatus. More than ever before, the agents of the Church are preaching Christian humiliation and submission. And when this is not enough, the Church denounces the nationalists, handing them to the colonialist police agents, sending them to torture chambers and to death. Many Catholic priests took up arms and went to the battlefield, side by side with the colonialists who were soldiers, against the Angolan nationalists who were fighting to liberate themselves from oppression.

When some African Catholic priests began to manifest themselves actively against the Portuguese colonialists, they were thrown into jail and expelled from Angola. Faced with this, the Catholic Church abstained from taking a position defending the right of these priests to express their patriotic views.

Therefore, the Catholic Church has not been defending justice and liberty for men. Rather it has been serving as an instrument of domination. The Church has been used as a means to perpetuate the regimes of oppression by defending the fascists and the colonialists.

Upon paying a visit to the Portugal of Salazar, Pope Paul VI has only taken off the mask — shown his true face. The face of a man and of an institution that defends — the institution and the man — the interests of the colonialists, that blesses the cruel war of repression against the people and which acts accordingly in order to perpetuate the domination and the oppression of man by man.

Appeal to the Bishops
CONCP

> *An open letter sent on 5 July 1969 to the African Episcopal Conference, meeting in Kampala, and signed by Uria Simango (member of Presidential Council, FRELIMO), Agostinho Neto (President, MPLA), and Amilcar Cabral (Secretary-General, PAIGC).*

Most Reverend Excellencies,

The peoples of the Portuguese colonies are aware that Paul VI will visit Uganda later this month. As you know, our peoples today are engaged, amidst difficult conditions, in a struggle for national liberation against Portuguese colonial domination.

The armed struggle which we are required to pursue is the only historical path open to us that may allow our peoples to fulfil their aspirations for freedom, justice and human dignity. It is the result of Portugal's obstinate and criminal refusal to recognize our people's rights to national independence.

In fact, in 1951, Portugal unilaterally decided, without consultation with the interested parties, that the Portuguese colonies would be named Overseas Provinces. Obviously, this decision was intended solely to mystify, and reality has proved that nothing was changed and that our countries are still colonies pure and simple.

In 1963, the OAU sent a special committee to New York in order to meet the Portuguese delegation to the UN about the problem of the Portuguese colonies, so as to create a climate which would allow for negotiations between the Portuguese Government and the leaders of the nationalist movements of our countries. The meeting was held, but it was a total failure due to the Portuguese Government's obstinate desire to continue its domination of our peoples.

Previously, our organizations had made several unilateral gestures, but Portugal always refused to agree to our demands. Instead, Portugal increased its repression of our peoples. Today Portugal is engaged in a colonialist, criminal, cruel war against our peoples in Angola, Mozambique and Guinea-Bissau.

To justify such wars, Portugal invokes the defence of the West and of Christian civilization. Cardinal Goncalvez Cerejeira himself, head of the Roman Catholic Church in Portugal, declared in Lisbon in 1967 that the day of peace proclaimed by His Holiness Pope Paul VI in *Populorum Progressio** should in no way be interpreted as being an invitation to pacifism in Africa, since that would mean an abject abdication of Portugal's sacred rights.

The war which Portugal is conducting in our three countries is thus being supported explicitly by the Roman Catholic Church of Portugal. The collective massacres, assassinations, deportations, the arrests and the torturing of thousands of men, women and children, the constant plane bombings, the napalm bombs, the burning or poisoning of the crops, in short, all the crimes which are being committed daily receive the benediction of the Roman Catholic Church of Portugal.

Repression affects even those African priests who share the daily sufferings of the people. We, peoples of the Portuguese colonies, realize that such crimes are in direct contradiction to the principles of Christian morality established by the Roman Catholic Church. The truth is that several Christian voices have already protested against the barbarous colonial war which the Portuguese government is conducting. In Portugal itself, some Portuguese Catholics, openly opposing the Catholic hierarchy, have held various kinds of demonstrations against the colonial war.

But it is just as true that we cannot dissociate Rome from the Portuguese Catholic Church, if Rome itself does not do it. This is why we are addressing ourselves to your Most Reverend Excellencies. It is our sincere conviction that the Church, particularly in Africa, shares in the heavy respon-

---

* A decree making January 1st officially the day of peace.

sibility of the defence of justice and the dignity of the peoples of Africa.

For this reason, we, FRELIMO, the MPLA, and the PAIGC, on behalf of the peoples of Mozambique, Angola, and Guinea and Cape Verde, respectively, and in particular on behalf of the hundreds of thousands of Catholics of our countries, direct this appeal to your Most Reverend Excellencies so that, in the name of the Roman Catholic Church in Africa, you may intercede with His Holiness Pope Paul VI, in order that on the day he will for the first time tread the soil of our continent, he may take an open and clear position in condemnation of Portuguese colonialism, and that he may contribute to a final negotiated solution of the conflict which opposes the Portuguese Government and the peoples of our countries, a solution based on a solemn recognition on the part of Portugal of the legitimate right of our populations to autonomy and national independence.

There is no doubt that the future position of our peoples vis-a-vis the Roman Catholic Church will greatly depend on the position which the latter takes in relation to the fundamental problem which our peoples face, that is the problem of the reconquest of our dignity and of our sovereignty as African peoples.

We are certain that Your Most Reverend Excellencies, aware of the magnitude of the role which you may play, will know how to contribute to the realization of the deep aspirations of our peoples to freedom, justice, and human dignity. We are at your disposal, as well as of His Holiness Pope Paul VI to furnish any further information you may need to clarify our views.

For FRELIMO	For MPLA	For PAIGC
Uria T. Simango,	Agostinho Neto,	Amilcar Cabral,
Member of the	President	Secretary-
Presidential		General
Council		

Change of Policy in the Vatican?
FRELIMO

Article in Mozambique Revolution _(FRELIMO),_
No. 49, July—September 1970.

On July 1st, 1970 at 12.30 p.m. Pope Paul VI received in private audience leaders of the Liberation Movements of the 'Portuguese' colonies, FRELIMO was represented by Comrade Marcelino dos Santos, Vice-President; PAIGC by its Secretary-General, Comrade Amilcar Cabral; and MPLA by its President, Comrade Agostinho Neto.

In principle, there is nothing strange in this audience. FRELIMO, MPLA and PAIGC are the organizations which truly represent the peoples of

Mozambique, Angola and Guinea-Bissau. Many countries recognize us as such. Many heads of state, not only in Africa but in Asia, Latin America and even in Europe, receive our leaders in their capacity as the only and legitimate representatives of our peoples and our countries. In principle, therefore, the audience granted by the Pope to our leaders was nothing out of the ordinary.

However, one circumstance of this act of the Pope caused multiple speculations. It is the fact that the Catholic Church has always, consistently and openly, supported Portuguese colonialism. Considering the agreement between the Holy See and Portugal, statements of high dignitaries of the Catholic Church, concrete acts of support from the Vatican to the Portuguese Government, we see that no other power has ever so unabashedly supported the colonial fascism of Portugal. The high point of this support was the visit of the Pope himself to Portugal in 1967. During that visit, the Pope made a gift of $150,000 to the Portuguese Government to be specifically used in the 'Overseas Provinces'. He decorated the head of the Portuguese Gestapo (PIDE), Major Silva Pais, and his very presence in Portuguese territory implied approval by the Catholic Church of the policy of the Portuguese Government which is fundamentally characterized by colonialism.

In this context arose the speculations regarding the Pope's action of receiving leaders of the Liberation Movements of the 'Portuguese' colonies. Two positions basically developed: one pretended to divest the Pope's act of all its political meaning; thus, the Pope would have been deceived by his advisers who did not inform him as to the quality of the persons he was going to see; or the Pope decided to receive them as religious persons and not as politicians. Others defended the idea that the Pope received our comrades fully conscious of the fact that he was receiving leaders of the Liberation Movements of the Portuguese colonies; and that he received them in that capacity, not as religious persons; through this act the Pope wanted to indicate his condemnation of Portuguese colonialism and his recognition of the right of the people of Angola, Guinea-Bissau and Cape Verde, and Mozambique to independence.

It is impossible to decipher the real intention of the Pope. However, an objective analysis of the facts leads us to the conclusion that *at least* the Pope could not deny that he was receiving leaders of the Liberation Movements: the fact that the preparations were underway for about one month and that in the request for the audience it was specifically declared that it was the leaders of FRELIMO, MPLA and PAIGC who were seeking an audience with the Pope; plus the fact that at that moment a Conference of Solidarity with the peoples of the 'Portuguese' colonies of international significance had just taken place in Rome in which hundreds of delegates participated. The Pope obviously knew whom he was receiving. To think otherwise would be to offend the Pope and to insinuate that he does not know what he is doing, that he does not assume his responsibility. Another proof, although more indirect, was the sabotage attempt made by a Monsignor of Portuguese nationality a few moments before the audience. He talked to our comrades in the waiting room at the Vatican and advised them not to address the Pope 'because you do not know our protocol and surely you will not know exactly what to say; or if you absolutely want to speak to the Holy Father, let me serve as interpreter because he does not speak Portuguese.' Our comrades replied that they would address the Pope and that they would use French which is a language that the Pope knows, and therefore they would not need an interpreter. Not giving up his sabotage attempt the Monsignor then said: 'Well then, in order to save you from a blunder, you must look at me during the audience; when you say something which must not be said, I will give you a sign for you to stop.'

But if it is so, if the Pope voluntarily and intentionally received our comrades, having to overcome the opposition of some of his staff, knowing that the visitors were leaders of Liberation Movements fighting against Portuguese colonialism, what then was the significance of his gesture? We are inclined to think that it was a political gesture of condemnation of Portuguese colonialism, and recognition of the right of our peoples to independence. Despite the fact that *'Osservatore Romano'*, the official organ of the Vatican, tried to minimize the importance of the audience, certain other facts suggest that very political intention of the Pope:

(a) Radio Vatican itself declared, commenting on the meeting, that 'the pacification — or the liberation through arms according to the sides on which we find ourselves — is a source of misery and death as any other form of war. May Angola, Guinea and Mozambique know *peace in justice*. The problem is posed again to the Christian conscience.' Radio Vatican stressed further that: (i) the audience with leaders of the three most important movements fighting against the Portuguese authorities in Africa was possible only because the Pope agreed to such an audience; (ii) Delegates of the Decolonization Committee of the United Nations as well as delegates of innumerable countries participated with the three leaders in the Anti-Colonialist Conference which had taken place in Rome a week before (Radio, press and TV gave enormous coverage of the Conference); (iii) The position of the Church concerning the independence of the new nations is constant and well known, expressed in the documents of the Council, in the encyclicals and the addresses of Pope Paul VI.

(b) The Sunday following the recall of the Portuguese Ambassador to the Vatican by Lisbon, the Pope, addressing the people in St. Peter's Square said: 'How can one close his eyes on what is going on in the world, on what is weighing on our society, on the equilibrium necessary to progress and peace? Grave thoughts are mixed with good hopes; for both of them we cannot neglect the help of God.' On that day, the Pope was acclaimed with particular warmth by the thousands of pilgrims among whom were many Africans.

(c) The tone of the Portuguese protest itself may help us also to find out the real intentions of the Pope. Words like 'deep wound' and 'terrible insult' are used to qualify the act of the Pope or its consequences. And the Pope was surely conscious of this reaction when he behaved as he did against his traditional ally.

(d) The words addressed to our comrades by the Pope are conclusive, too. He declared that 'the Catholic Church is concerned with all those who are suffering, particularly the African peoples, and that *she supports the struggle for justice, for freedom and national independence.*' When our comrades told him of the massacres that the Portuguese carry out against the people, the Holy Father answered shocked: 'I will pray for you!' Obviously, only a deliberate misinterpretation might claim that these words of the Pope referred only to the three persons in front of him and not to the peoples and to the cause they represented.

All in all, we are led to believe that the Vatican's position of support for Portuguese colonialism is now experiencing the influence of the evolution of the times. It was in this light that FRELIMO interpreted the gesture of the Pope, using it as an instrument to mobilize our people:

> Therefore, Comrades, let us continue and intensify the struggle, being certain that our struggle causes even those traditional allies of Portugal, such as the Holy See, to initiate changes in their position and to condemn the Portuguese colonialist policy. The struggle continues!

The Christian Church and the Freedom Struggle
ZAPU

Commentary by ZAPU on the Audience given by Pope Paul to the leaders of FRELIMO, PAIGC and MPLA. Published in Zimbabwe Review *(Lusaka), No. 9–10, September–October 1970.*

Eye-brows were raised in Lisbon and there was going and coming to and from the Vatican by the Portuguese envoy to the Holy See. The Portuguese are predominantly Catholic in religion and ruthlessly imperialistic in politics. Economically they are die-hard capitalists whose basic and unadulterated wish is to retain their colonies for merciless exploitation. They were, therefore, surprised that the leader of their Church should intimate that he sympathised with the noble cause of the violently oppressed African masses.

What must have surprised most people who profess to be Christians was the alleged surprise of the Portuguese fascists. The Church, as we understand it, stands for equality, justice and complete harmony among mankind.

We felt that the Pope's expression of his understanding of the problem of the oppressed masses was a revelation of his understanding of these three cardinal virtues which the Church should or, rather, purports to represent.

The Portuguese, as members of this same Church and reading the same religious material read by the Pope, should have understood why the Pope expressed his understanding of the plight of the oppressed people of Mozambique, Angola and Guinea-Bissau.

It is a known and historically proved fact that imperialists use religion only as a vehicle for their inhuman ideas. Religion is used in colonised African countries as a kind of mental anaesthetic whose effect renders the colonised docile to their oppressors because they have been made to believe that what matters is the life hereafter.

The present trend by young militants to despise and, in many cases, dislike the propagators of the Christian faith is caused by atrocities perpetrated on the majority by fascists like Caetano, Vorster and Smith who profess to be acting on behalf of Christianity.

It should be pointed out that those who feel strongly that the Christian Church should be protected and promoted must take a decisively strong stand against these fascists and not hide behind excuses about why they do not call a spade a spade.

We differ with some Church leaders in Zimbabwe because they wish to settle for what they term a moderate racial policy (this means moderate oppression, if such a practice can exist) while we demand the complete and unconditional destruction of all forms of oppression.

The Roman Catholic Church had better take stock of its activities not only in Mozambique, Angola and Guinea-Bissau but also in South Africa and Zimbabwe with a view to establishing whether its activities are more in keeping with Christian principles and teachings than with those of the temporal powers of the day.

Its stand must be made clear to all and sundry vis-a-vis oppression.

It would be unjust and base not to point out that the recent conference of Roman Catholic bishops from Tanzania, Uganda, Zambia and Malawi in Lusaka made a laudable stand against oppression in their communique.

Those short-sighted people who indulge in wishful thinking to the extent that they say the Church should concentrate on ecclesiastical matters and leave temporal affairs to politicians should realise that man is man irrespective of whether he is a clergy or a politician.

His feelings when he is praying before an altar are not different from when he is sitting in a national assembly. If they are, then that individual is a downright sinner and hypocrite who has no moral right to pretend to be a defender of the Christian faith.

The line often, if not always, followed by the fascists is exactly like that of Nazi Germany when most churches where the clergy opposed Hitler's tyranny were objects of attack by the politicians.

South Africa's Vorster's attitude towards the Church is that, if the religious leaders strongly criticise his inhuman racialist policies and practices, he will deal with them by silencing them once for all or deport them if they are not South African citizens.

Smith, for his part, pretends to be negotiating with Church leaders in order to reach an agreement acceptable to his dictatorship and the clergy. We fail to see how this is possible. If it is possible, then we dare say it is also possible for Christ to strike a modus vivendi with Satan — absurd!

Church leaders have betrayed the very principles they profess to stand for in Zimbabwe by failing to stand firm against injustice and political intimidation.

None of them in Zimbabwe (we are referring mostly to the white clergy) has come out strongly enough to such an extent as to embarrass the Smith regime internationally in the circles of Christian churches.

We do not underestimate efforts of people like Bishop Skelton who, until recently, was based in Bulawayo to head the Anglican Church in Matebeleland. His voice was brave but it was too weak to be heard as he was virtually alone.

His colleagues in Salisbury, Umtali and elsewhere, refrained from standing out openly and bravely against the sad state of affairs. They acted as if they did not really care.

They behaved as if they were scared of Smith and his bunch of racists. They disgraced themselves and their faith.

Had Jesus been alive today, they would cowardly abandon him at the crucial time of reckoning.

We condemn them but call them at the same time to live up to their teachings if what they preach really comes from their hearts and not just from their heads.

We draw their attention to the Lusaka communique of the Roman Catholic bishops, a part of which states: 'We deplore the creation of an atmosphere of fear in which citizens are afraid to raise their voices in opposition to policies in their own countries . . . No member of the human family can claim authority before God to deny human rights and social justice to another member of that human family on the grounds of race, colour, tribe, religion, political views or conditions of life in any country . . . .'

We regard these to be great words which are pregnant with wisdom and reality. We believe that Rhodesian Church leaders ought to remember and propagate them to their congregations instead of behaving as if they do not want to displease the fascist members of their congregations.

It is only when the Church leaders practise and suffer for what they preach that the oppressed masses can ever regard that institution with respect.

Many a time it has been stated that the young generations have chosen a path leading to what church leaders call darkness because they have turned their backs against the Church.

This assertion ignores the fact that the Christian Churches (their leaders) have failed themselves by not acting bravely and correctly in times when the oppressed masses expected them to come to their aid.

We have experienced incidents in which most of these leaders act so opportunistically that, when they think that the wind is blowing in favour of the oppressed masses, they begin to use their pulpits as platforms to denounce the fascists.

They never denounce these racists when it is clear that the situation is under their (the racists') control. This is a shameful attitude which is not in keeping with what the world understands to be Christian teachings.

It is very important for these Church leaders to realise the fact that future relations between a free Zimbabwe and the Christian (and other religious) institutions will depend to a very large extent on the performance against and attitude of these organisations to the fascists in Zimbabwe at this very difficult period.

11. Economic Inter-relations of Southern Africa

Editors' Introduction

The national liberation movements believed it was no accident that the last major territories in Africa struggling for their liberation were virtually all in Southern Africa. They shared many features: the presence of white agricultural settlers, the importance of mineral wealth, the unviability for those in power of decolonization. But in addition, they were in fact linked economic-ally, and especially in recent years.

Traditionally, the economic links consisted largely in the fact that various areas served as manpower pools for the South African mines. This was (and is) notably the case for Mozambique. Dr. Eduardo Mondlane had explained this in considerable detail to the United Nations in 1962, even before he had become the president of FRELIMO, which did not yet exist. At that time, he was still a professor of anthropology at Syracuse University.

Far from lessening, these economic inter-relations grew enormously in the period 1960–74, precisely concurrently with the wars of national liberation in Portuguese Africa. In part, this was an outgrowth of these very wars. But the major factor was more fundamental. It had to do with the economic growth of South Africa and the fact that the system of *apartheid* served as a severe constraint on the potential growth of an internal market. If *apartheid* and economic growth were to be compatible, South Africa had to locate nearby, politically accessible markets. It found them in the surrounding areas of Southern Africa.

SWAPO's article analysed the basic 'sticks and carrots' weapons of South Africa. The two FRELIMO articles showed the links between Mozambique and Rhodesia on the one hand, and Mozambique and South Africa on the other, including the crucial economic role of Cabora Bassa for the Southern Africa complex. The ANC report further spelled out South Africa's stake in Angola. But the MPLA analysis showed the degree to which Portuguese and South African interests diverged within the framework of their common military front.

Mozambican Contract Labour in South Africa
Eduardo Mondlane

*From testimony by Dr. Eduardo C. Mondlane to the
UN Special Committee on Territories Under
Portuguese Administration, 10 April 1962.*

The annual emigration of Mozambicans to South Africa, is estimated at
500,000 able-bodied men between the ages of 18 and 55, and is governed
by a series of agreements between South Africa and Portugal, beginning from
the year 1897. In that year an agreement was made between Portugal and the
then Republic of the Transvaal, followed by the *Modus Vivendi* of 1901,
the Transvaal-Mozambique Convention of 1909 and the Portuguese-South
African Convention of 1928, revised in 1934, 1936, and 1940. All of these
agreements between Portugal and South Africa were that the gold and diamond mine interests of the Transvaal are to be granted large-scale labour
recruiting privileges in at least the southern province of Mozambique, in
return for guaranteeing that a certain proportion of the seaborne traffic of
the industrial centre of South Africa, which includes Pretoria and Johannesburg, must pass through the Port of Lourenco Marques rather than through
the South African ports of Durban, East London, Port Elizabeth and Cape
Town. Other benefits to accrue to Portugal are: direct monetary payments
per African recruited, guaranteed repatriation of all clandestine emigrants,
maximum contract time, and permission to establish Portuguese Native
Affairs inspection and tax-collecting facilities (*curadorias*) on South African
territory.

At the turn of the last century about three-quarters of the total Afrcan
labour force on the mines of the Transvaal were from Mozambique.[1]
According to a Transvaal Labour Commission report, for the first twenty
years of the industry's development the gold mines were almost entirely
dependent upon the East Coast for their labour. As another reporter puts it,
'The Mozambique boy (*sic*) may, therefore, be described as the pioneer
coloured labourer of the Witwatersrand.'[2]

Since then, the African people of Mozambique have spent the most
productive years of their lives helping to develop an economy for which
they themselves received almost nothing, but which has, as is well known,
enriched and continues to enrich the white people of South Africa and, to a
certain extent, has profited and continues to profit the Portuguese Government.

Without going into the details of hazards through which generations of
Mozambicans have gone and in which thousands of our people have lost their
lives, we would like to underline a few points.

In the twelve years between 1902 and 1914, over 43,000 Mozambicans
dies as a result of mining accidents and diesase while employed by the
Chamber of Mines of the Rand.[3] It is quite likely that a greater number of
our people died at home as a result of diseases and accidents incurred in the

mines. All through my experience in Mozambique I cannot recall a single family that does not count the loss of at least one man who either died in the mines of South Africa or came home with an illness contracted in the mines and died a few years later. According to the 1954 annual statistics of Mozambique, the total number of Mozambican people who died in South Africa in the years between 1902 and 1940 stands at 81,166.[4]

Even if this great loss of our people were related to the economic development of our own country and for the benefit of our own people, it would be greatly deplored. However, the situation is worse. These thousands of Mozambicans have died to satisfy the economic greed of both the South African whites and the Portuguese.

Having grown up in the area where most of the people who compose this labour force come from, I should like to indicate in a few words some of the consequences of this migratory system of labour to their families back home. Most of the labourers stay an average of fifteen months in the mining areas, even though the contract allows for a maximum sojourn of eighteen months. During those fifteen months their services are lost to their wives and children. So that, while normally men help to build the huts and granaries of the family, besides clearing the forests and thickets to enable the women to cultivate the land and sow the seeds, they also provide an important element in the total life of a family. The many emotional problems which the wives of these men have to face as a result of their husbands' absence from home for so long cannot be told in a statement of a few minutes.

Nor is this all. In order to make certain that a large number of men leave their homes to work either in South Africa or in Mozambican plantations, industries and government projects, the Portuguese Government has from time to time passed laws to force Africans to leave. These are the so-called *contract labour* laws. In order to justify this, of course, the same kind of arguments and rationalizations, which we have already pointed out, are brought forth. Even as late as the 1940s a Portuguese governor stated the following:

> The problem of native manpower . . . is probably the most important preoccupation of European agriculture. Generally speaking, throughout the various seasons of the year, there is an insufficient number of workers for the accomplishment of the undertakings which have been planned. The recruiters struggle with great difficulties to engage the needed numbers of workers . . . The supply of labour in Africa cannot continue to depend upon the whim of the black man, who is by temperament and natural circumstances inclined to expend only that minimum of effort which corresponds to his minimum necessities.[5]

Forthwith, the governor went on to define the conditions under which Africans are considered to be idle and, therefore, obliged to seek employment. In subsequent circulars, the governor reaffirmed the principle that all

African males are presumed to be idle unless they can supply proof to the contrary, thus:

1. All active native males between the ages of 18 and 55 years of age are obliged to prove that they live from their work.
2. The required proof is satisfied in the following ways:
(a) Be self-employed in a profession, in commerce, or industry, by which he supports himself.
(b) Be employed permanently in the service of the State, administrative corps or private persons.
(c) To have worked for at least six months in each year as a day labourer for the State, administrative corps or private persons.
(d) To be within the period of six months after having returned from the Union of South Africa, or the Rhodesias, from a legal contract in conformity with international agreement.
(e) Be a cattle-raiser, with at least fifty head of cattle.
(f) Be registered as an African farmer under the terms of the Statute of the African Agriculturist approved by the Legislative Diploma No. 919 of 5 August 1944.
(g) To have completed military service and be in the first year of reserve status.

Africans who cannot supply proof in any of the above terms are considered to be idle and as such are subject to recruitment by the Government for six months of labour in the public interest.

Since, as is obvious from the above, the standards by which 'being employed' are given by a government whose cultural values are different, most able-bodied Mozambicans can never supply sufficient proof that they are gainfully employed. Consequently, Mozambicans are constantly pushed from one situation into another. They either have to offer their services to South African, Rhodesian, Tanganyikan mining, farming and plantation interests at very low wages, or face the Portuguese police and be sent to government projects, or be made available for local economic interests which often pay much less than mining interests in South African and the Rhodesias.

As can be seen from the above, an African worker is not allowed to stay more than six months in his own home. This conclusion arises from the fact that most Africans live in areas where there are no industries or European agricultural projects which can offer permanent employment or which can enable them to be employed while living at home. The South African mines have strict regulations against employing individuals who can bring their families. So that all of the estimated 400,000 Mozambicans who are out of their country at any given time have left their families behind. More than this, the above regulation means that a whole range of an African's traditional family responsibilities are expected to be fulfilled within six months (of any given year).

It is clear from this that the Portuguese Government wishes to gain something out of the migratory labour to South Africa, as well as to make certain that the conquered people of Mozambique are exploited as much as possible by white people within the country. An analysis of the conditions acceptable as proof of significant economic activity reveals a deep politico-economic commitment to the international *status quo* first established in 1897, and then to the perpetuation of the migratory flows to both foreign and domestic destinations at the expense of the development of African agriculture. Out of the seven acceptable proofs of significant economic activity, only two refer to activities which can normally be carried out within the precincts of the traditional African homestead. Five of these conditions involve the male either in migratory forms of employment or in activities requiring the removal of his family to an urban environment. The two exceptions, items (e) and (f), are conditions which can be met only in an insignificant percentage of cases.[6]

According to the instructions supplied with the 1950 Census Form, the occupation of all active African males who had no specific kind of employment was to be denoted by the term 'worker'. In the southern province alone, 183,294 males were so designated. Those, together with the 157,000 men registered in the Curadoria do Transvaal, constituted about 85% of the active male population of the southern area. For the same year, the census lists 1,246 southern males as exercising the profession of cattle-raiser, while 23,473 were classified as farmers. Most of the men classified as agriculturists or farmers by the census were probably merely engaged in the production of rice or cotton, both of which enjoy special status in the economy of the country. This means that in 1950 only some 25,000 or 7% of the southern male work force was in a position to provide proof of not being 'idle' by citing activities which did not involve urban or migratory wage employment. The remaining 93% constitute the pool from which foreign and domestic wage labour requirements are being met.

The control of our working people in Mozambique by Portugal and their use in the mines of South Africa is one of the most shocking examples of man's inhumanity to man. So long as we remain under the iron hand of Portuguese colonialism, we will continue to be used by both the Portuguese and the South African whites, and by whatever outside groups have invested capital in South African gold mining.

When discussing the problems hinted at above with those Portuguese who have never lived in any of the Portuguese colonies, one is struck by the insistence on quoting the various legal measures which the Portuguese Colonial Government has from time to time felt embarrassed enough to enact against those whites who are likely to abuse their privileged position. Often foreigners are taken in by the same trick. It is interesting to note here that practically all important labour legislation in Portuguese Africa came soon after an uproar had occurred against slave labour practices, during which Portugal claimed that there had been no forced labour. Yet each one of these laws is aimed at discouraging the same practices which the Government so loudly denies.

The African worker in Mozambique has never had and will never have protection against the Portuguese exploiters so long as the people have no voice in the government of the country . . .

In this connection, I should like to call attention to the fact that, under the terms of the already mentioned Portuguese-South African Agreement, the South African Chamber of Mines is granted permission to recruit in Mozambique an average of 100,000 labourers per annum. In exchange, South Africa pays Portugal some $6 per labourer, and allows the Portuguese government to collect head taxes directly from the labourers, and guarantees that a minimum of 47.5% of the seaborne import traffic to, and exports from, the area of Johannesburg-Pretoria will pass through the port of Lourenco Marques. When one adds to this those remittances which derive from Africans working in the Rhodesias, and Africans who have non-conventionally entered South Africa, proceeds from African emigrants compose a large proportion of Portuguese wealth.

No wonder, then, that Portugal is not only unwilling to give up her colonial empire, but also refuses to give information on her Territories in Africa. She is afraid that once the rest of the world comes to know the truth about her colonial practices, she will not be able to resist the furore that would result.

Consequently, Portugal is devising every means she can go keep the Africans of Mozambique ignorant, and oppressed.

Notes

1. Transvaal Labour Commission, 1904, p. 28.
2. *The Gold of Rand*, 1927, p. 58.
3. Louta Ribeiro, 1902, *Annaro de Mozambique*, Lourenco Marques, Impressa Nacional.
4. *Anuario de Mozambique*, 1940; *Anuario Estatistica*, 1940, 1954.
5. J.T. Bettencourt: Circular 818/D-7, 7 December 1942.
6. Harris, Marvin, 'Labour Emigration among the Mozambique Thonga: Cultural and Political Factors', *Africa*, Journal of the International African Institute, pp. 50–66.

Apartheid Expansionism
SWAPO

> *Article in* SWAPO Information *Bulletin (New York), II,*
> *3, Feb.–Mar. 1969.*

The nature of apartheid as a system of oppression and exploitation of African people in South Africa is notorious enough. But recently, it has become clear that the Republic of South Africa has embarked on a complex and many-sided offensive against the liberation movements and the independent African states. The policy of South Africa has been a carrot and stick policy.

On the one hand, South Africa has absurdly presented itself as an altruistic state interested only in developing friendship with African independent states with the intention of promoting trade and technical aid. Despite all the inherent absurdities of a policy of oppressing Africans at home while making friendship with them across borders and abroad, white South Africa is pursuing its aims skillfully and relentlessly. The strategic object of this aspect of South African government policy is to create a series of client states which will provide a base directed against the liberation movements and the independent states of Africa. So that in fact the aid and trade ultimately have military and strategic aims in view . . .

The above excerpt is from a joint statement by the following supreme leaders of the fighting liberation movements of Southern Africa and Guinea-Bissad; Amilcar Cabral of PAIGC (Guinea-Bissau), Agostino Neto of MPLA (Angola), James Chikerema of ZAPU (Zimbabwe), the late Eduardo Mondlane of FRELIMO (Mozambique), Sam Nujoma of SWAPO (Namibia) and Oliver Tambo of ANC (South Africa). The statement was presented by Mr. Tambo to the Fifth Assembly of the Heads of States and Governments of the OAU in Algiers, September 1968.

The facts outlined in the excerpt are of central importance in understanding South Africa's current moves to extend her margin of manoeuvres for regional hegemony. Through a host of intriguing schemes, Pretoria has managed to woo Banda's Malawi into the white-dominated zone whose northern buffer Malawi now provides.

In March 1967, Malawi ministers were flown to Pretoria. They were dined, wined, and accommodated in Pretoria's all-white hotel. Subsequently, a trade agreement was concluded between Malawi and the apartheid Republic. By the terms of this agreement, South Africa agreed to permit Malawi to export 500,000 pounds of tea to South Africa, duty free. Malawi in return, granted South Africa preferential tariffs for all South African goods imported into Malawi. In June 1967, South Africa announced the plan to build a 'diplomatic village', a special location a distance away from Pretoria, to house the 'kaffir' diplomats from Malawi who could not live in the usual Corps Diplomatique area of Cape Town because of residential apartheid practised in South Africa. In September of that year, diplomatic relations were officially established between Malawi and South Africa at the charge d'affaires level. By the end of that year, the South African Import-Export Corporation had obtained a contract to build a new capital for Malawi at Lilongwe in Central Malawi. Subsequently, this corporation formed a joint company with the Malawi Development Corporation. Banda first sought British help regarding the idea of building a new capital. The British, however, declined to help with the scheme after an economic mission reported that it was wasteful and unproductive in terms of the capital expenditure involved. Banda then turned to South Africa. In 1967, a team of South African physical planning specialists, headed by L.S. Rautenbach, one of Vorster's top rational strategists, completed a report in which they hailed the plan as the most important aspect of Malawi's development planning. Why South Africa was so readily receptive to the scheme deserves closer examination. Lilongwe, which is situated in Central Malawi, is in flat country which is well suited for the construction of an airport. Some observers of Southern Africa believe that the South African Airways, which is barred from using the East African Coast air route to Europe, could benefit from an airport at Lilongwe. These observers think that, for the South African airlines, such an East Coast air route would be both cheaper and quicker to Europe than the Angola-Canary Islands route now used by the South African Airways.

From a logistic point of view, Malawi will become an important staging ground for aggressive military moves against the fighting liberation movements in Southern Africa, as well as for military threats against the neigh-bouring countries which are supporting those liberation movements. Pro-fascist Banda will readily guarantee South Africa such a right. Furthermore, the South African fascists are aware that Malawi's integration into the South African trade network will make things harder for even a progressive government in Malawi after Banda. Experience has shown in Africa how hard it has been for the newly independent nations to break economic ties with their former colonial masters because the colonial economic set-ups were so neatly anchored to the economies of 'mother countries'. By 1968, Malawi had drifted deeply into the zone of white domination.

The dependence of the former High Commission territories is obvious and somehow understandable. Botswana, for instance, depends to a large extent on the 394 miles of the Cape Town to Rhodesia line. About two-thirds of Botswana's imports come from the Republic. Most of Botswana's meat, her main product, goes to South Africa. Both Botswana and Lesotho's road networks are embedded in the mass of South Africa. Malawi's situation regarding the apartheid Republic is not comparable. Britain takes nearly one-half of Malawi's exports and supplies one-third of her imports. Like the former British High Commission territories, the labour market constitutes Malawi's important link with South Africa The picture is generally drawn, in an exaggerated fashion, that these countries are helpless before their economically powerful neighbour, South Africa. But a common policy between Malawi and the former High Commission territories could be an important bargaining card with South Africa. A well-coordinated policy could enable Malawi and the former High Commission territories to compel South Africa to at least improve the conditions of workers and increase their wages. This could equally reveal the fact that economic cards are not so one-sidedly stacked, as it is usually made to appear. The South African economy requires a constant flow of labour supply from these countries. Any tactical halt on this supply would be economically unbearable to South

Africa.

The docility of these countries is a remarkable gain, so far, in the South African strategy of regional domination. Today these countries, especially Malawi and Lesotho, are giving active diplomatic support to South Africa. When the Afro-Asian delegates made an attempt at the U.N. early this year to suspend South Africa from the United Nations Conference on Trade and Development because of her racist policy of apartheid, it was these client states' delegates who were lobbying against the Afro-Asian attempt. The client states have also gone on record to condemn 'terrorism' — the South African label for the freedom fighters. They echo Pretoria's trite propaganda of 'good neighbourliness' among all the states of Southern Africa.

The two most important weapons of apartheid expansionism are 'sticks and carrots,' i.e. threats and bribery. They are being used at home and across the borders with the same vigour and intensity. In South Africa proper, as well as in the occupied territory of Namibia, most of all the able and pro-gressive spokesmen of the African populations are either in prisons or forced underground or into exile.

South Africa is now carving up the territory of Namibia into 'Bantu nations' and an economically dominant white nation, over which South Africa will have total political control. The resulting political arrangement would effectively place the richest portion of Namibia under the direct administration of South Africa and leave the 'Bantu nations' as puppet enclaves, economically dependent on the 'mother country'. Domestically, the frustrated traditionalists, who view the rise of African Nationalists and their liberation movements as a threat to their 'power', are the ones in which South Africa finds its staunchest allies. The political leadership of the newly created 'Bantu nations' is drawn from these traditionalists who are usually outspoken in their embrace of 'separate development' as well as in their opposition to progressive African Nationalism.

There are instances where South Africa has managed a successful flirta-tion with disgruntled opposition leaders abroad. Nkumbula of Zambia is one such opposition leader whose political fortunes have long been sagging. It has recently been established that South African and Rhodesian money has found its way into Nkumbula's campaign funds during the election of December 1968, in Zambia. On the other hand, Kenneth Kaunda and his UNIP government have been the constant targets of South Africa's vitupera-tion, threats and intimidation; that being the other factor in the 'carrots and sticks' policy already mentioned.

Smith, Sanctions, and Salazar
FRELIMO

Article appearing in FRELIMO Information *(Algiers) in July 1968. Translated from French.*

The question about Portugal and its territories was noticeably avoided during the loud debate over Rhodesia. In January 1966, the Lonrho-Beira pipeline was but a temporary solution, and in April of the same year the Joanna V became the headline issue. More recently, however, the bonds between Rhodesia and Mozambique, as well as those between Portugal and Great Britain, were kept as silent as possible by the latter's government and the press, even if next to South Africa it is the Mozambican colonial government which is the most important support of Smith's regime, the one which enables it to survive even today.

The following are some of the facts which have a tendency to be overlooked:

The Economic Alliance
Portugal has largely complained over the fact that it has lost 15,000,000 pounds sterling in Mozambique as a result of sanctions, which illustrates sufficiently well the closeness of the Rhodesia-Mozambique interdependence. This leads us to ask what is the significance of what Portugal does not lose and of what these bonds provide once again Rhodesia with.

Transportation of Goods
Ten per cent of the gross national revenue of Mozambique comes from the transportation of goods forwarded to Rhodesia, or coming from Rhodesia. Actually, since Mozambique lies between Rhodesia and the sea, it has always been the main outlet of Rhodesia's commerce. Beira is by far the closest port to Salisbury and Bulawayo. These cities are connected to Beira by means of roads or railways. A railway line connects them also with Lourenco Marques.

Manpower
Even if the largest emigration of Mozambican workers is toward South Africa, that towards Rhodesia still is significant. In 1963, 119,871 Mozambican workers were at work in Rhodesia and 6,387 of them were employed in (U.N. statistics). Mozambique profits from the taxes sent back by these emigratn workers.

Rhodesia thus gains from having a supplementary manpower source which is even more vulnerable to police operations than its own manpower due to continuous threats of deportation. The importance of this fact could increase if the Zimbabwe people become involved in the economic war, in the future.

It is in Mozambique that one can find the beaches closest to Rhodesia

Each year nearly 80,000 white Rhodesians spend their vacations in Mozambican seaside resorts. It is probable that Mozambique may see its popularity increase now that neither money or Rhodesian passports are valid in a number of countries. Mozambique, however, still accepts them. Its friendly relations with Rhodesia thus softens considerably the effects of the sanctions war.

Finances
Since Mozambique accepts Rhodesia's illegal money, it can be utilized in a more general way as an outlet of Rhodesia's finances.

Commerce
In 1965 commerce between both countries was not significant; Rhodesia accounting for only 1.9% of Mozambican imports and 3.1% of its exports. In the past two years commercial relations have become more significant, and certain signs lead one to think that they will develop considerably in the future.

In 1964 a pact was signed which would come into effect in 1965 according to which Rhodesia was granted the status of most favoured nation. The consequences of such an agreement should not appear in the 1965 figures. In 1966 a group of envoys made up of Portuguese bankers and industrialists came to Rhodesia to check the possibility 'of an increase in industrial and commercial exchanges between Portugal, its colonies, and Rhodesia' (*Tribuna*, 20 November 1966).

B.H. Musette, Rhodesian Minister of Commerce and Industry, had previously declared, in July, at the time of the Mozambique's commercial fair, that 'the main object of the Rhodesian minister's visit was to stimulate economic relations between Mozambique and Rhodesia.' (*Diario Popular*, Lisbon, 8 July 1966).

The Political Alliance
If the Portuguese authorities do their best in Mozambique to help Rhodesia blunt the impact of avoiding sanctions, it is for clear economic reasons, but this co-operation is also based on a similarity of political interests.

In 1965 *Le Monde* stated that 'according to information received from Lisbon's diplomatic circles, an agreement had been secretly concluded among Portugal, Rhodesia, and South Africa, for the defence of white Africa . . . The agreement foresees the organization of a common defence against nationalist and Communist subversion.' (*Le Monde*, 14 September 1965). Such fraternal co-operation has certainly evolved since U.D.I., and both the PIDE (the Portuguese secret police) and the Rhodesian police work together.

If the British Government really wanted the fall of the Smith regime, it would seek among other things to separate Smith from such a useful ally. The surest way of arriving at such a goal would be to help the formation of a nationalist government in Mozambique.

However, while a clear majority supports the will to independence of the

Mozambican people at the United Nations, Great Britain persists in voting against the resolutions pertaining to this question.

In its relations with Portugal, England, Smith's main ally after South Africa, has been satisfied with minimal reprimands on the subject of pipelines and tankers. Besides this, both commercial and diplomatic relations are still maintained as cordially as ever. It seems that Portugal will remain as Englan's oldest ally, its partner in EFTA, and in NATO; and protected in this way by so-called ties of friendship, Portugal will continue to make sanctions inoperative and make Smith's dictatorship a success.

Even if Great Britain pretends to overlook the Smith-Salazar bonds, the real enemies of both dictatorships do not. We, in FRELIMO, we are quite aware that our fight against Salazar is closely associated with that against Smith, and that a blow directed at one dictator is one brought against the other. While those who call themselves champions of Western democracy pretend otherwise, and support and appease the rising forces of Fascism in Southern Africa, the peoples of Africa rare fighting and will continue to fight.

South Africa's Stake in Angola
ANC

Article in Sechaba *(ANC), III, 2, February 1969.*

Since the armed struggle in Southern Africa began gathering momentum, South Africa has shown unusually keen interest in the anti-guerilla operations of Rhodesia and Portugal. Whereas her stake in Rhodesia is widely known, her interest in the Portuguese colonies is less well known and understood.

Examples of this concern are many. Some months ago United Party Leader, Sir De Villiers Graaff, issued a policy statement which warned that, if the Portuguese troops failed in their operations in Angola and Mozambique, South Africa could be faced with a guerilla war within weeks. He then urged that the Portuguese be given help since 'in a sense they are fighting our battles and they are acting as most effective buffers for us.' *Sunday Express*, 4.8.68). Was the U.P. man exaggerating or was he trying to outflank Vorster?

The fact is that he did not do his homework well. Vorster and Co. have long advocated this line. Since last year, one of Vorster's close associates has been prominent in this respect. In November 1967, Theo Gerdener, the Administrator of Natal, initiated the Mozambique Soldiers' Comfort Fund. Using the same words as Graaff, he said that, if Portugal withdrew her 80,000 soldiers, South Africa could become involved in a 'terrorist' war within weeks.

How does this concern apply to Angola? First of all, Angola is the fascist Republic's next-door neighbour because Namibia (South West Africa) is virtually the fifth province of South Africa. The Republic thus fears that, if Angola became free, she herself would be exposed to attack on this flank. For her security South Africa, therefore, supports Portugal against the guerillas. In short, Angola is one of South Africa's strategic buffers.

Secondly, Angola produces a highly strategic commodity: *Oil*. Since the United Nations and the Anti-Apartheid Movement began advocating sanctions against the racist regimes, South Africa's greatest worry has been her vulnerability to an oil embargo. Highly industrialised, she cannot do without oil. Frantic searches and prospecting within her borders have proved fruitless. Then this previous liquid was found in Angola — in fact, in the enclave of Cabinda, separated from main Angola by the Congo River. There, the Gulf Oil Corporation of Texas discovered rich offshore deposits. By 1970, Angola is expected to pump out 150,000 barrels of oil a day! And by 1971 she will be getting 25% of her foreign exchange earnings from oil.

Obviously, this oil is a godsend to the Unholy Alliance. As the *U.S. News & World Report* (10.6.68) said, Angola 'is the only country with major oil reserves, and in a showdown with African nationalists this would be vital to the White-ruled nations.' It is clearly in Vorster's interests to be on good terms with Caetano.

The third point is related to the previous one, Angola's wealth finances Portugal's anti-guerilla operations in Mozambique. Guinea-Bissau and, of course, in Angola itself. This, too, is in the Republic's interests, And Angola is a country rich in mineral and other resources!

Since 1960, Angola has been enjoying an economic boom. In the tear 1962–63, her exports were valued at 135,440,000 U.S. dollars; and the imports, 112,240,000 dollars; a favourable trade balance of over 20 million dollars. Also in 1962, her Industrial Production Index stood at 100; by 1966 it had soared to 222.

In the industrial sector, Angola has sizeable deposits of diamonds, iron and copper. Plans are afoot to open a tyre factory (U.S. capital), and a motor-car assembly plant. And a whole range of secondary industries is sprouting.

In the agricultural sector, Angola is just as well endowed. She is the fourth biggest coffee producer in the world, and her fishing industry is said to be the fourth largest in Africa. No wonder then that foreign corporations are tripping over one another in their haste to invest there. These come mostly from Britain, West Germany, U.S.A., Denmark and South Africa.

Two examples clearly show the Republic's economic stake. *Defence and Aid Information Service* (Jan.–June 1967, p. 9) published in London reports that in 1967 a South African manufacturing firm, Bondcrete Ltd., won a contract for laying a 13-mile pipeline from the Bengo River to Luanda. Moreover, in 1966, South Africa's imports from Angola were worth R3.5 million, whereas her exports were worth R2 million. That is, South Africa got more from Angola than did Angola from her.

Add this all up, and it is clear that Angola is a land far richer in resources than Portugal itself. It is not difficult to understand why Portugal is making such an effort to hold it.' So commented *U.S. News and World Report*

(10.6.68).

Now, Portugal's plunder of Angola does not merely fatten her. More importantly, it enables Portugal to fight our brothers in her colonies, and to perpetuate the rule of doddering Dan Salazar and the present President Marcello Caetano and their cohorts. And on the ability of this regime to fight the guerillas depends South Africa's security from attack.

Can Portugal hang on indefinitely in Angola? The answer is a big *No*. This is not just because the cause of our brothers is just and victory certain. Fresh and convincing evidence has come to hand — from the enemy itself.

Earlier this year, a South African journalist, one A.J. Venter, visited Angola and returned with a remarkable story. It was published by *News-Check* (12.7.68), the *Sunday Times* (14.7.68) and the *Sunday Express* (14.7.68). It should be remembered that these publications support White supremacy in Southern Africa and abhor armed struggle — the only means left by which we can attain power and human dignity.

What did Venter discover in Angola? With regard to our comrades-in-arms, he learned from Portuguese officers that their calibre has improved tremendously. 'The type of "terrorist" we get these days knows exactly what he is doing,' a Colonel told him. This skill appears in the character of the war itself. Venter describes it as 'Thrust by the enemy and swift counter-measures by the Portuguese . . . only the thrusts are becoming more commonplace and more widespread, while Portuguese counter-measures are proving more difficult against a better trained, better equipped and more tenacious enemy.' As a result, he says further, 'the Angolan war has taken a dramatic turn for the worse.'

What liberation movement is responsible for this 'dramatic turn' in Portuguese fortunes? Venter was told: MPLA which he describes as 'by far the more effective, efficient and better organised'. And, MPLA is looked upon by the Portuguese as the deadlier of the two factions. (May the O.A.U. note the admissions of the enemy on the revolutionary war waged by MPLA.

What about the calibre of the 60,000 Portuguese troops? Their morale is not terribly impressive. The biggest problem is that they spend 'two years at a stretch without wives or families'. One officer frankly remarked that this period is 'a long time for a man to be away from home — but they seem to manage even though *their morale drops a little towards the end*.' (our emphasis).

Concerning equipment, Caetano's boys lack 'heavy equipment, vehicles and helicopters,' and see a role for South Africa in this regard. However, Portugal views the Republic with jealousy and fear. Some officers felt that South Africa might be willing to help but that 'it could be Lisbon which was not eager to see South Africa increase its influence in this part of Southern Africa.' In other words, the ranks of the Unholy Alliance are not made of solid granite.

Of course, Lisbon's fears are justified. South Africa is itching to fight in Angola, just as she is doing in Rhodesia. She regards it as militarily and economically sensible to fight guerillas outside rather than inside her borders.

Being heavily industrialised, she can suffer immense damage from our forces. To prevent this, she would rather fight in Angola to the last Portuguese.

In short, Angola is of vital importance to South Africa. And now, she is beginning to doubt the staying power of Portugal. But Portugal in turn fears its stronger ally. The two countries are imperialist plotters. Such contradictions hasten the downfall of the enemy.

Portugal and South Africa: Competitive Monopolies
MPLA

*Excerpts from the MPLA Report to the International
Conference in Support of the Liberation Movements
of the Portuguese Colonies and Southern Africa, held in
Khartoum (Sudan), 18–20 January 1969. Translated
from French.*

South Africa has become a rather industrialized capitalist country, anxious to find external outlets for its manufactured goods, sources of raw materials it lacks such as petroleum, and new investments for its capital.

Nothing is more natural, therefore, than that the primary objectives of South African expansionism are racist Rhodesia and the Portuguese colonies. The goal of a 'Common Market for Southern Africa' proposed by Pretoria is to eliminate Portugal from the region.

But we must place this struggle for hegemony in Southern Africa in the context of imperialism. In fact, Portugal is relatively dependent on imperialist powers. It is calculated that two-thirds of the capital invested in Portugal are tied, directly or indirectly, to international monopoly capital.

A study on Portugal and her colonies published recently by the French financial review *Enterprise** came to this conclusion: 'While, in 1959, long-term foreign capital came to only 1% of private investment, they represent 20% of the total in 1965.' Naturally, the review refrains from noting that this 20% is far from the whole story, since all the nominally Portuguese companies are already penetrated to a lesser or greater degree by foreign capital. Nevertheless, these figures have the merit of showing us the increasing dependence of Portugal on the imperialist powers.

South Africa, too, cannot be considered an independent economic power. A U.N. study+ asserted that foreign investments in South Africa resulted in $362 millions in profits, of which 175 million went to Great Britain and 101 million to the United States. Foreign assets in South Africa reached $4.8

* No. 655, 30 March 1968.
+ *Marches Tropicaux*, 1967.

billion in 1965, Great Britain and the United States controlling 70% between
them. And we are sure the U.N. study is far from being complete.

The economic war between South Africa and Portugal has all the signs of
a competition between monopolies, occasionally difficult to follow, since the
trusts are linked or divided in complex games of multiple interests. But this
economic struggle has been relegated to the second level for the needs of the
cause, in fact of the nationalist forces . . .

South Africa is today torn by its own contradictions. If she wishes to
maintain her system of ultra-exploitation and apartheid, she has to expand
beyond her frontiers seeking to occupy neighbouring countries and thus
creating a 'political void' around her. South Africa's policy is similar to that
of another equally virulent expansionism, that of Israel.

The South African Government can buy mercenaries but they will always
be insufficient to keep down the numerous peoples of the southern regions
of Africa.

Whatever they do to enlarge their frontiers, the racists forget that they
encounter always the resistance of other peoples, as was the case with the
Roman Empire.

All this shows that South African expansionism is insatiable — and has
reached a point of no-return. It thus represents a certain danger for all of
Africa. Furthermore, the economic penetration by South African monopolies in numerous African countries recalls the old story of the Trojan horse.

OTHER BOOKS AVAILABLE FROM ZED

On Africa

A. Temu and B. Swai
Historians and Africanist History
A Critique
Hb and Pb

Dan Nabudere
Imperialism in East Africa: Vols. I & II
Hb

Horst Drechsler
Let us Die Fighting
Namibia under the Germans
Hb and Pb

Chris Searle
We're Building the New School
Diary of a Teacher in Mozambique
Hb

Okwudiba Nnoli (Ed.)
Path to Nigerian Development
Pb

Robert Archer and Antoine Bouillon
The South African Game
Sport and Racism in South Africa
Hb and Pb

SWAPO Department of Information and Publicity
To Be Born a Nation
The Liberation Struggle for Namibia
Pb

Ben Turok (Ed.)
Development in Zambia
A Reader
Pb

Edwin Madunagu
Problems of Socialism
The Nigerian Challenge
Pb

Claude Ake
Revolutionary Pressures in Africa
Hb and Pb

Baruch Hirson
Year of Fire, Year of Ash
The Soweto Revolt: Roots of a Revolution?
Hb and Pb

Maina wa Kinyatti
Thunder from the Mountains
Mau Mau Patriotic Songs
Hb

No Sizwe
One Azania, One Nation
The National Question in South Africa
Hb and Pb

Albert Nzula and others
Forced Labour in Colonial Africa
Hb and Pb

Justinian Rweyemamu (ed.)
Industrialization and Income Distribution in Africa
Hb and Pb

Ann Seidman and Neva Makgetla
Outposts of Monopoly Capitalism
Southern Africa in the Changing Global Economy
Pb

Elenga M'buyinga
Pan Africanism or Neo-colonialism
The Bankruptcy of the OAU
Hb and Pb

Faarax Cawl
Ignorance is the Enemy of Love
Pb

Mohamed Babu
African Socialism or Socialist Africa?
Hb and Pb

Aquino de Braganca and Immanuel Wallerstein (Eds)
The African Liberation Reader
Documents of the National Liberation Movements (3 vols.)
Hb

Basil Davidson
No Fist is Big Enough to Hide the Sky
The Liberation of Guinea and Cape Verde: Aspects of an African Revolution
Hb

Eduardo Mondlane
The Struggle for Mozambique
Hb and Pb

Yolamu Barongo (Ed.)
Political Science in Africa
A Radical Critique
Hb and Pb

Bade Onimode
Imperialism and Underdevelopment in Nigeria
The Dialectics of Poverty
Hb and Pb

Ronald Graham
The Aluminium Industry and the Third World
Hb and Pb

Henrik Marcussen and Jens Torp
The Internationalization of Capital: The Prospects for the Third World
A Re-examination of Dependency Theory
Hb and Pb

Louis Wolf and others (Eds.)
Dirty Work: The CIA in Africa
Hb and Pb

Peder Gouwenius
Power to the People
South Africa in Struggle: A Pictorial History
Pb

Zed Press titles cover Africa, Asia, Latin America and the Middle East, as well
as general issues affecting the Third World's relations with the rest of the
world. Our Series embrace: Imperialism, Women, Political Economy, History,
Labour, Voices of Struggle, Human Rights and other areas pertinent to the
Third World.

**You can order Zed titles direct from Zed Press, 57 Caledonian Road,
London, N1 9DN, U.K.**